BY THE SAME AUTHOR

The City of the Gods

A Search for God in Time and Memory

THE WAY OF ALL THE EARTH

THE WAY OF ALL THE EARTH

Experiments in Truth and Religion

JOHN S. DUNNE

Macmillan Publishing Co., Inc.
NEW YORK

Collier Macmillan Publishers
LONDON

Macmillan Publishing Co., Inc.
866 Third Avenue, New York, N.Y. 10022
Collier Macmillan Canada, Ltd.

Library of Congress Catalog Card Number: 78–167928

First Macmillan Paperbacks Edition 1972

SIXTH PRINTING 1978

Printed in the United States of America

Contents

Preface

Is a religion coming to birth in our time? It could be. What seems to be occurring is a phenomenon we might call "passing over," passing over from one culture to another, from one way of life to another, from one religion to another. Passing over is a shifting of standpoint, a going over to the standpoint of another culture, another way of life, another religion. It is followed by an equal and opposite process we might call "coming back," coming back with new insight to one's own culture, one's own way of life, one's own religion. The holy man of our time, it seems, is not a figure like Gotama or Jesus or Mohammed, a man who could found a world religion, but a figure like Gandhi, a man who passes over by sympathetic understanding from his own religion to other religions and comes back again with new insight to his own. Passing over and coming back, it seems, is the spiritual adventure of our time. It is the adventure I want to undertake and describe in this book.

The course such an adventure follows is that of an odyssey. It starts from the homeland of a man's own religion, goes through the wonderland of other religions, and ends in the homeland of his own. Much depends, if this is true, on the religion where it starts and ends. Gandhi began and ended with Hinduism; he passed over to Christianity particularly, and Islam too, but he always came back again to Hinduism. A Christian, in accordance with this, would begin and end with Christianity, a Jew with Judaism, a

Muslim with Islam, a Buddhist with Buddhism. If we examine the matter more deeply, though, we find that there is a more ultimate starting and ending point, and that is the person's own life. One has to pass over, to shift standpoints, in order to enter into the life of Jesus, even if one is a Christian, and then one has to come back, to shift standpoints again, to return to one's own life. From this point of view all the religions, even one's own, become part of the wonderland in this odyssey. One's own life is finally the homeland.

Lives too are the wonderland, especially the lives of figures like Gotama and Jesus and Mohammed. It is by entering into their lives, by examining the pattern of their lives, I believe, that one learns the real meaning of their words. Let us begin our odyssey in this book by passing over to the life of Gandhi. He called his adventures "experiments with truth." Let us call ours that too, though we may come to somewhat different results. When we pass over to his life, we find that he was led by his experience to a renunciation of sexuality and violence. When we come back to our own lives, we may be led to a somewhat different ideal, an ideal perhaps of transforming instead of simply renouncing the dark forces in man, transforming sexuality into love and transforming violence into action. A life of transformed sexuality and violence could be a profoundly simple life, a life like that of Gotama given to insight and the sharing of insight with others. The experiences of Gotama's life are not uncommon: a life in the world, then a withdrawal into the wilderness, and then a return among men. What is uncommon is his insight into his own experience, his enlightenment. To pass over to his life we would have to examine our own lives, our own withdrawal, our own return. We could compare his life with that of Jesus and that of Krishna, figures who are considered incarnations of God. It was one of Gandhi's convictions that every man is an incarnation. If there is truth in this, it should be possible for us to find a basis within ourselves for understanding even such lives as these.

This is the test of the idea that every man is an incarnation, our ability to pass over to the lives of men who are considered human incarnations of God. A parallel idea that every man is a prophet is put to the test when we pass over to the life of a prophet like Mohammed. Passing over is essentially a matter of sympathetic understanding; a man must have within him somehow what he finds in another. As it turns out, our understanding is always partial; we gain some insight but not the enlightenment of the sage or the revelation of the prophet. We are left with the feeling, nevertheless, that further insight is always possible, that by continuing the process of going over to other lives and coming back to our own we would go from one insight to another. It may be that all the basic spiritual experiences of mankind can be re-enacted somehow in our individual lives. If this is so, then there is some kind of lesson to be learned about the course of human events from the individual's life story, and there is conversely a lesson to be learned about the individual's life from the story of mankind.

Does everything which belongs to the story of mankind come to light in the individual's life story? It all enters into his life, it seems, but it does not all enter into his consciousness. It enters into his life because he is a man and everything belonging to the story of mankind belongs to man's being. It does not all enter into his consciousness unless we suppose that at some point in his life he comes to know everything a man can know. This is why there are dark forces at work in a life, we can guess, forces which seem destructive but become creative when they are transformed and assimilated through insight. A dark and yet creative power seems to be at work in the life and time of man.

To gain insight into this dark and creative power is the object of the adventure we are now undertaking. Hence the titles of the two parts of this book, "A God in Disguise" and "A Journey with God." This book for me is the record of the third phase of a personal journey which I began some years ago. The first phase appears in my first book, *The City of the Gods,* where I was engaged in passing over to cultures. I compared cultures there in terms of their answers to death. The concern with death led me on to an interest in the life story. Thus in the second phase, in *A Search for God in Time and Memory,* I became engaged in passing over to lives. It was there that I began to use the term "passing over" and began to study the different standpoints, biographical and autobiographical, from which a life can be understood. Now in the third phase of my journey, in this book, I am engaged in passing over to religions. The influence of the second phase can be seen in my approach to the religions by way of the life story. The influence of both the first and the second can be seen in my effort to correlate the life story and the story of mankind.

The writing of the book was itself a journey for me in which I went from one insight to another. I wrote the book chapter by chapter, starting with the first and then retracing my steps in the last. This is the way I wrote the earlier books too. In each of them, as the reader can tell, I do not fully know what I am doing until the retracing of steps in the last chapter. All I have in the beginning is an image of what I am going to do along with chapter titles which work out the image in phases. The actual ideas come then in the process of writing. Originally I expected that experiments with truth would mean gaining new experiences by walking new paths, the "way" of which Jesus spoke, the "middle path" of which Gotama spoke, the "straight path" of which Mohammed spoke. As I went on, though, I began to realize that the experiences on which the religions were based were common experiences, and that the uncommon thing was the insight into the experiences, the "enlightenment" and the "revelation." I realized that I was engaged in a process of gaining new insight into experiences which I already had. Hence the title, *The Way of All the Earth*. The phrase "the way of all the earth" in the King James Version of the Bible (Joshua 23:14 and 1 Kings 2:2) corresponds to the phrase "the way of all flesh" in the Douay Version and means the way of common mortality. I use it to mean the common experience of mankind and wish to say by it that the religions consist of insight into the common experiences of mankind. There is a depth which can appear in the most common human experiences. It is an abyss which opens up like a narrow and bottomless crevice at crucial points in a human life. A man leaps over it when he goes from one stage of life to another, from childhood to youth, from youth to manhood, from manhood to age. He crosses it in passing over by sympathetic understanding to another human being and crosses it again in coming back to himself. He goes down into it when he withdraws from the cares of his existence and comes back out of it again when he returns to them once more.

What we will be doing in this book, therefore, is leaping over this abyss, crossing it and crossing back again, going down into it and coming out of it again. Or we will be remembering the times when we did all these things, and we will be reflecting on what happened to us when we came to and from the abyss and on what happened to others, on what we have seen in the abyss and what others have seen.

I would like to thank the friends who helped me with this book, especially David Burrell, Robert Meagher, and John Noonan, who read the manuscript in whole or in part and gave me valuable suggestions and criticisms.

Part One

A GOD IN DISGUISE

1

Experimenting with Truth

"How many centuries is it," Malraux has asked, "since a great religion shook the world?"[1] Buddhism, Christianity, Islam, each in its turn shook the world, but it has been some thirteen centuries now since the last great religion arose. Each of the religions brought with it a revelation about man. After the religions ceased to seem new and revealing, though, men began searching once again to find out about themselves, for themselves and from themselves. This led, at least in the wake of Christianity, to a multiplication of memoirs and autobiographies. Thus the newest disclosures of man, and of God too, seem to be found in personal documents rather than in scriptures. It is almost as though personal religion and personal creeds had replaced the great religions and the common creeds. There is a way, nevertheless, of finding out about man and God that seems to combine the way of religions and that of memoirs. It is the way of what Gandhi called "experiments with truth."

The life of Gandhi was a series of experiments of this kind. He called his autobiography *The Story of My Experiments with Truth.* He included there the story of his experiments with nonviolence, celibacy, truthfulness in word, truthfulness in thought, and other principles of conduct, but he wanted to embrace under the term *truth* "not only the relative truth of our conception, but the Absolute Truth, the Eternal Principle, that is God."[2] For instance, he experimented with the truth proposed in that central Hindu scripture, the *Bhagavad-Gita.* The sovereign remedy, according to the Gita, is renunciation of the fruits of action. If a man were to actually try renouncing the fruits of action, he would be experimenting with the truth of a great religion, even with the truth of its God. Gandhi made a translation of the Gita and wrote a commentary on it, grounding his work not on scholarship but on forty years of experience in trying to put the teaching of the Gita into practice. This suggests an approach which could be taken to all the great religions, Buddhism, Hinduism, Judaism, Christianity, and Islam. Gandhi's own life involved persistent endeavors to "enforce the meaning,"[3] as he said, of both the Gita and the Sermon on the Mount.

Enforcing the meaning of scriptures like these in one's life amounts to turning poetry into truth, making the poetry of the religions come true in one's life. It is the reverse of writing an autobiography, putting the truth of one's life into words, turning truth into poetry. Gandhi evidently did both: first he turned poetry into truth, enforcing the meaning of the Gita and the Sermon on the Mount, and then he turned truth into poetry, writing the story of his experiments. If we are going to follow Gandhi's cue in approaching the religions, therefore, maybe we should begin by experimenting with truth and poetry. This seems particularly necessary since Goethe maintained in his autobiography, *Poetry and Truth in My Life,* that it is good to turn the truth of one's life into poetry but very destructive to try making poetry come true in one's life.[4] Cervantes too has left us in *Don Quixote* the satirical portrait of a country gentleman who, crazed by his reading of the books of chivalry, sallies forth to make poetry come true. Because of and in spite of these warnings, let us experiment with the process of turning poetry into truth, and when we have seen what happens let us then experiment with the reverse process of turning truth into poetry.

1. Turning Poetry into Truth

Imagine a Don Quixote who as a child read more than an ordinary share of fairy tales, then as a youth read ancient epics and modern epic novels. It is not easy to classify all the stories our Quixote will have read, but the categories of epic poetry may serve: war epics, journey epics, and creation epics.[5] We could imagine a less bookish Quixote who has encountered the poetry of war and journey and creation simply by hearing stories told or by seeing them enacted. Since this is a book, though, let our Quixote be as bookish as the original of Cervantes, who spent all his leisure time reading books of chivalry, neglecting the management of his affairs for them and wasting his means on them, bringing home as many of them as he could get. Suppose too that our Quixote, like the original, has become so crazed by his reading that he has hit upon the idea of putting what he has read into practice.

How he ever hit upon this idea it is hard to imagine. For there is a pessimistic wisdom in the epics which discourages any attempt to carry them out in practice. The war epics seem to say that it is possible to win battles but not to win wars, that wars end in the mutual destruction of those who fight them. The journey epics seem to say that it is possible to come home from the journey but not to bring home immortality, that the journey ends in the human situation from which it began. The creation epics seem to say that it is possible to subdue the power of evil but not to destroy it, that the attempt to destroy evil ends in being destroyed by evil.

It is conceivable, though, that a man might act upon this very wisdom itself, however pessimistic. Maybe this is the way to turn poetry into truth. Instead of enacting the story, one could act upon the moral of the story. This could mean not entering into the wars and journeys of mankind and the struggles of God against evil. Or it could mean, realizing that one is already involved in all these things, withdrawing from them. Or it could mean, knowing that one is so involved in these things that one cannot truly withdraw from them, playing one's part in them without illusion. Nikos Kazantzakis, who wished to be a man of this last sort, wanted the inscription on his tombstone to read "I have no hope, I have no fear, I am free."[6] Living this out would mean being free to fight battles without hope of winning wars or fear of losing them. It would mean being free to go upon the journey without hope of bringing home immortality or fear of coming home to die. It would mean being free to struggle against evil or join God's struggle against it without hope of destroying it or fear of letting it survive.

This is the kind of thing advocated in the Gita, renouncing the fruit of action without withdrawing from action. The Gita itself is a discourse placed in the midst of a great war epic, the *Mahabharata,* but its message could be generalized and applied to the poetry of journey and creation as well as to that of war. Enforcing the meaning of the Gita, as Gandhi endeavored to do, would be more like acting upon the moral of the story than acting out the story itself. The *Mahabharata* was the story; the Gita was really a statement of the moral of the story. The question for experiment is "What would happen to a man if he were to act upon the moral of the story?" Would his story be essentially the same as the original recounted in the epics or would it be quite a new and different story?

As it is told in the *Mahabharata* the story of war is a tale of mutual destruction. There are winners, to be sure; the five brothers who are the chief heroes of the epic destroy their enemies, but their entire army is destroyed afterwards in a night raid by the survivors of their enemies. This appears to be typical of epic literature on war. In the *Iliad* the Achaians are to defeat the Trojans and burn their city, but they themselves are to be decimated in the war and in the voyage home.[7] The tale of mutual destruction is not only the story of war, perhaps we could say, but also the history of war, whether we think of ancient wars like these or medieval wars like the Crusades or modern wars like the religious wars of early modern times or the revolutionary wars and the world wars of more recent times. The inner logic of the story and the history seems to be that the purposes and cross-purposes of the opposing sides cancel one another out and the outcome is something intended by neither, mutual destruction in whole or in part. There is an ancient human wisdom here, venerable and traditional, but surprisingly little known or little perceived even where the story is told and the history recounted.

Still the moral of the story and the lesson of history is not obvious. It is left unstated in most of the epics. The Gita is an exception, but however late it may have been composed it has become an integral part of the epic, a deeper reflection upon the situation of man at war. The moral which it draws from the story of mutual destruction is not what one would expect, that a man should withdraw from war or never enter into it in the first place. It is rather that he should rise above the purposes and cross-purposes involved in the conflict. This is not immediately persuasive. Looked at from below, from the viewpoint of the purposes and cross-purposes themselves, a man who rises above them cannot seem admirable. He appears to be either indifferent to the fate of the antagonists or else bent upon their mutual destruction. Krishna, the incarnate God who is the main speaker in the Gita, is accused of both of these things in the course of the epic. Yet once a man has stepped out of the framework of purpose and cross-purpose and no longer has to see everything in these terms, he can begin to see Krishna's way in its own right.

An objection, nevertheless, can be leveled at this doctrine also by the man who has risen above purpose and cross-purpose. It is that warfare becomes meaningless if its fruits are renounced. This is Gandhi's own criticism of the Gita.[8] Gandhi agreed with the principle of renouncing the fruits of action while not withdrawing from action, but he held that there were some kinds of action, among them all actions entailing violence, which could not be performed at all if their fruits were renounced. A man cannot do violence, according to this, without becoming a violent man within. So Gandhi held for the renunciation of all violence. The only kind of action which can be performed while renouncing its fruits, he believed, is nonviolent action. To replace violence and warfare in the ordinary sense, therefore, he developed the theory and practice of *Satyagraha,* "truth-force" or nonviolent resistance.[9]

It may well be, though, that there is really no question of entering or not entering into warfare, that a man is already so involved in the struggles of mankind that he cannot truly extricate himself from them. If this is true, then the doctrine of the Gita looks more feasible than it would if a man had to have a motive for entering into those struggles or for not withdrawing from them. Gandhi's nonviolent action, in fact, is a way of being involved in the struggles of mankind without doing violence. Instead of regarding it as a renunciation of violence and a replacement of violence by something else, as Gandhi himself regarded it, we could regard it as a transformation of violence into action the essence of which is communication. Regarding it this way could make a difference. Instead of trying to suppress what is violent within himself a man could be seeking to transform it. Both suppression and transformation would lead to nonviolent action, to communication instead of violence, but suppression would leave part of the man behind while transformation could bring the whole man into action.

Whether violence is transformed or whether it is suppressed the story of war is considerably changed. Let us see now if something similar happens to the story of the journey. The central role played by violence in the story of war seems in the story of the journey to be played by sexuality. If the war epics tell of the sorrows of war, the journey epics tell of the sorrows of love. The *Ramayana* tells of the sufferings of Rama and his wife Sita, what Rama must go through to win back Sita from the demon-king Ravana, and what Sita must go through to remain faithful to Rama during her captivity. The *Odyssey* tells of the sufferings of Odysseus and his wife Penelope, what Odysseus must go through to reach home again and what he must then go through to win back Penelope from her suitors, and what Penelope must go through to remain faithful to Odysseus during his absence. The great temptation against love, according to these stories, is demonic, the desire, as it were, to be more than mortal man or woman. Sita must resist the allurements of a demon; Odysseus must resist the allurements of goddesses and the offer of immortality.[10]

The moral of the story of love is as difficult to draw as that of the story of war, and here we have no Gita to draw it for us. Insofar as the story of love, and the history of love too for that matter, is a tale of suffering, a man might conclude that it would be better for him never to engage in love, much as he might conclude from the story of war that it would be better for him never to go to war. Or, if he is already involved in love, he might conclude that he should withdraw from it, much as he might conclude that he should have nothing further to do with war. On the other hand, he might realize that he is so involved in love that he cannot truly withdraw from it or avoid entering into it, that fleeing from sexuality is tantamount to fleeing from mortality and attempting to be more than mortal man. This would be like realizing that he is so implicated in the wars and struggles of mankind that he cannot really escape them or stand aloof from them. The only way of rising above the sorrows of love after he realized all this would be to love and yet renounce the fruits of love, like the Gita's way of rising above the sorrows of war, to act and yet renounce the fruits of action.

Gandhi's approach to sex was the same as his approach to violence—total renunciation. He was married at the age of thirteen and he had four children, but he began to abstain from intercourse at the age of thirty-one and vowed celibacy at the age of thirty-seven. His term for celibacy, *Brahmacharya,*[11] suggests a comparison with *Satyagraha,* his term for nonviolent action. Apparently the idea was not simply to renounce sexuality but to replace it with another form of love. Certainly his idea with regard to violence was not simply to give it up and practice nonresistance but to replace it with a nonviolent form of resistance. Judging from his life and paralleling the Gita's doctrine on action, we could define his *Brahmacharya* as love renouncing the fruits of love, pleasure, and procreation. If a man were to love and yet renounce pleasure and procreation, his love would become more and more universal, extending to ever-widening circles until it embraced all mankind. This is what was supposed to happen, according to Gandhi's views, and it is what seems actually to have happened in his own life.

The question remains, analogous to the one we asked about action, whether renouncing the fruits of love has to mean suppressing sexuality or whether it can mean transforming it. There are three acts, it seems, which can have a place in any human interaction: giving, receiving, and taking. Renouncing the fruits of action means abstaining from taking what is not given, for in taking one is intent merely on obtaining the fruits and not on the quality of one's action. It does not mean abstaining from giving and receiving. Thus it does not mean that the action will be fruitless but only that the fruit will be measured by the nobility of the action, and not vice versa the action by the desirability of the fruit. Human intercourse is a giving and a receiving; it does not have to be a taking of what is not given. Sexual intercourse too, we could say, is a giving and a receiving, and it can be a giving and receiving without taking. To seek the fruits of love would be to measure love by its fruits, pleasure and procreation. To renounce the fruits would be to measure the fruits instead by the love, by the giving and receiving. It would not have to mean suppressing sexuality itself, therefore, and rendering it fruitless.

If sex and violence were to be transformed like this, by renouncing their fruit, the story of the journey and the war would perhaps be changed as much as if they had been totally renounced. The question as to what should be done about them, whether to transform them or to abolish and replace them or to leave them be, is linked to the question as to whether they are ultimately evil and hurtful to man. Let us consider in this light the struggle against evil described in the epics of creation. In the most ancient tales, such as the Babylonian creation epic the *Enuma Elish,* the struggle is a combat between a god and a monster: the god may suffer temporary defeat but in the end he subdues the monster and establishes the present order of the world. There are comparable tales, however, in which the hero is a human being. In a modern version of the story, Melville's great novel *Moby Dick,* the hero is a human being and is killed in the act of killing the monster.

Perhaps we can take the monsters of these tales to embody the dark forces of sex and violence. The nonhuman character of the monsters and their divine antagonists would be explainable, on this hypothesis, by the fact that none of these forces, neither the evil nor the good, is the human being but only a power at work within him. Man is the battleground of these powers and so cannot identify himself with one of them nor truly side with one of them. He cannot take sides in the struggle without part of himself being on the other side. If he were to take sides, then he would be destroyed himself in the very moment of destroying the monster, as Melville's hero Ahab is killed in the very moment of killing the great white whale Moby Dick. So it would seem that his aim should be to resolve the struggle by renouncing the fruits of a victory for either side, even for the side of good. This would be analogous to the doctrine of the Gita on renouncing the fruits of action, except that it would refer to the struggle going on within man rather than to the struggle between man and man.

The lesson of these tales makes one wonder about Gandhi's experiments with truth, whether Gandhi was not trying like Ahab to kill the monster. Gandhi's aim in all his experiments, he said, was "self-realization, to see God face to face, to attain *Moksha*";[12] to resolve, perhaps we could say, the struggle going on within man. *Satyagraha* was an experiment in action without violence, *Brahmacharya* an experiment in love without sex, both of them experiments dealing with the struggles and relations between man and man, between man and woman. *Moksha,* on the other hand, was not so much peace among men as peace within man; it was the achievement of the *Sat* or "truth" in *Satyagraha* and the *Brahman* or "prayer" in *Brahmacharya*; it was the liberation of man from the overpowering influence, from the illusions, from the turmoil of violence and sex. The liberation of India for which Gandhi lived was primarily this inner liberation of the Indian and of Gandhi himself in particular, though it meant a transformation of human relations and hence a political and economic and social revolution in which human relations would no longer be based on sex and violence. It was to be, as in the creation story, a killing of the monster and an establishment of the new order.

The alternatives we have considered to Gandhi's action without violence and love without sex, namely a transformed violence and sexuality, would also lead towards a resolution of the struggle within man. It would be more like the fairy tales, though, where the monster proves to be an enchanted prince than the creation epics where the monster is killed. Or it would be like the creation epics in which the world is not simply purified of the monster's presence but a new world is built out of the monster's slain body.[13] Sex and violence, according to our alternatives, would be essentially good and integral to man. The enchantment which turns them into monsters would be the spell cast by seeking their fruits. Violence, when its fruits were renounced, would turn into action; sex, when its fruits were renounced, would turn into love.

It would be an experiment with truth to determine whether violence really could be transformed into action and sex into love. So far, instead of actually transforming them, we have merely been carrying out a "thought experiment." In physics a thought experiment is an imaginary experiment carried out with imaginary apparatus under imaginary conditions but with no violation of the basic laws of physics. It is this last stipulation, "with no violation of the basic laws of physics," that makes the thought experiment actually pertinent to physical reality. The corresponding stipulation for our experiment would be "with no violation of the basic limits of the human condition." Turning poetry into truth, as we have set out to do, requires us to begin in imagination but to end in reality. We have begun in imagination with the poetry of war and journey and creation. But we have not ended in the truth of life. Rather we have ended in imagination too, imagining what it would be to enact these stories and what it would be to act upon their moral. The pertinence of our imaginings to the truth of life depends on their not violating the limits of the human condition, the limits which appear in "limit situations"[14] such as death, suffering, guilt, strife, and chance.

The pessimistic wisdom which we have found in the epics is a possible definition of the human condition and its limits: the mutual destruction involved in strife, the inevitability of death, the impossibility of eliminating death, suffering, guilt, strife, and chance from human life. To imagine, as we have, a man acting upon this wisdom is of course to imagine something compatible with it, something which does not violate the limits it defines. Yet the thing we are imagining is really a testing of the limits of the human condition. So we cannot simply assume that we already know the limits and proceed to think within them.

To see what really is possible in love and action we must go beyond imagination to actual practice. We have so far a promising thought experiment, but there is no substitute for something like the "forty years' unremitting endeavor" which led Gandhi "in all humility" to disagree with the Gita.[15] Maybe we will find that love and action as we have imagined them cannot really exist, that sexuality and violence belong to the human condition in such a way that man is only deceiving himself when he attempts to renounce their fruits. Maybe we will find that this kind of love and action can exist but only under Gandhi's conditions, that renouncing the fruits of sexuality and violence amounts to renouncing sexuality and violence themselves. Maybe we will find that the love and action we have imagined can exist, that sexuality and violence can be transformed. Even then we will learn something unexpected and unimagined. We will learn what a transformed sexuality and violence are actually like.

Let our first step be the inverse experiment of turning the truth of life into poetry. This sounds like another thought experiment and indeed it is an experiment in imagination. The effect of turning the truth of one's life into poetry, though, should be to transform the truth of one's life. If a man were to make poetry out of his experience of love and war, this should have a transforming effect on love and war in his life. Let us see what this effect would be and how near it would come to the transformation of sexuality into love and of violence into action.

2. *Turning Truth into Poetry*

"You know my uttermost when it was best," wrote Donne, "and even then I did best when I had least truth for my subjects. In this present case there is so much truth as it defeats all poetry."[16] I am afraid that may be so in this present case too. We have set ourselves the formidable task of somehow making poetry of the truth of our lives and times. One way of going about it would be to make stories of our experience of love and war, stories of war and journey and creation such as we found in the ancient epics. After what we have seen, though, about acting upon the moral of the epics instead of enacting the epics themselves, a more promising way would be to turn our truth into poetry like that of the Gita, the poetry of the moral rather than the story. The limitation of the Gita was that it dealt only with war and not with love. We must attempt something of its kind, but dealing with love as well as with war. Perhaps we should try to combine the Hindu story of incarnation with the Christian story, for what the Gita does with war, the Gospels do with love. This, if we do it, will amount to transforming poetry into poetry, to be sure, but it will also mean transforming truth into poetry insofar as our own experience of love and war will have to guide us in making over the poetry.

Let the literary form of our poetry be that of an essay of the imagination rather than that of verse. Kierkegaard drew upon the poetry of the Gospels in what he called "an essay of the imagination,"[17] his famous parable of the king who loved a humble maiden. Let us go and do likewise, but with the Gospels and the Gita, with love and with war.

Consider the following parable. I call it the Parable of the Mountain. Man, let us say, is climbing a mountain. At the top of the mountain, he thinks, is God. Down in the valley are the cares and concerns of human life, all the troubles of love and war. By climbing the mountain and reaching the top man hopes to escape from all these miseries. God, on the other hand, is coming down the mountain, let us say, his desire being to plunge himself into the very things that man wishes to escape. Man's desire is to be God, God's is to be man.[18] God and man pass one another going in opposite directions. When man reaches the top of the mountain he is going to find nothing. God is not there. Let us suppose that man does reach the top and does make this discovery. Or suppose that he passes God on the way, or finds God's tracks leading downwards, or hears a rumor that God is descending the mountain. One way or another man learns that climbing was a mistake and that what he seeks is to be found only by going down into the valley. He turns around, therefore, and starts going down the mountain. He sets his face towards love and war, where before he had turned his back upon them.

The experience or "truth" to which this parable gives expression is twofold. There is the experience of climbing and the experience of going down the mountain. The one is the experience of escaping, or at least attempting to escape, the troubles of love and war. The other is the contrary experience of deliberately plunging oneself into those troubles. Earlier we said that a man cannot "truly" withdraw from the troubles of love and war. Here we are saying that there is a "truth" of withdrawal and a "truth" of return. What we said earlier is perhaps what a man might say on his return, comparing the experience of withdrawal with that of return. Maybe to say that he cannot truly withdraw is the same as saying that he does not find God at the top of the mountain or that the God he finds is not the true God. He would only say this after he had somehow experienced an emptiness at the top of the mountain and a fullness at the bottom of the valley.

It might be illuminating to compare and contrast our story with Plato's well-known Parable of the Cave.[19] According to Plato's parable man lives in an underground cave and sees only by firelight. If a man were to climb up into the world above and see by sunlight, he would realize that he had been living in a world of shadows; if then he were to descend once more into the cave underground, he might try telling the men still living there about the daylight world. There is an ascent and a descent in Plato's story as in ours, but the truth is found in his by ascending; the only purpose of descending again is to bring the truth to others. Thus it could seem that our Parable of the Mountain is the exact reverse of the Parable of the Cave. Yet this is not quite so. If the wisdom which is found at the top of the ascent is a negative wisdom, a "knowledge of ignorance"[20] like the wisdom of Socrates, then it might well compare with the experience of emptiness at the top of the mountain. If, on the other hand, the experience of fullness at the bottom of the valley arises from a sharing of truth with others, then it might well compare with the experience of returning to the cave. What our parable would be saying that Plato's parable does not say is, first of all, that the ascent is at once a pursuit and a flight, that in climbing the mountain a man is pursuing the truth but he is also fleeing from the things he dreads in the valley, love and war.

The fear of love drives a man to the pursuit of autonomy. He desires to be so self-contained, to have such inner wealth that he will need no other person outside of himself. He fears needing another, having his happiness depend on another, having to bring along others with him wherever he goes. It is like the "many-body problem" in physics and mathematics. The motion of one body is a simple matter; the two-body problem is much more complex and much harder to solve; the three-body problem is thought to be insoluble. The happiness of one person likewise seems quite feasible; that of two is considerably more difficult to achieve; that of more than two seems almost unattainable. Thus a man could well be afraid of involving himself with others in the pursuit of happiness. This would be the thing he dreads in love. Still, the fear of love is as ambivalent as the fear of falling. A man clings to the side of the mountain for fear of falling and yet he is tempted to look down, and the fascination of it may actually cause him to fall. He desires autonomy and he fears losing it, and yet there is another side of him which is fascinated by the thought of losing autonomy and of taking away the autonomy of others.

The ambition to which the fear of war drives a man is much akin to that of autonomy; it is that of power. He desires to have such power as to be unassailable, such strength that no one would dare attack him. He fears being involved in any kind of conflict with others, being in danger of losing his life or his reputation or whatever else he holds dear, being compelled to fight for these things and to gamble with them. Climbing the mountain in fear of love, a man is searching for solitude. Climbing it in fear of war, he is searching for a vantage point, a retreat, a fastness. The fear of war is as ambivalent as the fear of love. It is not at all peaceful. It drives a man to stockpile weapons, to make himself ever more powerful and ever less assailable. What he would want most of all, it is true, is a perfectly bloodless victory in which he would so terrify his enemy as to make him surrender or flee or never even approach. The dread of actually being attacked, of actually having to fight, of actually risking defeat, though, can fascinate him with the weapons of war. It can fascinate him with power and lead him into the very thing he fears. It is like the vertigo we find in the fear of love. It will not lead him to climb down; it will lead him to fall down the mountain.

Let us suppose, nevertheless, that he does not fall, that he actually reaches the top, that he achieves autonomy and power, that he is safe at last from the troubles of love and war. What is it like there at the top? The essence of both autonomy and power, I would say, is knowledge: it is knowledge that gives a man a rich interior life, so that he is less in need of friends outside of himself; it is knowledge that gives him the tactics and strategy to defeat any enemies. He will probably never reach the top of the mountain if he tries to achieve power and autonomy through something more external than knowledge, for instance through money. For this would make him dependent on things outside himself and would leave him weak and insufficient in himself. Yet even his knowledge, however interior it is to him, is knowledge of something and to that extent is dependent on the outside. The only way we can make him completely autonomous and get his power completely inside of him is to make his knowledge its own object. This is Aristotle's definition of God, "a knowing of knowing,"[21] and it became Hegel's definition of the autonomous human spirit.

A knowing of knowing would be like a view from a mountaintop. By knowing all about knowing itself one would know in some manner everything there is to know. It would be like seeing everything from a great height. One would see everything near and far, all the way to the horizon, but there would be some loss of detail on account of the distances. The knowing of knowing would mean being in possession of all the various methods of knowing. It would mean knowing how an artist thinks, putting a thing together; knowing how a scientist thinks, taking a thing apart; knowing how a practical man thinks, sizing up a situation; knowing how a man of understanding thinks, grasping the principle of a thing; knowing how a man of wisdom thinks, reflecting upon human experience. It could mean being able to think in all these ways, being an artist, a scientist, a practical man, a man of understanding and a man of wisdom all in one. What it could not mean, if we are to make it humanly possible, is actually having put all things together, taken all things apart, sized up all situations, grasped all principles, and reflected upon all human experience.

Of course we could imagine a God who had equivalently done all these things, a God who by the knowing of knowing would, without any restriction, know all there is to know. He would have the richest imaginable interior life and so would have no need of anyone or anything outside of himself. Also, insofar as knowledge is power, he would have the greatest imaginable power, and his power would be the power of knowledge. His also would be a view from the mountaintop, but his sight would be keener than man's and would not be obscured by the distances. He would be the envy of man, the implicit ideal of all man's striving in climbing up the mountain.

In Zen tradition there was a mad poet called Han-shan, "Cold Mountain." He is pictured dressed in rags and leaning on a broom. To those who thought he was crazy his advice in one of his poems was "Try and make it to Cold Mountain."[22] Perhaps we should say the same about our mountain. It is all very well for us to say that ultimately the thing for man to do is turn around and go down the mountain into the valley. Only one who has climbed the mountain and seen what there is on top can understand what this is all about. One would have to know what things look like from the mountaintop, what the knowing of knowing is like, what peace of mind there is in being somehow beyond the troubles of love and war, before one would know what one is doing, deliberately going down the mountain and entering into the valley. Maybe the only thing that can be said to a man before he has finished climbing is "Try and make it to Cold Mountain."

At the top of the mountain, as we have been describing it, there is a kind of madness—not the madness that consists in having lost one's reason, but a madness that consists in having lost everything *except* one's reason.[23] The knowing of knowing, to be sure, seems worthy of God and worthy of man. The only thing wrong is that man at the top of the mountain, by escaping from love and war, will have lost everything else. He will have withdrawn into that element of his nature which is most characteristic of him and sets him apart from other animals. It is the thing in him which is most human. Perhaps indeed he will never realize what it is to be human unless he does attempt this withdrawal. Even so, the realization that he has lost everything except his reason, that he has found pure humanity but not full humanity, changes his wisdom from a knowledge of knowledge into a knowledge of ignorance. He realizes that he has something yet to learn, something that he cannot learn at the top of the mountain but only at the bottom of the valley.

Once a man has been to the top of the mountain he can never be the same. He will inevitably be something of a Han-shan, a Cold Mountain, for the rest of his life, and he will always retain the ability to return once again to Cold Mountain if he finds the valley intolerable. He cannot simply forget what it is like up there and plunge into the affairs of the valley, as if he could be transported from the top to the bottom without actually climbing down. Rather he must descend the mountain, step by step, perhaps by the same paths as he ascended. If at the summit he experienced a knowing of knowing, he will be unable simply to forget his knowledge and turn to love and war. He will have to come to love and war by means of knowledge. He will have to make his way to them through the art, the science, the prudence, the understanding, the wisdom of loving and of warfare. He will have to think his way through autonomy in order to plunge himself into love. He will have to think his way through power in order to plunge himself into war.

Going from an ideal of autonomy to one of love, he will probably have to think of love as the love of autonomous persons for one another, a love in which autonomy is not violated. A love in which he were to give up his autonomy or take away that of another person would appear evil to him. He would describe it, no doubt, as "using" another person or "being used" by another. His ethic will be the rule that a person is to be treated as an end and never as a means to an end.[24] The art of loving for him will be the art of making love within the limits imposed by the ethic of autonomy, loving and yet not enslaving the other person, being loved and yet preserving his own freedom. In analyzing his relations with others, as he will be very prone to do, he will tend to be suspicious of any taint of using or enslavement.

These will be the terms in which he will tend to size up situations of love, for instance triangles in which two persons are in love with one. The principle of love as he understands it will be distance in intimacy, rather than pure intimacy. The lessons he will learn from the experience of love, however, with such ideals, will probably be somewhat discouraging lessons; how the distance between two persons can abolish their intimacy, or how the intimacy between them can abolish their distance.

When it comes to war he will be torn between using violence to do away with the enslavement of some human beings by others and abstaining from violence as itself a violation of the autonomy of others. Coming from an ideal of power to one of struggling for freedom, he will probably have to think of freedom as power, especially the kind of power he has known, the power of knowledge. War he will see as being much more a battle of wits than a clash of brute forces. This will be partly a carry-over from his old desire for bloodless victories and his fear of bloody fighting, partly a result of his new desire to avoid doing violence. The science of war for him will be the analysis of every battle into a battle of wits. The art of war will be in turning every clash of brute forces into such a battle; the prudence of war will be in sizing up a struggle and seeing what is possible and what is impossible in it to force and to wit; the understanding of war will be in grasping the principle at work in human struggles, that the outcome is never victory for one side but a resultant of the opposing purposes. But the wisdom of war, the lessons he will learn from it, like those he learns from love, may turn out to be somewhat discouraging, how the clash of brute forces is not easily changed into a battle of wits and how the result is likely to be mutual destruction rather than the realization of some higher good.

These discouraging lessons which he learns about love and war will show him that he is still climbing down the mountain, that he hasn't yet reached the bottom. There is a wisdom at the bottom of the mountain, let us say, just as there is at the top. The God we imagined at the top had a wisdom which amounted to a knowing of knowing, a knowledge which gave him complete and inviolable autonomy. If we were to imagine a God at the bottom, we would have to imagine him possessing a wisdom which could see through autonomy itself. He would be like the incarnate God of Christianity and Hinduism. He would know, like Jesus, that love means giving up autonomy, giving it up autonomously maybe ("No one takes my life from me; I lay it down of myself"),[25] but giving it up nonetheless. He would know, like Krishna, that war means being in real opposition to other persons; perhaps without seeking thereby to make them means to an end ("renouncing the fruits of action"), but being in opposition to them nonetheless.

When autonomy is still the prime value, giving it up can only seem to be masochism, taking it away can only seem to be sadism. This is the way things appear to a man fleeing from the affairs of the valley and trying to make his way to the top of the mountain. He is indeed tempted to masochism and sadism. This is the way love and war look to him when he looks at them over his shoulder, fleeing from them. The masochism he is tempted to does indeed amount to giving up personal autonomy; the sadism amounts to taking away the autonomy of other persons. But the perverse pleasure which tempts him in the thought of these things is nothing more than the perverse fascination contained in his fears. His temptation to masochism is the fascination which accompanies his fear of love and sexuality; his temptation to sadism is the fascination which accompanies his fear of war and bloodshed. Coming down the mountain, he will see these same things ahead of him that he formerly saw behind him, but they will look different when he faces them squarely from the way they looked when he glanced at them backwards and asquint.

As he enters the valley, let us say, he sees that he must relinquish the solitude he enjoyed on the mountaintop, give up his autonomous existence and make himself available to others. Once he had thought availability to others a kind of masochism inspired by greed for the pleasure of giving. It would be a life in which there would be no receiving and no willingness to receive but only to give; it would have the effect not of enriching others but only of tainting them with the same greed; it would lead ultimately to giving his life in a kind of suicide, but this death too, like the life, would be fruitless to others, would only burden them with obligation to a similar death. Autonomy, on the other hand, he had conceived to be an ideal state in which giving and receiving would be in balance. There would be no greed, neither that of receiving nor that of giving; if he gave it would be freely and without obligating the other person; if he received it would be equally freely, without feeling any obligation to make a return. Now it seems to him that in fact there is no real giving or receiving in autonomy. (Now he is looking back over his shoulder at autonomy.) For real giving means giving himself and thus, it seems to him, giving up his autonomy, making himself available to others, putting himself at the service of others, willingly becoming a means to the ends of others; and real receiving means letting another person do all this for him.

He had considered war to be essentially a struggle between masters and slaves, or a struggle in which each side was attempting to make slaves of the other. Having no desire to be either a master or a slave, except for that perverse fascination, that sadism and masochism, in his fear of both, he had tried to rise above both of them and live an autonomous existence.[26] Autonomy would be a state, he had thought, in which he would neither be dependent on others nor have others dependent on him. Actually it proved to be a state in which he was *unrelated* to others, in which he had neither friends nor enemies, not to mention masters or slaves. Coming back down from the mountain into the life of the valley, he makes friendship and love possible once more, but by the same act he also makes enmity and war possible. On this second look, however, war does not appear so thoroughly evil as it did before. It seems to him now that it is not merely a struggle between masters and slaves or a struggle to master and enslave. Rather it is a human relationship, the relationship of enmity. A man can be at variance against another man without being either his master or his slave and without eventually becoming either his master or his slave. Instead he can become his friend, or he can remain his enemy. Mastery and slavery are fruits of warfare which can be renounced.

Renouncing mastery and slavery as fruits of warfare perhaps amounts to loving one's enemies: to love one's enemies implies that one has enemies but, if love really means anything here, that one treats them differently than one would otherwise. Only a man who had been to the top of the mountain and had the taste of autonomy would think of doing this. The same is true of sacrificing one's autonomy and receiving the sacrifice of another's autonomy in mutual love and friendship. Only a man to whom autonomy had been a value could value such a sacrifice.

By going to the top of the mountain and coming back down again, therefore, a man does not simply waste his time. He ends up where he began, in the valley, but not in the same state of being. He climbed the mountain to escape from love and war, for he feared that love might so encumber and complicate his pursuit of happiness that he could never be happy, and that war might bring on the loss of everything he already possessed and of his hopes for the future besides. At the top of the mountain he found a self-sufficiency through knowledge, a knowledge which so enriched his inner life that he had no more need for other persons, and which made him so resourceful that he had nothing more to fear from others. When he realized that all he had was knowledge, though, that he had lost everything else by escaping from love and war, he turned around and started to make his way down into the valley again. At first he tried to enter into love and war without losing the self-sufficiency he had gained, but ultimately he found that he had to leave it at the top of the mountain. All he could bring with him was a memory of it and a sense of its relative value. Yet this in itself was enough to work a change for him in love and war down in the valley.

His story is the story of a life and of a time. We have been telling of the withdrawal and return that can take place in an individual life, but simultaneously we have been telling of the historic withdrawal and return that seem to be taking place in our time. Gandhi's "experiments with truth," if we do not reflect on them very deeply, can seem a part of the withdrawal. His *Brahmacharya* can seem a flight from love and his *Satyagraha* can seem a flight from war. Considered more carefully, though, his experiments appear to be rather a part of the return. The flight from love as we described it is a flight from the complications of pursuing the happiness of more than one person. Gandhi's celibacy was not a retreat from the two-person to the one-person situation so much as an advance from the two-person to the many-person situation; his *Brahmacharya* was an experiment in universal love. The flight from war we spoke of is a flight from the struggles of mankind and from the personal risks they involve. Gandhi's nonviolence was not a refusal to fight so much as a willingness to fight with a handicap, namely without using violence, and to run thereby a greater personal risk in the struggles of mankind; his *Satyagraha* was an experiment in courage.

Although it has been many centuries since a great religion shook the world, maybe one is rising now out of the meeting and confluence of the religions of the past. Gandhi's "experiments with truth" are perhaps an indication of what this religion may be like. Its truth need not be simply the common ground of the previous religions. Rather it may be a more comprehensive truth like that to which Gandhi was led by trying to live both the Gita and the Gospel. The God we told of in the valley of love and war seemed to resemble both the incarnate God of love in the Gospel and the incarnate God of war in the Gita. Gandhi went on and tried to combine the truth not only of Christianity and Hinduism but also of Islam and Buddhism. Now let us in our turn, in our own experiments with the truth of the religions, work towards this comprehensive truth step by step. Or if we cannot reach a truth which embraces all the religions, let us try at least to embrace them all in poetry.

NOTES

1. André Malraux, *Anti-Memoirs,* tr. by Terence Kilmartin (New York, Holt, 1968), p. 2.
2. Mohandas Gandhi, *An Autobiography: The Story of My Experiments with Truth,* tr. by Mahadev Desai (Boston, Beacon Press, 1968), p. xiii.
3. Cf. Mahadev Desai (ed. and tr.), *The Gospel of Selfless Action or The Gita According to Gandhi* (Ahmedabad, Navajivan Publishing House, 1956), p. 127.
4. Cf. my discussion of this in *A Search for God in Time and Memory* (New York, Macmillan, 1969), pp. 131 ff.
5. For this classification of epic poetry cf. G. Rachel Levy, *The Sword from the Rock* (London, Faber & Faber, 1953).
6. This is inscribed on his tombstone at Herakleion in Crete. Cf. Kimon Friar in the introduction to his translation of Kazantzakis, *The Saviours of God* (New York, Simon & Schuster, 1969), p. 36. Kazantzakis was something of an epic man, turning poetry into truth, but even more of an epic poet, turning truth into poetry. Cf. his great epic poem *The Odyssey: A Modern Sequel,* tr. by Kimon Friar (New York, Simon & Schuster, 1958).
7. Cf. my discussion of the *Iliad* in *The City of the Gods* (New York, Macmillan, 1965), pp. 29 ff.
8. Cf. Desai, *The Gita According to Gandhi,* pp. 133 f.
9. Cf. Gandhi, *The Story of My Experiments with Truth,* pp. 318 f.
10. Cf. my discussion of the *Odyssey* in *The City of the Gods,* pp. 67 ff.
11. Cf. Gandhi, *The Story of My Experiments with Truth,* pp. 204 ff. and 316 ff. Note, however, that *Brahmacharya* is a traditional term, whereas *Satyagraha* is a word coined by Gandhi himself. Erik Erikson's book on Gandhi, *Gandhi's Truth* (New York, Norton, 1969), being the work of a psychoanalyst, is especially interesting on Gandhi's approach to sex and on the relation of this to his approach to violence.
12. Gandhi, *The Story of My Experiments with Truth,* p. *xii.*
13. Cf. my discussion of transforming the dark forces in *A Search for God in Time and Memory,* pp. 175 ff.
14. This is Karl Jaspers' term. Cf. his *Philosophie,* vol. 2 (Berlin, Julius Springer, 1932), pp. 201 ff.
15. Cf. Desai, *The Gita According to Gandhi,* pp. 133 f.
16. John Donne in the letter to Sir Robert Carr accompanying his poem "An Hymne to the Saints, and to Marquesse Hamylton" in Herbert Grierson (ed.), *The Poems of John Donne,* vol. 1 (London, Oxford University Press, 1953), p. 288.
17. Soren Kierkegaard, *Philosophical Fragments,* tr. by David Swenson and Howard Hong (Princeton, N.J., Princeton University Press, 1962), the title of Chapter Two, p. 28.
18. Cf. my discussion of man's passion to be God and God's passion to be man in *A Search for God in Time and Memory,* pp. 20 ff.
19. Plato, *Republic,* VII, 514 ff.
20. Plato, *Apology,* 21 ff.
21. Aristotle, *Metaphysics,* Λ, 1074b34. Cf. also *ibid.,* 1072b18–31, which Hegel quotes to conclude his *Encyclopedia.*
22. This is Gary Snyder's translation in *Evergreen Review,* vol. 2, no. 6

(autumn 1958), p. 79. Cf. also Arthur Waley's translation in *Encounter,* vol. 3, no. 3 (September 1954), p. 6, and Burton Watson's translation in *Cold Mountain* (New York, Grove, 1962), p. 75.

23. This is Chesterton's definition of a madman, "the man who has lost everything except his reason," in *Orthodoxy* (New York & London, John Lane, 1909), p. 32.
24. This is Kant's formulation in *Fundamental Principles of the Metaphysics of Ethics,* tr. by Otto Manthey-Zorn (New York & London, D. Appleton-Century, 1938), p. 47. Observe how Kant comes to this idea after an experience of the "knowing of knowing" in his *Critique of Pure Reason.*
25. John 10:18.
26. Cf. my discussion of Hegel on the masters and the slaves in *The City of the Gods,* pp. 189 f.

II

The Simple Life

THE STORY IS TOLD of Tolstoy that he was walking in a forest one day when he came into a clearing and saw a lizard sitting upon a stone, sunning himself. Tolstoy began speaking to the lizard. "Your heart is beating," he said, "the sun is shining, you're happy." After a pause, he added, "I'm not."[1]

Why is it not enough for a man that the sun is shining and his heart is beating? "Everything is burning," Gotama said in his famous Fire Sermon.[2] A man's flesh is burning, his spirit is burning, burning with desire. It is not merely a matter of the flesh and the spirit being in conflict. A man can go the way of luxury, trying to satisfy the desires of the flesh; he can go the way of asceticism, trying to satisfy the desires of the spirit. The point of Buddha's parable of fire is that it does no good to try and satisfy desire; this simply feeds the fire with more fuel. The desire that was satisfied yesterday arises again today and is stronger and more insistent for having been satisfied yesterday. Man, according to this, will never reach the point where he is content, where it will be enough for him that his heart is beating and the sun is shining.

Maybe there is some bliss for him, nevertheless, other than mere contentment. Imagine a burning hunger and thirst. There is such a thing as food which gives nourishment without satisfying hunger and drink which gives strength without quenching thirst. Maybe there is, analogous to such food and drink, a whole way of life which leads to well-being even though it does not lead to contentment.

Gotama seems in his own life to have found such a way. At the age of twenty-nine he renounced luxury and became an ascetic. After seven years of searching he discovered a way to bliss, a way midway between luxury and asceticism. Moved by compassion he spent the remainder of his life, over forty years, sharing his discovery with others. Perhaps this could be a guiding image for a man: first he must find the middle way, and then he must spend the rest of his life sharing the insight with others. The life of Jesus has this same simple structure, only it is greatly telescoped. Instead of seven years in the wilderness Jesus spent only forty days. Instead of some forty years of public life Jesus had only one year or perhaps three.

These lives may be deceptively simple. Other men, even very great ones, seem never to have found the kind of peace which Gotama and Jesus apparently enjoyed. One of Augustine's biographers speaks of his "lost future,"[3] the peace of mind which Augustine had hoped to attain by his conversion and never did. Goethe, in spite of all the optimism which appears in his writing, says that he experienced hardly four weeks of genuine well-being in his entire life.[4] Tolstoy admitted to the lizard that he was not happy. Gandhi, who incidentally was greatly influenced by Tolstoy, endeavored throughout his life to free himself of the passions of sex and violence but acknowledged in his autobiography that he had not succeeded.[5] Wittgenstein, also considerably influenced by Tolstoy, said on his deathbed, "Tell them I've had a wonderful life," but his biographer expresses astonishment at this, saying that Wittgenstein's life appeared to him "fiercely unhappy."[6]

We may already have the answer to this in Gotama's Fire Sermon: desire cannot be satisfied and so happiness or peace in the form of contentment is not possible. Bliss, nevertheless, is still possible, the bliss of Gotama's middle way and of Jesus' beatitudes. The inner peace of Gotama and Jesus themselves was apparently not one of contentment—consider, for instance, the agony of Jesus in the Garden of Olives. This makes it all the more mysterious and tantalizing. It is truly a "peace that passeth understanding."[7] Evidently the only way to taste it is to follow their paths, to experiment with their ways. Gotama's seven years in the wilderness were indeed seven years of experimenting with truth. They are the prototype of Gandhi's experiments. Jesus' forty days in the desert may have been a greatly foreshortened but similar venture. Let us see to what extent we can rediscover the paths they followed.

1. The Way of the Individual

The remarkable thing about Gotama the Buddha was that he walked alone, without a friend, even without a God. Without a friend, though he was very ready to share with others everything he had discovered—without a God, though he seems to have enjoyed an inward bliss like that of a man at peace with God. He would not allow anyone to call him "friend"[8]: he had many disciples and admirers, but there was no one with whom he had enough in common to be an intimate friend. There was no personal God in his teaching, although Nirvana as he described it has many of the attributes of God, but there was no God to whom one could pray and whose companionship one could enjoy in life. Gotama's way, at least from this point of view, presupposes less than any other great religion, Hinduism, Judaism, Christianity, or Islàm. It is the simplest and starkest way of all.

This makes it very helpful for purposes of experiment. It adds an element of control which would otherwise be largely missing in experiments with the truth of the religions. What is called a "controlled experiment" in science is a complex set of tests, some of which simply repeat the main test with one alteration in order to determine what role a given factor may have played in the main test. For example, a chemical substance may be tested and then another test may be performed called a "blank determination" in which the substance is omitted in order to ascertain the effect of the other factors involved (such as impurities in the reagents). Gotama's way, for our purposes, is like a "blank determination" in which divine and human companionship is omitted in order to ascertain the effect of the other factors involved in a great religion. Other religions promise man the attainment of bliss, but they assume that he will walk with God along the way to it. We can learn from Gotama's way whether a man can attain bliss who walks alone.

There is a parable in which Gotama explained why he refused to speak like other religious teachers about God and the soul. It is his Parable of the Arrow.[9] A man, he said, was shot with a poisoned arrow. When others wanted to pull out the arrow and tend the wound, the victim refused them. He would not have the arrow pulled until he knew who shot the arrow, what kind of arrow was used, and what kind of poison was put on it. Before all this could be learned, of course, the man died of the poison in his wound. It is similar, Gotama said, with the man who wants to know all about God and the soul before he will do anything about his own suffering and misery. He will die before he learns all he wants to know. The Buddha's teaching, therefore, has nothing to say about God and the soul and such matters. Its purpose is simply to instruct a man about suffering and about bliss, about the way that leads to suffering and the way that leads to bliss. Thus Gotama did not deny the existence of God or the existence of the soul (although his refusal to talk about the soul has ordinarily been interpreted this way); he simply refused to offer any teaching on them.

He found his own way to bliss by a method of trial and error, so to speak, trying the way of luxury and finding it unsatisfactory, then trying the way of asceticism and finding it unsatisfactory too, and finally, through insight into his failure, discovering a middle way between luxury and asceticism. The first thing one would think of doing would be to learn from his mistakes and not attempt to find bliss along the way of luxury or that of asceticism, but to enter immediately upon the middle way. This is what his disciples tried to do. His descriptions of the way, however, are not that helpful. He called it the Eightfold Path of "right view, right resolve, right speech, right action, right livelihood, right effort, right thought, and right meditation."[10] It makes one feel like Pilate asking Jesus "What is truth?" but the inevitable question is "What is right view, right resolve, right speech, right action, right livelihood, right effort, right thought, and right meditation?" Maybe there is no way of finding out except by trial and error, by trying the ways of luxury and asceticism, and by discovering and eliminating the causes of their failure to lead man to bliss.

The way of luxury, as far as Gotama's personal experience went, was not the life of an adventurer but simply childhood and youth in well-to-do circumstances. The personal experience of Jesus before going out into the desert was childhood and youth in rather poor circumstances. For our purposes an experience of childhood and youth is sufficient. The problem is not to gain complete experience of all the ins and outs of self-indulgence, to live the life of an adventurer like Casanova, but to examine the experience we already have to the point where it becomes clear to us why a young man like Gotama went into the forest and why a young man like Jesus went into the desert.

There are many facts in a man's experience which he will ordinarily dismiss as mere "coincidences," such as the persons he happens to meet, the course which events happen to take in his life, the words which happen to be spoken to him, the thoughts which happen to occur to him. The facts of his life, on the other hand, which are regular occurrences in every human life, such as birth and death, childhood, youth, manhood and age, love and war, he will ordinarily take in stride. He dismisses the coincidences because, however appropriate and significant the concurrence of events may be, there is no apparent causal connection among them. He takes the regular occurrences in stride because the very fact that they occur regularly seems to him to imply that they should not change the normal pace of his life or cause him to lose his equilibrium or interfere with his regular activities. In both cases he gives no further thought to his experiences. The coincidences do not make sense anyway, he believes, and so there is no use trying to understand them. The regular occurrences make sense by virtue of being regular and so, he believes, he understands them already and need not look into them further.

Now if there were a man who never dismissed a fact of his experience as a mere coincidence, he would have difficulty taking in stride the facts which regularly occur in human lives. The regular occurrence of a fact would not constitute an explanation in his eyes. For instance a young man, let us say, is confronted with the fact that men grow old, take sick, and die, and that this will eventually happen to him too, though he is now young and healthy and alive. If he is accustomed to finding significance and appropriateness in the coincidences of his life, in the persons he meets, in the course events take, in the words that are spoken to him, in the thoughts that occur to him, he is likely to look for significance and appropriateness also in these other facts of his life. He is not likely to be satisfied with the thought that old age, sickness, and death are things which happen to everybody. Instead of taking them in stride he is likely to let these prospects change the normal pace of his life, to upset his equilibrium and interfere with his regular activities. He will not be able to continue his life as before like the man who never gives such things a second thought.

We can imagine something like this happening to Gotama. According to tradition the experience which decided him to leave home and enter the forest was the sight of a sick man, an old man, and a dead man.[11] We can verify the experience for ourselves. The mere sight of a sick man, an old man, and a dead man, to be sure, is not enough. But if we break the habit of dismissing the individual facts of our lives as mere coincidences and make a habit of treating them instead as significant and appropriate events, then the common facts of life, the ones which recur in every human life, will acquire a power to upset us. The prospect of sickness, old age, and death will make it impossible to continue living as before and will make it seem necessary to enter upon a new way.

But why should the new way be the way of asceticism? "What did you go out into the wilderness to see?"[12] Jesus asked the multitudes, speaking to them of John the Baptist. We could ask the same question of Jesus himself and of Gotama. If one were to treat the individual facts of one's life as significant and appropriate events, as we have recommended, one's life would be so enriched that one could bear going out into the desert or forest and following the way of asceticism. On the other hand, a man who ordinarily dismissed the individual facts of his life as coincidences and took the rest in stride would have such an impoverished inner life that he could hardly bear impoverishing his outer life too. Still this doesn't tell us positively what the man with the rich inner life would go out into the wilderness to see. Perhaps he would go out to see what significance and appropriateness he could find in the common facts of life like sickness, old age, and death. Going out into the wilderness would strip him to his bare humanity and enable him to see what man is like without any external aids.

Or so he would think. Actually the experience of thinking, fasting, and waiting, if one tries it, does not bring the kind of insight one would hope for. Meditation, it is true, brings a peace of mind, but meditation on the teachings of others is not the same as personal insight. A simple experiment in meditation of this kind would be, for example, the repeated reading of some work which contains an entire worldview, such as the *Summa Theologiae* of Aquinas or the *Ethics* of Spinoza or the *Phenomenology* of Hegel. When one reads again and again through this sort of book, if one enters into it fully and sympathetically, one can experience a great peace of mind, lifting one out of moods of depression and loneliness and pacifying all one's emotions. It is almost like a vision in which one can see God and see everything else proceeding from God and returning to God. One could well believe, at these times, in Aquinas' doctrine that bliss is to be found in the vision of God, or in Spinoza's doctrine that freedom from the bondage of the emotions comes from contemplation of God, or in Hegel's doctrine that autonomy of spirit consists in a knowing of knowing like that traditionally ascribed to God. And yet in each instance it is not one's own vision but Aquinas' or Spinoza's or Hegel's that one experiences. What one has is at best a vicarious experience of another man's vision.

This may have been the kind of experience which led Gotama to be dissatisfied with the teachers he encountered in the forest. He attached himself first to a teacher named Alara Kalama and then to one named Uddaka Ramaputta.[13] He seems not to have disagreed with their teachings but only to have been dissatisfied with the degree of personal insight which he attained under their tutelage. So he gave up following the teachings of others and decided to go his own way. The first thing he tried on his own initiative, however, can seem rather a surprising way of trying to gain insight. It was to engage in the most severe austerities and fasting. Apparently he believed that his body was holding his mind back and that he must win a complete victory of mind over body before he could attain insight.

The effect of bodily deprivation, as one can verify from experience, is to create wild fantasies of fulfillment and generally of the opposite of whatever one believes in and is pursuing. Jesus went into the desert to be tempted by Satan; Gotama went into the forest to be tempted by Mara. The most lurid description of these fantasies is probably that of Flaubert in his *Temptation of St. Anthony*. Flaubert has Anthony tempted in his desert solitude first by memories, especially of a girl who attracted him and a young disciple who abandoned him; then by fiery imaginings of possessing power and doing violence and being seduced; then by doubts about his faith and his ideals of martyrdom and the hermitic life; then by imaginary conversations with the great heresiarchs expounding the alternatives to his own faith, discouraging visions of martyrs who do not want to die, superstitious women debauching at tombs; then uncomfortable visions of other gods and other saviors who parody his God and his Savior, the death of the gods preluding the death of God; then an initiation by the devil himself into the scientific view of the universe and the impersonal character of God in such a view; and finally a vision of death and lust, the chimera and the sphinx, and a whole menagerie of monsters which give him a kind of pantheistic feeling of being one with all matter and life.

Fantasy seems to have a balancing effect both on the way of luxury and on the way of asceticism. Eating, drinking, and making merry along the way of luxury tends to be balanced by grim fantasies of sickness, old age, and death, as in the proverb "Eat, drink and be merry, for tomorrow we die" or the song "Let us rejoice now while we are young, for after a pleasant youth and an unpleasant old age the ground will have us."[14] Thinking, fasting, and waiting along the way of asceticism tends to be balanced by wild fantasies of sex and violence, doubt and despair as in the temptations of Anthony, or of dread and fascination as in the temptations of Gotama, or of satiation, presumption, and power as in the temptations of Jesus. Each kind of fantasy points towards a whole man who is greater than the part of man which is being realized along the way he is living. To learn what he really is a man would have to put together what he is doing with what he is imagining.

Approaching wholeness from the side of luxury, he has the problem of putting together the individual and the common facts of life. If he considers the individual facts of his life fortunate, luxury will consist for him in taking advantage of his good fortune. If he considers them unfortunate, it will consist in making up for his bad fortune. T. H. White, who considered himself very unfortunate in parents and upbringing, advises (or has Merlin advise) that when one is feeling unhappy the thing to do is to learn something. The many things that he himself learned in the course of his life—archery, flying, plowing, falconing, diving, sailing, swimming, fishing, shooting, racing, gaming, painting, carpentry, and odd bits of scholarship—were a measure of his own very great unhappiness.[15] Beyond these many things there seems to be one thing that a man can learn only by fitting together his individual lot with the common lot of mankind. It is perhaps the thread which runs through the whole series of his enthusiasms. It is his heart's desire and his personal destiny. As long as he compares his lot only with the individual lot of other persons it will tend to appear fortunate or unfortunate. If he compares it with the common lot of mankind, though, it will no longer seem fortunate or unfortunate but simply individual. It will appear as something beyond good and evil fortune, something which places him beyond the reach of good and bad luck.

Approaching wholeness from the other side, that of asceticism, he has the problem of putting together mind and body. The mind is cultivated at the expense of the body along the way of asceticism, and yet the works of the mind in this condition, as we have seen, tend to lack originality. At the same time the deprived body gives rise to wild orgies of imagination. Perhaps the solution is to apply one's mind to one's temptations and make them the material of insight. By attaining insight into the images thrown up in his temptations and then acting upon that insight, a man might remedy both his mental and his bodily difficulties with one stroke. Flaubert in the course of his life wrote three different accounts of Anthony's temptations: the first (1849) he felt was lacking in plan and connection, the second (1856) had a plan, but the third (1873) had a new plan, and he endeavored there to come up at last with "a logical link among the different hallucinations of the saint."[16] Flaubert's problem in composing his account reflects the problem a man encounters in trying to understand his own temptations. If he could only find the link among the images, he would attain to a personal vision of things, and at the same time he could understand and live out his own wholeness.

The two approaches to wholeness, uniting individual and common facts of life, uniting mind and body, seem to converge upon a single point, the concreteness of the individual man. This appears to have been the point which Gotama reached when he attained his enlightenment and became the Buddha, the "awakened one." He must have comprehended both the common facts of life which originally drove him into the forest and the temptations which he experienced after he had become a forest-dweller. Whatever it was that he found, sitting under the bo tree, it filled him with a lifelong assurance and confidence. This apparently is what gave him such inner resource that he could walk alone through life, without an intimate friend, without a personal God.

There is an extant discourse in which he enumerated the sources of his assurance, his "four confidences."[17] The first is that he saw no ground for anyone to reproach him legitimately with not having perfect comprehension of those things which he claimed to comprehend. He could be confident of this because he did not claim to comprehend everything, only the middle way between luxury and asceticism. Actually this seems like very little to claim. Doesn't everyone know that virtue lies in the middle between the extremes, that moderation is the way of wisdom and excess the way of foolishness? As an abstract doctrine it is indeed common knowledge, but the actual mean between the extremes is concrete rather than abstract. To find the concrete mean is the same as finding one's own concreteness and wholeness, one's own way between the extremes. Only a man who has personally tried the extremes can find this mean.

On the other hand, trying the extremes will not necessarily lead to finding the mean. Only the man who perceives the shortcomings of the extremes will find it. The method of trial and error requires not only that one try different ways of reaching the desired result, but also that one discover and eliminate the errors or causes of failure. Thus the second of Gotama's four confidences was that he saw no grounds for anyone to reproach him legitimately with not having destroyed the *asavas,* the errors and causes of failure of the ways of luxury and asceticism. Now his claim looms larger. We have been able to describe these on the level of imagination. The grim fantasies of sickness, old age, and death which bother a man living the life of luxury are clues to the failure of luxury to lead man to bliss. The wild fantasies involved in the temptations which bother a man living the life of asceticism are corresponding clues to the failure of asceticism. To actually discover the errors and the causes of failure, though, one would have to attain insight into these images; to eliminate them one would have to act upon such insight.

Now Gotama claimed to communicate just such an insight. His third confidence was that the "hindrances" (*nivaranas*) of which he spoke were really hindrances, and that he saw no ground for anyone to assert that there was no harm in practising them. No doubt they were hindrances and there was harm in practising them, but the various traditional lists of hindrances are not very enlightening. For instance, the five *nivaranas* were lust, ill-will, torpor, worry, and skeptical doubt. This hardly gives one a profound insight into the errors and causes of failure of luxury and asceticism. Perhaps the only thing that can be said is that luxury and asceticism themselves are the hindrances. There is harm in practising them in that they lead to misery rather than bliss. The paradox is, nevertheless, that one cannot find the way to bliss except by trying these ways and learning for oneself, as Gotama did, that they are ways to misery.

The fourth confidence was that the way he taught, the middle way, would lead anyone who followed it to the perfect destruction of misery. He was confident of this because this is where it led him. What he was not confident of was his ability to communicate his own insight to others. After attaining his enlightenment he debated seriously whether or not he should try to teach his way to others. "Must I preach to others now what I have so hardly won?"[18] There was good reason for doubt if what we have said is correct, that the mean between the extremes is concrete. For if the mean is concrete, each man has to find his own middle way. If the mean were abstract, then it could be adequately described in a general doctrine intended for any and every man. If it is concrete, then the best one man can do for another is help him find his own way between luxury and asceticism. This, I believe, is what Gotama ended up doing. The decision to do this, though, launched him upon a way which was less solitary than the way he had traveled till then.

2. *The Way of Conscious Individuation*

The life of Jesus presents a difficulty to those who would be his followers. Dying as young as he did, at the age of thirty or thirty-three, he did not show us how to live the second half of life. Or so it seems until we compare his life with that of Gotama. The two lives have a similar structure: first childhood and youth, then withdrawal into the wilderness, then return and a life of teaching. Gotama lived to an advanced old age, dying at eighty, and he spent the whole second half of life doing what Jesus did in his short public life, communicating to others the insight he had found in the wilderness. Evidently, therefore, the ultimate length of the life does not matter; the important thing is to find one's way to bliss and then spend the remainder of one's life, long or short, sharing one's insight with others. But what of the man who has already lived the first half of life and entered upon the second half without discovering the way to bliss? Should he spend the second half of life communicating whatever limited insight he has found, or should he spend it searching for the way?

Communicating whatever limited insight he has found might in fact be the best method of searching for the way. This would be in accord with the maxim "Give away everything that you have, then shall you receive."[19] As one communicates the limited insight one has, one receives further insight. It is like driving on a highway at night: the headlights illuminate only a portion of the road ahead and one guides the course of the automobile by the limited vision which this gives, but the road goes on, further and further portions of it appear, and one is confident that one will eventually reach a destination which cannot as yet be seen. What one is doing, in effect, is discovering the way as one travels it. This supposes, it is true, that one is on the right way. Yet this may not be too much to suppose, for, however Gotama and Jesus may have described the way, what they did with their own lives after discovering it was this very thing, share their insight with others. So maybe this *is* the way, to share one's insight with others. At least it is an experiment worth trying.

The reason it just might work is the process of what Jung called "individuation." According to his idea there is a natural process of development which takes place as a man goes from childhood to youth to manhood to old age, a process which goes on independently of whether or not the man himself understands what is taking place. If this is true, then maybe there are events in every human life analogous to those in the lives of Gotama and Jesus. Maybe in every human life there is, after childhood and youth, something analogous to the withdrawal into the wilderness and then something analogous to the return and the life of teaching. The difference would be that ordinarily the process is not understood, ordinarily there is no great enlightenment or revelation, and so ordinarily there is no great sense of a mission to communicate what one has found to others. If, nevertheless, a man were at some point in his life to become aware of what was going on, then his individuation would become thereafter what Jung called "conscious individuation."[20]

The completely individuated man, as Jung envisions him, would be free from emotional ties. This sounds indeed like a description of Gotama after he was enlightened and had become the Buddha. Here is how Jung puts it in his autobiography, after having related a dream about his dead wife and a series of visions he had experienced during an illness:

> The objectivity which I experienced in this dream and in the visions is part of a completed individuation. It signifies detachment from valuations and from what we call emotional ties. In general, emotional ties are very important to human beings. But they still contain projections, and it is essential to withdraw these projections in order to attain to oneself and to objectivity. Emotional relationships are relationships of desire, tainted by coercion and constraint; something is expected from the other person, and that makes him and ourselves unfree. Objective cognition lies hidden behind the attraction of the emotional relationship; it seems to be the central secret. Only through objective cognition is the real *coniunctio* possible.[21]

Perhaps we could relate "objective cognition" here with what we are calling "insight," and say that the "real *coniunctio*" of which he speaks would be a union of persons which comes about in the sharing of insight.

When individuation is still unconscious, a man finds himself in a position like that of King Lear, liable to great suffering at the hands of others, especially at the hands of those closest to him, because "he hath ever but slenderly known himself."[22] It is as though each man had a tragedy of his own to undergo like Lear's, starting with the stage where his self-knowledge is slender and his suffering can drive him to madness, then entering a period of conscious individuation where he begins attaining insight into his relationships and sharing this with others, and ending in a state of completed individuation where he is free of emotional ties and his relationships are based on a sharing of insight. The starting point would be the state that Jung describes in which a man is bound by emotional ties, where his ties with other persons still contain projections of himself, where his relationships are relationships of desire, tainted by coercion and constraint, in which something is always expected of others, leaving them and himself unfree. The temptation at this point is inevitably to flee from his relationships, for instance to withdraw into thought as we described in the previous chapter in the Parable of the Mountain, but this is quite different from working his way through his relationships by means of insight. To search for insight into one's relations with others is more like a deliberate descent into hell.

If one undertakes this deliberate descent into hell, the first thing one comes upon, it seems, is the fact that one's feelings towards other persons are mixed. This is a hard thing to admit, especially when it comes to one's most important relationships such as those to one's parents, one's children, one's friends. The circles in which a life moves, from this point of view, are circles of hell, the least intimate being the outer circles and the most intimate being the inner circles of that hell. Whenever one loves a person, it seems, one also is likely to hate that person; for whenever a person can cause great joy in one's life he can also cause great pain and usually does, and so he becomes simultaneously the object of hope and of disappointment, of confidence and of fear, of trust and of mistrust, of affection and of resentment.[23] This is hard to admit to oneself: the reality of one's love tends to make one deny the dark side of the relationship and to expect pure and unadulterated love from the other person. Insight into the ambivalence has something of a liberating effect, especially if it is accompanied by the realization that genuine emotional ties are always ambivalent, for it tends to take away the self-righteousness and the expectations which cannot but be disappointed.

The desire for an unambivalent relationship is overpowering, though, so overpowering that one is sometimes ready to settle for a breakup of the actual relationship. One desires a relationship of pure and unadulterated love but, if this cannot be, one would rather break off the relationship than live in the intolerable uncertainty that it brings. This can lead one in imagination to envision the triumph of the dark side of the relationship: it seems as if it would be better to be enemies or mere acquaintances than to be such ambiguous and unreliable friends. It can lead, on the other hand, to envisioning a situation in which one has complete control of the other person so that the relationship is assured. Or it can lead to envisioning relationships with people outside the circles in which one's life ordinarily moves, in the hope that these people will somehow prove less ambiguous than the people one knows. What the desire is at bottom is a hunger and thirst for certainty, for certainty at almost any cost. It has the self-defeating quality that the pursuit of certainty always seems to have: the more desperately one seeks for certainty the more intensely one is plagued by uncertainty.

Is it possible to give up the pursuit of certainty? If it were possible, this would be the thing to give up rather than the relationship with the other person. When an emotional tie with another person is tormenting and one feels that it has got far too much hold upon one's life, then it would seem better, if possible, to let go of certainty than to let go of the relationship. If it is not possible to let go of certainty, then the only way one can go oneself and be free is to break off the relationship. It does seem possible, however, to let go of certainty. At least it is possible to see how one's pursuit of certainty is self-defeating, how it turns one's relationships into a torment, how there really is no situation in which one could control the other person and be sure, how one would run into the same impasse with people outside the circles in which one's life presently moves. The pursuit of certainty may be an obsession and a compulsion in one's life, something which no amount of reasoning can change. Abstract reasoning about the futility of seeking for certainty will leave it unchanged, but concrete insight which recognizes the particular form which the pursuit of certainty takes in one's own life, which sees how this and not merely the pursuit of certainty in general is self-defeating, may have some effect.

If one succeeds in giving up the pursuit of certainty, one's individuation begins to be a conscious process. Before this point one was striving to attain a goal quite different from that of individuation, and so the goal of individuation and the process leading towards it were unconscious. One's goal had been to be sure of oneself and of others, to escape from the terrible uncertainty in which one found oneself and to attain assurance and peace of mind. The incompatibility of this goal and this pursuit with the ambivalence of one's actual relationships turned life into a hell. Giving up this goal and this pursuit, paradoxically, brings a certain peace of mind, not the peace of assurance but the peace that comes when some great striving ceases. The uncertainty still remains and pervades all the circles in which one's life moves, but the striving for certainty and all the anxiety and depression which it brings have ceased. One is no longer anxiously trying to make sure of other persons; one is no longer depressed by one's failure to be reassured by them.

This is a far-reaching change, and yet it seems to be initiated simply by acknowledging the ambivalence of others towards oneself and one's own ambivalence towards them. The insight into the ambivalence of one's relationships is so shattering that one will ordinarily resist it as long as one can and by every means at one's disposal. To admit this insight, one might think, would open the door to a profound cynicism in which one would no longer be able to believe in the sincerity, the benevolence, the rectitude of other persons, nor in one's own. Actually cynicism represents a disappointed quest of certainty in which only the dark side of the ambivalence is taken to be real. When one recognizes both sides of the ambivalence, the dark and the bright, the attitude one tends to take is not cynicism so much as understanding and forgiveness. If a man is able to forgive, then no one, it seems, can make him unhappy. The practice of forgiveness is itself an experiment with truth, an experiment in which one attempts to replace the pursuit of certainty by a pursuit of understanding.

Going over from the pursuit of certainty to the pursuit of understanding can be a change of mind as well as a change of heart; it can occur in the realm of pure thought and intellectual endeavor as well as in the realm of human relations. The possibility of doing it in the sphere of the mind may actually occur before that of doing it in the sphere of the heart.[24] As a purely intellectual experiment one finds it very rewarding, for it leads to adventures of the mind which would never be undertaken if one's mind were still gripped by the need for certainty. For instance, trying to arrive at a sympathetic understanding of cultures other than one's own, lives other than one's own, religions other than one's own, are adventures of the mind which would probably not be undertaken for fear of unsettling one's confidence in one's own culture, one's own life, one's own religion. Or if one's confidence in these things were already shaken and these adventures were undertaken in order to find some new basis of certainty, they would probably be abandoned, for the divergence of cultures and lives and religions would seem to indicate that no agreement could ever be reached on these matters. When one is no longer concerned about reaching agreement, however, and restoring confidence, but simply about attaining insight and understanding, then one can enter freely into other cultures, lives, and religions and come back to understand one's own in a new light.

As an experiment in human relations, although it is much more difficult to carry out, going over from certainty to understanding seems to lead towards parallel results, towards turning life itself into an adventure or a series of adventures; risks that would never be run if one's heart were still set upon being secure in one's human relations. These adventures seem connected very closely with the ages of life, childhood, youth, manhood, and old age. It is difficult to grow out of the relationships formed in one period of life and to enter into those appropriate for the next period, to leave behind those of youth for those of manhood, to leave behind those of manhood for those of old age, to leave behind those of old age for those of the dead. It is also difficult to allow someone else to leave a relationship with oneself behind as he grows and moves onward, because a familiar relationship is being abandoned for an unknown one. The pursuit of certainty would pull one back into the familiar; the pursuit of understanding would push one forward into the unknown.

One passes to "objective cognition" and the "real *coniunctio*" as each stage of individuation is completed and one becomes free of the emotional ties characteristic of that stage. In youth the individuation that goes on in childhood can reach completion and the young person can become free of the emotional ties proper to childhood; in manhood, similarly, one can become free of those proper to youth; and in age one can become free of those proper to manhood.

This can happen, but very frequently one fails to outgrow some of the ties appropriate to earlier stages. Moreover, the freedom from emotional ties which one does attain, if the individuation of any one state is successfully completed, is only relative. The young person may have outgrown the relationships appropriate to childhood, but he is involved in those appropriate to youth, and these too are relationships of desire, containing demands and expectations which leave him still unfree and incomplete. So also with the man and the old man. Each may be free with respect to the ties of the previous stages of life, but he is bound by those of the stage which he is in. At each stage one is faced with the task of working one's way through the relationships of that time of life and not giving in to the temptation of avoiding them or breaking them off. The price of avoiding them or breaking them off is failure to achieve the growth proper to that stage. The only way one can become genuinely free of an emotional tie, it seems, is to outgrow it, and even then the relationship is not broken so much as transformed.

What usually happens is that one finds oneself at a later stage of life, such as manhood, and realizes that one has not yet worked one's way through problems of the earlier stages, childhood and youth. One finds oneself entering into the kind of relationships a child would have with a grownup or an adolescent would have with another adolescent, or experiencing a child's fears and an adolescent's sexual turmoil. This is not quite the same as the continued presence of the child and the youth in the mature man. In the man who successfully completes the individuation of childhood and youth the complete child and the complete youth live on; the child's wonder and the youth's quest do not die. In the man who has not yet worked his way through the problems of the earlier stages it is rather the incomplete child and the incomplete youth that live on, the childishness of the child and the adolescence of the youth. Once a man has become aware of the child and the youth in himself, nevertheless, he can still work to perfect his childhood and youth, to bring the child within him to the point of balance that one can sometimes observe in children just before the onset of adolescence, and to bring the youth within him to the point of balance that one can observe in young persons when they have worked through the initial chaos of adolescence.

The opposite can happen too—a young man can work his way through the problems of later life. This appears to be what happened in the lives of Gotama and Jesus. The life of Jesus, as we saw, was more telescoped than that of Gotama. The life of Gotama, however, was itself very accelerated by comparison with the traditional scheme of life in India. The Brahmanic tradition on the ages of life divides a man's life into four periods: first the student, then the householder, then the forest-dweller, and finally the sage.[25] Ordinarily the householder would not become a forest-dweller until his children were grown and self-sufficient; then he would leave home and go into the wilderness, and come back again as a sage only towards the end of his life. Gotama left his young wife and child when he was twenty-nine and thus became a forest-dweller when he was still a young man, instead of waiting until he was a seasoned householder. He came back again as a sage when he was only thirty-six. So he had over forty years in which to communicate his wisdom to others, instead of merely a few years at the end of his life.

If the problem at each stage of life is to go over from the pursuit of certainty to the pursuit of understanding, each time at a different level, then one can see how it might be possible to work through the problems of later life in youth, and vice versa, to work through the problems of earlier life in manhood.[26] In childhood the problem lies on the level of the here and now. The child's fear of the dark, of being alone, of strangers, and the like, has to do with the uncertainty of the immediate situation; the child's wonder about the unknown, his playing alone, his curiosity about strangers, is correspondingly a seeking to understand the immediate realities of his life. In youth the problem lies on the level of life considered as a whole with a past and a future. The adolescent's insecurity is an uncertainty about his future, a lack of confidence in his past, a loneliness which both desires and fears the presence of other persons; the youthful quest, in turn, is an adventure which begins when the young person gives up trying to make sure of his future and his past, of himself and others, and tries instead to live by insight. In manhood the problem lies on a level which reaches beyond the self and its life to other persons and other lives. The man's cares are cares not merely for himself but for his children and for all who are committed to his charge; the pursuit of understanding for him means giving up the attempt to plan the lives of those for whom he cares and, without ceasing to care for them, letting them follow out their own destinies.

The life of the forest-dweller, in the tradition of India, seems to begin at this point, where the man who has been a householder lets go of his children and allows them to live their own lives. Perhaps we can suppose that Gotama had reached this point prematurely in his own inner development, that he had outgrown his domestic relationships, when he left his wife and child and entered the wilderness. Gotama's search, nevertheless, has many of the qualities of the youthful quest. By going into the wilderness as early as he did, he anticipated the events of later life but he anticipated them in a youthful manner. In the more ordinary life, accordingly, there is something in youth itself that corresponds to his search. The sharing of insight to which he devoted the remainder of his life was the existence of a sage, but doing this as he did, in his late thirties, he almost inevitably did it somewhat in the manner of the householder instructing his sons. There can be a sharing of insight at this time in the more ordinary life too, a sharing of the limited insight which a man will have obtained from his youthful quest. Further insight awaits the ordinary man when his children outgrow his fatherhood and he finds himself almost unwillingly plunged into the wilderness of later life.[27] The extraordinary thing about Gotama's life is that he seems to have attained the fullness of insight in the middle of life.

The further insight which a more ordinary man will attain when his children have left him to undertake their own lives or, if he is a teacher, when pupils of his have outgrown their relationship to him, will be, first of all, the realization that human beings outgrow their relationships to one another. With this he will begin to experience the freedom from emotional ties of which Jung speaks. It is interesting to note that Jung was an old man in his eighties when he wrote the words about this which we quoted above. He had in his own way already become a forest-dweller and returned as a sage; he spoke as a sage standing at the end of life. At an earlier period in one's life the prospect of emotional ties being outgrown is difficult to contemplate. The experience of outgrowing relations, to be sure, comes early, when the youth ceases to be a child, and when the man ceases to be a youth, but the experience of being outgrown by others generally comes later when one has children or pupils or other persons committed to one's charge and they become eventually independent or when one's wife or husband dies or when one's friends die; it comes earlier mainly in the estrangement of friends and lovers.

Sharing insight becomes rather a different matter after this. One seeks to move the hearts and illuminate the minds of others, but, knowing that the relationship must eventually be outgrown, one tends to be less possessive. Seeking to move and illuminate, one can be keenly disappointed when others fail to respond. Giving up the pursuit of certainty, though, one finds a kind of certainty after all, an increasing confidence as one goes from insight to insight on the pursuit of understanding. It is a confidence which allows one to be outgrown without being shattered. It appears very clearly in the lives of Jesus and Gotama. Jesus is keenly disappointed when others fail to respond, but he seems willing enough to be outgrown. He tells his disciples that it is better for them that he go away, for if he does not go the Spirit of Truth who is to lead them in the future will not come.[28] Gotama tells his disciples that his teaching is like a raft which they are using to cross a river: once they have reached the other side of the river, it would be foolish to lift up the raft and carry it away on their shoulders out of gratitude for its aid in crossing. Rather, they should leave it there on the riverbank and walk away unburdened.[29]

The completely individuated man, according to this, would be a man who relates to other persons by illuminating their minds and moving their hearts. No deeper relationship than this, it seems, can be imagined. In spite of its depth and its importance to lives, though, such a relationship is not what Jung called an "emotional tie." It is emotional, to be sure, in that it involves the heart as well as the mind, but it is not emotional in the sense of being a relationship of desire in which something is demanded of the other person. The completely individuated man's willingness to go away and let his disciples be led simply by the spirit of truth, his willingness to have them leave behind his teaching as a raft which has served its purpose and is no longer needed, implies that his relationship does not contain the element of desire and demand which would leave him and them unfree. His state is not one of mere autonomy and unrelatedness, for he has touched their minds and their hearts. It is a state of freedom and relatedness; it is a state in which freedom and relatedness can go together.

3. The Insight into Suffering

"Hell is other people,"[30] Sartre has said; and yet compassion and forgiveness have a power, we have found, to abolish that hell. Gotama, we could say, went into the wilderness and learned compassion; Jesus went into the desert and learned forgiveness. Still the harrowing of hell remained incomplete somehow, for suffering seems to have occurred in the life of Gotama even after he had learned compassion; it surely occurred in the life of Jesus after he had learned forgiveness. This suffering which comes after appears to be compatible with bliss, the bliss which arises when compassion and forgiveness abolish hell insofar as it is due to other persons. Gotama, if this is true, must have been talking about the suffering which comes before, since his Four Truths about suffering, its origin, its end, and the way to end it, clearly suppose that suffering can be ended. Jesus, on the other hand, must have been talking about that which comes after, since his Beatitudes ascribe bliss to those who suffer. Up till now we have been looking mainly to what Gotama and Jesus did, rather than to what they said. This time let us start with what they said, specifically with the Four Truths and the Beatitudes.[31]

Instead of simply applying their teachings, however, let us turn their answers into questions. Instead of enunciating the Four Truths, let us ask the four questions which Gotama was answering:

> What is suffering?
> What is the origin of suffering?
> What is the end of suffering? (i.e. What is bliss?)
> What is the way to the end of suffering? (i.e. What is the way to bliss?)

Instead of repeating the Beatitudes let us ask the question about the blessed and the question about blessedness which Jesus was answering:

> Who among men are blessed?
> In what does their blessedness consist?

By turning the answers of Gotama and Jesus into questions we turn from their teaching to our own experience for answers. There is a learning that comes from suffering, a learning that can come to each from his own suffering. This will have to be the source of our answers. It was a major theme of Greek and Shakespearean tragedy. Aeschylus actually used the phrase "the learning that comes from suffering" in *Agamemnon,* meaning that wisdom comes to human beings only through bitter experience.[32] Shakespeare made much of the theme in *King Lear:* Lear learned by bitter experience that the daughters whom he had believed faithful were unfaithful and the one whom he had rejected as unfaithful was really faithful, and Gloucester learned a parallel truth about his sons. The learning in instances of this kind is an insight into the hell of other people, being mistaken about others and coming to the truth about them and about oneself in relation to them. It could, in fact, become an insight not only into one's own relationships and one's own life but into all human relations and into human life as such. At this point it would begin to become comparable with the insight into suffering attained by Gotama and Jesus.

The experience out of which Gotama spoke was an experience of compassion, it seems, a sympathetic experience of the suffering which human beings undergo, not merely his own private suffering.[33] Yet the subject matter of his teaching is the private suffering of the individual man. The compassionate man, by the very fact that he is in sympathy with the sufferings of others, is not enclosed in the hell of private suffering. This is what enables him to map that hell. If he were enclosed within it, he would be unable to see its limits and describe its boundaries. Where his wisdom begins to fail is in the attempt to understand the suffering that comes to him after he has risen to compassion and forgiveness. Thus Jesus cries out on the cross "My God, my God, why have you forsaken me?"[34] He is enclosed in the world of this suffering and cannot see its limits or describe its boundaries. The end is like the beginning, a darkness in which suffering seems incomprehensible. There is a day between the two nights, nevertheless, in which a bliss is found which takes away the darkness of the first night and is not taken away itself by that of the second.

The learning that first comes from suffering is likely to be the simple realization that the wheel of fortune turns. A man who knows that the wheel turns can be a kind of prophet. When everyone else hopes he despairs; when everyone else despairs he hopes. His personal experience of the turning wheel is likely to be an experience of the ages of life, finding himself too old for things he was once young enough for, and finding himself old enough for things he was once too young for. His wisdom is also likely to come from comparing his life with that of others, seeing for instance another man who was once successful in the very way that he himself is now, but who now is too old and has been passed by and forgotten. Comparing his life with others' may also lead him to believe that he will not always be breaking ground the way a younger man does but will someday be taking a more definitive stand, living and speaking out of a more definitive wisdom. At each of these stages, he realizes, certain human relations are possible which are impossible at others: he can have loves, for instance, at an earlier stage that he will be unable to have at a later one, and disciples at a later stage that he was unable to have at an earlier one. On a larger scale of time he can see how movements once in the ascendant are no longer so and movements not yet in the ascendant are likely to be so, and how those associated with the former have declined and those associated with the latter have not yet risen to eminence.

The wisdom of the turning wheel is common and ancient. It appears in literature in many of the places where the idea of learning from suffering appears.[35] One might think at first that it even encompasses the insights of Gotama and Jesus. The man who knows that the wheel turns seems at first to have the answers to all the questions we posed. If he is asked "What is suffering?" and "What is the origin of suffering?" he can point to the wheel. So also if he is asked "What is bliss?" and "What is the way to bliss?" Bliss and suffering from the viewpoint of his wisdom are fortune and misfortune; the way to the one and the way to the other are the way up and the way down on the wheel. The turning of the wheel seems to allow him to speak paradoxically like Jesus about the blessed and their blessedness. He can say "Blessed are the poor, the hungry, the sorrowful, the persecuted, for they will be rich, satisfied, glad, triumphant," and vice versa "Woe to the rich, the satisfied, the glad, the triumphant, for they will be poor, hungry, sorrowful, persecuted,"[36] meaning simply that the wheel of fortune turns.

Somehow, though, this is a little too simple. Gotama is said to have attained his insight into suffering by recalling all his previous existences.[37] Recalling one's former lives, in a culture like India's where reincarnation is taken for granted, would be like learning all the turns which the wheel of fortune has ever taken. Remembering all the turns would amount to encompassing the wisdom of the turning wheel and seeing through it. According to tradition, what Gotama did was first recall his previous lives, then recall former epochs of history, and then finally discover the truth about suffering, its origin, its ending, and the way to end it. Given our background of Western culture, where there is no traditional belief in reincarnation, it is difficult to re-enact his experience of recalling former lives and times. Perhaps we can approximate it by substituting for the concept of former lives and times that of parallel lives and parallel times. This would change our task from one of remembering to one of comparing. We could compare our own lives and times with other lives and times, and perhaps awaken resonances within ourselves which would be like the resonances which occur when we remember things we have forgotten.

There is such a thing as an experiment in total recall, where a person strives to remember his past with complete clarity and in complete detail, but what is ordinarily envisioned in such an experiment is merely the past of one's current existence. To recall previous existences, if it were possible, would be a feat of memory to end all feats of memory. The nearest approximation which I can seriously envision would be to compare my life with other lives, especially with lives that appear to be somewhat similar to my own. I have developed in another book a method of "passing over," as I call it, to other lives.[38] It is a method of entering sympathetically into another person's autobiographical standpoint, seeing the whole world anew as that person sees it, and then coming back enriched to one's own standpoint and to a new understanding of one's own life. The technique of passing over is based on the process of eliciting images from one's feelings, attaining insight into the images, and turning insight into a guide of life. What one does in passing over is try to enter sympathetically into the feelings of another person, become receptive to the images which give expression to his feelings, attain insight into those images, and then come back enriched by this insight to an understanding of one's own life which can guide one into the future. We were doing something like this with the life of Gandhi in the previous chapter and are doing it with the lives of Gotama and Jesus in this one. Now let us imagine a man who has made a practice of passing over to other lives and times. Perhaps he will be in a position comparable to that of Gotama remembering his former existences.

The practice of passing over to other lives has the effect of extricating a man from the hell of private suffering and allowing him to move about in the larger world of compassion. The sympathetic understanding into which he must enter in order to pass over to another man's life is itself compassion, for it involves a sharing of feelings and images as well as insight into the images and feelings. The broadening and deepening of his experience to which this leads makes possible a more penetrating answer to the question "What is suffering?" Before passing over a man would probably say that suffering is misfortune; he might add that emotional maturity means being able to take one's bad luck in stride. After passing over he would be less harsh with others and with himself. It might appear to him after passing over that suffering is not merely the unfortunate moments of a life, not merely the moments when the wheel of fortune has carried a man's lot downwards, but the whole of his life insofar as it is bound to the wheel of fortune and is subject to its ups and downs.

He would have a different answer for the second question too, "What is the origin of suffering?" Before passing over he would probably have traced the origin of suffering to the turning of the wheel. Being on the wheel himself he would be mainly aware of the contrasts, sometimes seeing himself down and other persons up, sometimes seeing himself up and others down, and so he would naturally tend to ascribe everything to the fact that the wheel turns. After passing over to other lives, however, he would become more aware of the common lot and would tend to trace the origin of suffering to whatever it is that binds men to the wheel. His personal experience of emerging from the hell of private suffering by means of compassion serves as a clue. The privateness of private fortune and misfortune is the thing that compassion abolishes. The cause of suffering, therefore, is probably this very thing. The absorption in oneself that allows one to live in a private heaven at times and plunges one into a private hell at other times, that reduces one to the size of one's fortune and misfortune, is what rivets one to the wheel of fortune and renders one completely subject to all its turns. It is the obstacle to passing over to persons who occupy other positions on the wheel. It is the bondage which is broken by passing over.

Here he has the answer to the third question "What is the end of suffering?" or "What is bliss?" What has brought the hell of his private suffering to an end is compassion. Before passing over he would have thought that the only way out of this hell would be a turning of the wheel which would bring him around from bad to good fortune. After passing over he realizes that there is another and more drastic way, a way of disengaging himself from the wheel. It would be possible, it is true, to conceive the end of suffering simply as an abolition of the self or of selfishness or of absorption in oneself. This is the way it has been conceived in the tradition of Hinayana Buddhism. The ideal of compassion in Mahayana Buddhism, on the other hand, seems to be a more helpful clue in the light of our present experiment. For compassion *is* the abolition of the closed world of the self. Oftentimes a person will feel trapped in himself and unable to see beyond himself; he will feel driven into himself by his anxiety and his depression; he will desire most earnestly to rise above himself but will find no means of doing so. It does him little good to be told that he must forget himself and rise above himself and be selfless. This is what he wants to do, but he does not know how. The ideal of compassion is helpful at this point because it describes this selflessness in positive rather than negative terms; it indicates not only the goal but also the way.

If compassion is bliss and the ending of suffering, then the way to bliss must be the way to compassion. The answer to the fourth question, therefore, "What is the way to the end of suffering?" or "What is the way to bliss?" must be the way we have found to compassion, the process of passing over. This makes the third time we have tried to answer this question in the course of this chapter. In the first section of this chapter we described the way as the middle way between luxury and asceticism, repeating as it were the experiments of Gotama (and probably also of Jesus) with luxury and asceticism which led by trial and error to the middle way. In the second section we described it as the way which Gotama and Jesus actually followed during the remainder of their lives after discovering the way, namely the sharing of insight with others. Now in this third section we are describing it as the way which leads to compassion and forgiveness, the process of passing over to other lives. The connection between these answers seems to be as follows. Luxury and asceticism, as self-indulgence and self-torture, fail to lead one to bliss because they leave one absorbed in oneself. Passing over to other lives is the way leading to compassion; sharing insight with others is the exercise of compassion; and compassion is the only frame of mind, I believe, in which a man breaks out of the hellish world of the self without forgetting or denying that he has a self.

Because he still has a self, he can still suffer after he has attained compassion. This is partly a matter of slipping back from the high vantage point of compassion to the narrow perspective of self-centeredness: a man finds himself continually driven back into himself by anxiety and depression; he finds it necessary to pass over again and again to abolish the hell of other people. Besides mere slipping back, though, there is a return to self, which is an intrinsic part of the process of passing over. One passes over to the life of another, but then one comes back to one's own life enriched. This coming back is a return to self; it is necessary if the self is to be transformed and the course of the life changed by the experience of compassion, but it leaves a man open to suffering. The famous doctrine of *anatta,* "no-self,"[39] in Buddhism would be the final truth if compassion meant simply passing over to others and never coming back to oneself. Passing over to other lives is the only way I can see of achieving a state of "no-self," but coming back to one's own life makes the self reappear. So in the last analysis the self is enhanced, not destroyed. This seems to be the reason why suffering could still occur in the life of Jesus, and occur with supreme intensity, even after he had reached the heights of compassion and forgiveness.

This is where the questions to which Jesus was speaking in his Beatitudes seem to become pertinent. The question "Who among men is blessed?" really does not ask who among men is beyond all suffering; it asks who enjoys bliss in the midst of suffering. The question is so elemental that it can be asked without words, simply looking at faces to see if one can find someone who is happy or who enjoys peace of mind. Those to whom Jesus attributed bliss, the poor in spirit, those who mourn, the meek, those who hunger and thirst for righteousness, the merciful, the pure in heart, the peacemakers, those who are persecuted for righteousness' sake,[40] appear to be likely candidates only when one has come to the point of seeing bliss and suffering as compatible. It is true, one could take him to mean merely that those who suffer in this world will enjoy bliss when this world comes to an end. If one takes the question as we are taking it, though, "Who among men is blessed?" asks about a bliss which is now being enjoyed. Taking it this way, we could say "Blessed are the compassionate" or "Blessed are those who forgive."

"In what does their blessedness consist?" According to the Beatitudes they would be blessed because theirs is the kingdom of heaven, because they shall be comforted, because they shall inherit the earth, because they shall be filled, because they shall obtain mercy, because they shall see God, because they shall be called the children of God. All this lends itself easily to the interpretation which would paraphrase "Blessed are those who suffer, for they shall enjoy bliss when this world comes to an end." Our interpretation is possible, nevertheless, and seems to lead further towards an understanding of the actual experience of suffering. We could say "Blessed are those who forgive, for they shall be forgiven," and we could mean that they shall be forgiven now and that the difference will be felt now and not merely later. The experience of forgiving occurs in the moment of passing over to the other person's life; the refusal to forgive is the refusal to pass over which locks one into the hell of one's private suffering. The experience of being forgiven, by God let us say, occurs in the moment of coming back to oneself and one's life, to what was once a hell and is so no longer.

The experience of Jesus on the cross shows that this is not as simple as it sounds. After praying "Father, forgive them, for they know not what they do," he cried out "My God, my God, why have you forsaken me?"[41] Surely the hell implied in the phrase "Hell is other people" was abolished by his forgiveness. When he came back to himself from compassion and forgiveness, though, he was still liable to suffering, the suffering which arose from his fate at the hands of God. The harrowing of hell on the cross seems really to have gone much further than the abolition of the hell of other people. After Jesus had forgiven other people, there was still the God who had abandoned him to his fate. I hesitate to speak here of "forgiving God," a phrase foreign to ordinary religious language, and yet it seems the most appropriate way of describing what sometimes happens when a man makes peace with God. A person can suffer all through his life from resentment at his fate; this is especially so if he has some affliction from birth or if he has been maimed for life, but resentment tends to arise from every fate. To forgive God, to pass over to God, if that were possible, would be the only way to abolish the hell of this resentment. Maybe such a forgiving of God and such a passing over to God is implied in the last words of Jesus on the cross, "Father, into your hands I commend my spirit."[42]

We have come here unexpectedly upon a rather surprising way of responding to the Biblical problem of suffering. The problem is that posed in the Book of Job where the sufferings of an innocent man are described.[43] Job lost everything, his possessions, his children, his health. His friends "comforted" him by telling him that he must have brought it upon himself and that he should ask God for forgiveness. Now to say that Job should forgive God would be to take a view exactly opposite to that of his friends. Job dared to maintain his innocence against his friends, because he was truly innocent, but he did not dare even to maintain his innocence against God. When the voice of God came to him out of the whirlwind, Job stopped his mouth. Now we are suggesting not merely that he maintain his innocence against God but that he presume to forgive God!

Forgiving God, however, would be quite a different thing either from rebelling against his fate or resigning himself to it. In both rebellion and resignation man is set over against God or against whatever it is that determines his fate. Either he is fighting against God or submitting to God. In forgiving God he passes over to God, endeavors to enter into sympathy with God, to see things as God sees them. In the moment of passing over, if he were to succeed, there would be a oneness of God and man such that it would no longer seem appropriate to speak of a God existing apart from man or a human self existing apart from God. A man at this moment would find himself in a position like that of Gotama, refusing to speak of a God or a self. Perhaps this was, in effect, the position of Gotama. The attitude which he adopted towards human beings and, for that matter, towards all beings was a kind of divine compassion and mercy, a care for all creatures and a desire to lead them all to bliss. This attitude of his is what led later on in Mahayana Buddhism to the ideal of the Bodhisattva, the person who compassionately refrains from entering Nirvana in order to save others.[44] To adopt an attitude of universal compassion is to pass over, as it were, to the standpoint of God. One thinks of the words with which each chapter of the Koran begins, "In the name of Allah, the compassionate, the merciful."

The question which we must ask is whether it is really possible for a human being to stand in a standpoint such as this. What locates a person in a standpoint, it seems, is care or concern. When he is concerned only about his own life, he remains fixed in his own standpoint and finds himself unable to pass over to that of another person. The expansion of care which allows him to pass over to the standpoint of another human being would be the first step towards passing over to the standpoint of God. The care which would characterize the standpoint of God would be what is ordinarily called "providence," a care for all things in the universe, from the greatest to the smallest. To pass over to the standpoint of God a man would have to go beyond caring simply about his own life or about the lives of a small circle of family and friends to caring about the lives of all human beings, indeed of all beings human and nonhuman. The ideal of the Bodhisattva is the ideal of a human being who would do this, who would wait for all others to enter Nirvana before entering himself, who would be willing to wait "till the grass is enlightened." However the care is conceived, whether in terms of reincarnation and Nirvana or otherwise, the essential thing is that it be universal.

It does seem possible that a human being could come to care

about all beings and, to that extent, that a man could stand in the standpoint of God. In the standpoint of universal care, insofar as he could attain it, a man would see things as God sees them. The limitation on this, it seems to me, is that after passing over to God a man would have to come back again to himself. In the moment of passing over he would be in the position of Gotama, who found it superfluous to speak of a God apart from man or of a human self. This is because the moment of passing over is a moment of "ecstasy" in the literal sense of "standing outside of oneself." It is followed, though, by the moment of coming back to oneself, and in this moment, however enriched one is by the experience of passing over, one sees oneself as distinct from the One to whom one passed over. In coming back to oneself, therefore, it makes sense once again to speak of a self and a God. There is a care about one's own life from which one cannot finally escape, it seems, though one can take the narrowness and selfishness out of it by experiencing what it is to care about all things. I imagine that Gotama himself must have had to return to the cares of his own life and that he could not stand always in the standpoint of universal providence.

We began our experiment with Buddhism thinking that Buddhism was going to be simpler than the other great religions, Hinduism, Judaism, Christianity, and Islam, because it did not have any doctrine on God. Now we have found that the simplicity was deceptive. In our effort to re-enact the life of Gotama we have found it necessary to try passing over to a standpoint of providence or universal care. We might have suspected that God would figure somehow, just from the parallelism between the lives of Gotama and Jesus. Our endeavor to re-enact their lives, nevertheless, has enabled us to discover a number of things about the way to bliss. We described it first as "the way of the individual" and then as "the way of conscious individuation." Hegel said that two ideas are necessary to understand the history of philosophy, the idea of concreteness and the idea of development.[45] Our way of the individual is a way of concreteness; our way of conscious individuation is a way of development.

The idea of concreteness which we came upon was that of the concrete mean between the extremes of luxury and asceticism. We found that an abstract doctrine of the mean was of little help, for instance a list of virtues with opposing vices, placing courage between cowardice and rashness, temperance between profligacy and insensibility, liberality between stinginess and prodigality, and so forth. A man has to find his own way between the extremes, we concluded, going from an ordinary life to a life of thinking, fasting, and waiting as Gotama and Jesus did when they withdrew into the wilderness. Both the ordinary life of self-indulgence and the life of thinking, fasting, and waiting are balanced, we found, by a counterpoint of fantasy, the ordinary life by grim fantasies of decay and death, the life of thinking, fasting, and waiting by wild fantasies of fulfillment. What is revealed to insight in these fantasies is the whole man. The grim fantasies reveal the side of man that is neglected in luxury; the wild fantasies reveal the side that is neglected in asceticism.

The idea of development to which we came after this was an idea of what it would be like to live according to the whole man. We knew that in luxury and asceticism man lives only according to a part of his being, but we did not have any positive idea as yet of how he could live according to the whole of his being. Looking once again to the lives of Gotama and Jesus, we observed that when they returned from the wilderness they spent the remainder of their lives sharing their insights with others. Human development is largely a matter of human relations, and the sharing of insight, we surmised, is probably the essence of human relations at their highest and best. Looking to our own experience with human relations, we found that the ambivalence or mixture of feelings which pervades them and the pursuit of certainty to which this leads is a major source of human misery. The union of minds and hearts based upon the sharing of insight, we concluded, implies a compassionate understanding of the ambivalence of human feeling and a real conversion from the pursuit of certainty to the pursuit of understanding. It comes about as a person works his way through the human relations appropriate to each stage of life, childhood, youth, manhood, and age, and becomes willing to outgrow them and be outgrown in them by others.

The insight into suffering which all this yielded was an insight into the suffering that arises from lack of concreteness, when a man suffers from the inadequacy of luxury or asceticism as a way of life, and into that which arises from lack of development, when a man suffers from the inadequacy of his human relations. Passing over by sympathetic understanding from the standpoint of one's own life to that of other lives tends to alleviate suffering, we learned, for it awakens the latent possibilities in one's own life which are being neglected in one's way of life and it leads to a forgiveness that heals the hurts of one's human relations. There is a more ultimate source of suffering, however, which is not directly touched by passing over to the lives of other persons, and that is one's own concrete destiny. The whole man is a concrete individual and the road of his development is a singular path of individuation. There is a deep-running resentment which a man tends to feel at his personal fate. We ended with the possibility that this resentment might be healed by passing over to God and adopting a standpoint of universal care and compassion. Now we must see whether man really can pass over to God and whether God, in his turn, passes over somehow to man.

NOTES

1. Cf. Malraux, *Anti-Memoirs,* pp. 5 f. Malraux heard the story from Maxim Gorky who, unbeknown to Tolstoy, was following Tolstoy that day at a distance.
2. Cf. *Mahavagga,* I, 21, 1, tr. by T. W. Rhys Davids and Herman Oldenberg in F. Max Müller (ed.), *The Sacred Books of the East,* vol. XIII (reprinted at Delhi, Motilal Banarsidass, 1965), pp. 134 f. Cf. also T. S. Eliot, *Collected Poems* (New York, Harcourt, 1936), pp. 78 ff. Part III of Eliot's "Wasteland" is called "The Fire Sermon" and alludes to Buddha's sermon.
3. Peter Brown, *Augustine of Hippo* (Berkeley, University of California Press, 1967), pp. 146 ff.
4. Goethe is quoted to this effect by William James in *The Varieties of Religious Experience* (New York, Random, 1936), p. 135.

5. Gandhi, *The Story of My Experiments with Truth,* p. 505. On his reading of Tolstoy cf. *ibid.,* pp. 90, 137, and 160.
6. Norman Malcolm, *Ludwig Wittgenstein: A Memoir* (London, Oxford University Press, 1967), p. 100 (the last page). On the influence of Tolstoy which led Wittgenstein to give away his inheritance cf. the short biography by Von Wright under the same cover with Malcolm's memoir, p. 10.

   The reason I point out all these connections with Tolstoy is to raise a question about the apparent failure of the simple life advocated by Tolstoy and put into practice in different ways by Gandhi and Wittgenstein. I am implicitly answering this question in the next paragraph and in the whole chapter.
7. Philippians 4:7.
8. In his first sermon he tells the five ascetics with whom he had been associated before his enlightenment not to call him "friend." Cf. *Mahavagga,* I, 6, 11, and 12 in Müller, *op. cit.,* p. 92.
9. *Majjhima-nikaya,* I, 426 ff., tr. by Robert Chalmers, *Further Dialogues of the Buddha,* vol. I (London, Oxford University Press, 1926), pp. 304 ff.
10. *Mahavagga,* I, 6, 18 in Müller, *op. cit.,* p. 95.
11. Cf. *Jataka,* I, 58, 31 ff., tr. by Henry Clarke Warren, *Buddhism in Translations* (Cambridge, Mass., Harvard University Press, 1922), pp. 56 ff.
12. Matthew 11:7.
13. Cf. *Majjhima-nikaya,* I, 163 ff. in Chalmers, *op. cit.,* pp. 115 ff.
14. The proverb is quoted in I Corinthians 15:32. The song I am translating is the well-known medieval students' song:

    Gaudeamus igitur,
    Juvenes dum sumus.
    Post jucundam juventutem,
    Post molestam senectutem,
    Nos habebit humus.
15. Cf. Sylvia T. Warner's introduction to her biography *T. H. White* (London, Cape with Chatto and Windus, 1967), pp. 23 f.
16. Quoted by M. J. Durry, *Flaubert et ses projets inédits* (Paris, Nizet, 1950), p. 239. One can find the three successive versions of Flaubert's *Tentation de Saint Antoine* in Flaubert, *Oeuvres complètes,* vol. I (Paris, Editions du Seuil, 1964), pp. 375 ff.
17. *Majjhima-nikaya,* I, 71 f. in Chalmers, *op. cit.,* p. 48. Cf. also in F. L. Woodward, *Some Sayings of the Buddha* (London, Oxford University Press, 1960), pp. 294 f.
18. *Majjhima-nikaya,* I, 168 in Chalmers, *op. cit.,* p. 118.
19. Quoted by C. G. Jung in his autobiography *Memories, Dreams, Reflections,* ed. by Aniela Jaffé and tr. by Richard and Clara Winston (New York, Vintage, 1963), p. 186.
20. Cf. Jung, *Answer to Job,* tr. by R. F. C. Hull (New York, Meridian, 1960), p. 185, where he likens unconscious individuation to being dragged through life and conscious individuation to walking through life upright.
21. Jung, *Memories, Dreams, Reflections,* pp. 296 f.
22. *King Lear,* Act I, scene 1, line 293.
23. Cf. Erik Erikson, *Gandhi's Truth,* pp. 235 and 243 f. on the ambivalence in Gandhi's relationship to his wife Kasturbai and his son Harilal.

24. Cf. my discussion of it in *A Search for God in Time and Memory,* pp. 217 ff., where it is primarily a change of mind but already to some extent a change of heart.
25. Cf. Erik Erikson's discussion of this scheme, *op. cit.,* 36 ff. and 176 ff. Cf. Gandhi's own account of his transition from householder to forest-dweller in *The Story of My Experiments with Truth,* p. 206.
26. Cf. my theory of the ages of life in *A Search for God in Time and Memory,* pp. 126 ff., where the child is the "immediate man," the youth is the "existential man," and the man is the "historic man."
27. Cf. my preface to Eugene Geissler's *There Is a Season* (Notre Dame, Ind., Ave Maria Press, 1969) and the view he develops in the book on the two confrontations with life, first in one's own youth and then in the youth of one's children.
28. John 16:7.
29. *Majjhima-nikaya,* I, 134 f. in Chalmers, *op. cit.,* pp. 94 f.
30. Jean Paul Sartre, *No Exit and Three Other Plays* (*No Exit* tr. by Stuart Gilbert) (New York, Vintage, 1956), p. 47. Sartre's sentence is "L'enfer, c'est les autres."
31. The text of the Four Truths is in *Mahavagga,* I, 6, 17 ff. in Muller, *op. cit.,* pp. 94 ff. There are two versions of the Beatitudes, one in Matthew 5:1 ff. and the other in Luke 6:20 ff.
32. Aeschylus, *Agamemnon,* 187. Cf. also Homer, *Iliad,* XVII, 32; Hesiod, *Works and Days,* 218; Herodotus, *Histories,* I, 207; Plato, *Symposium,* 222B.
33. Cf. my discussion of this in *The City of the Gods,* pp. 123 f.
34. Cf. my discussion of this in *A Search for God in Time and Memory,* pp. 12 f., 75, 113, and 193 ff. I am aware of the possibility that Jesus was simply reciting Psalm 22, which begins with these words. Even so, he could have really meant these words and felt them as eminently appropriate.
35. E.g. in Herodotus, *Histories,* I, 207, and in Shakespeare, *King Lear,* 2, 2, 180, and 5, 3, 176.
36. I am thinking here of the Beatitudes in Luke rather than of those in Matthew. Note how in Luke they are followed by the corresponding Woes.
37. Cf. *Majjhima-nikaya,* I, 22 f. in Chalmers, *op. cit.,* pp. 15 ff.
38. This was in *A Search for God in Time and Memory*. Cf. especially the preface and the first chapter.
39. Cf. the various sources of the *anatta* doctrine tr. by Warren, *op. cit.,* pp. 129 ff.
40. Here I am thinking of the Beatitudes in Matthew rather than of those in Luke. Instead of the poor in spirit Jesus speaks in Luke simply of the poor, instead of those who hunger and thirst for righteousness he speaks simply of the hungry, and he says "Blessed are you who hunger *now,* for you shall be filled. Blessed are you who weep *now,* for you shall laugh." The Beatitudes in Luke do seem to mean "Blessed are you who suffer, for you shall enjoy bliss soon, when the kingdom comes."
41. Here I am putting together different accounts of the passion of Jesus. Luke is the one who has Jesus say "Father, forgive them, for they know not what they do," while Matthew and Mark have him say, "My God, my God, why have you forsaken me?"
42. Luke 23:46.

43. Cf. my previous discussion of this in *A Search for God in Time and Memory,* pp. 179 ff. There I did not speak of forgiving God, but I did speak of the change in religious thought which has taken place in the nineteenth and twentieth centuries, going over from answering Job to taking Job's part.

44. On the ideal of the Bodhisattva cf. the Diamond Sutra tr. by Edward Conze in *Buddhist Wisdom Books* (London, Allen & Unwin, 1958), pp. 21 ff.

45. Hegel, *Lectures on the History of Philosophy,* vol. I, tr. by Elizabeth S. Haldane (London, K. Paul, Trench, Trubner and Co., 1892), pp. 20 ff.

III
The God in Disguise

"ONCE UPON A TIME there was a great king over many realms, and he was just and wise and a strong young man; by day and night he used to go round his dominions to see how they were being managed and governed. And many times he used to travel simply dressed and not to be recognized, in order that he might better see and learn about affairs."[1]

This is the beginning of a folktale. Let us turn it into a story of God. First let us take up the idea which arose towards the end of Chapter Two, that a man tends to resent his personal fate. A man, let us say, tends to desire the impossible: the old man may want to be young, the short man to be tall, the black man to be white, the woman to be a man. Let us add also the idea which came up in Chapter One, that man's desire is to be divine, and God's desire is to be human. Let us imagine that God often comes among us, that he comes among us whenever we need him. We could also say, following the folktale, that he comes among us to see how things are going among us, to see for himself with the seeing that comes from sharing human experience. Whenever God comes among us, it is, let us suppose, "without rank, without office, without temporal honors, almost without a name," as Rilke said in one of his *Stories of God*.[2] It would seem inappropriate, if we consider how the king in the folktale used to travel simply dressed and not to be recognized, for God to come among us as a "very important person." And what then would he do if he came among us? He would show us how to live, how to be old, how to be small, how to be black, how to be human.

The God in disguise figures in several of the great religions. In Mahayana Buddhism there are the Bodhisattvas, human beings, to be sure, but human beings who care for all beings and who refrain from entering Nirvana in order to save others. In Hinduism there are the Avatars, the incarnations of God, who act without seeking the fruits of action. In Christianity there is the incarnate Logos, who reveals to men what God is. All of them correspond in some degree to the God of our story, for they all come in human guise and show men how to live. There are some differences too. The God of our story comes whenever we need him; the Bodhisattvas appear in every age; the Avatars come "whenever righteousness declines and unrighteousness prevails";[3] the Logos is incarnated "once and for all."[4] Let us see now if we cannot attain some understanding of each of these versions of the God in disguise, including the one in our story. Our method of experimenting with truth would require us to re-enact, as far as we can, the doings of God in each of his disguises and thus to pass over, as it were, to the standpoint of God. This is not as impossible as it sounds. Insofar as these doings were in human guise and were meant to show men how to live, they were meant to be re-enacted.

1. To Care for All Beings

Imagine a man who cared for all beings. One way of imagining him would be to envision a person greatly burdened with cares. The care for all beings would be the heaviest burden imaginable. If we were to compare all the human emotions with one another, joy and sorrow, love and hatred, fear and anger, desire and disgust, hope and despair, we would find that there is one thing common to them all, and that is care. Even joy would not be possible if one were completely carefree, if one cared about nothing, for then there would be nothing to be joyful about. Thus the existentialists have said that care is the essence of human existence.[5] It is certainly the heart of every human feeling. Because it is the essence of human existence, though, human life is pervaded by suffering. There is an axiom in both Buddhism and Hinduism to the effect that existence is pain.[6] The pain of human existence, it seems, is the care which is its essence. The careworn face is the very image of human suffering. Now if we imagine a person who is burdened not merely by the ordinary cares of human life, care for himself and for his family and friends and for whomever else is committed to his charge, but by care for all beings, we are imagining, it would seem, a person in great pain.

What we are imagining, though, is really no more than an extension of ordinary human care. It could be, in fact, that care changes qualitatively as well as quantitatively when it is extended from some to all. On the one hand, it could be that care cannot be extended without diluting it, that to care for all is to care for none. On the other hand, it could be that to care for all is to care for whatever it is that all beings share—call it Being. Let us explore this last possibility. What would it be to care for Being? "Man," Heidegger has said, "is the shepherd of Being."[7] Heidegger said this in his *Letter on Humanism* to contrast a concern for Being with a humanism that would be concerned only about human beings and human existence. He had in mind a concern for Being that would pervade man's thinking. What would it be, though, for such a concern to pervade man's living? What would a shepherd of Being be like?

The kind of thinking to which an interest in Being leads seems to be very similar to the wisdom that is to be found in Buddhist wisdom books like the Diamond Sutra and the Heart Sutra. The kind of living to which it would lead is probably the life of the wise man described there, the Bodhisattva, the man "whose essence is enlightenment," the man who cares for all beings. What makes a Bodhisattva is the resolve to lead all beings to Nirvana. "As many beings as there are in the universe of beings," he vows, "all these I must lead to Nirvana, into the realm of Nirvana which leaves nothing behind."[8] This is his burden. But then, according to the Diamond Sutra, he adds "And yet, although innumerable beings have thus been led to Nirvana, no being at all has been led to

Nirvana." His burden turns out to be light, to be no burden at all; his task turns out to be no task.

The pain and the burden of existence, we said, is care, the care for beings. Nirvana, literally "extinction," would be the extinction of that pain, the lifting of that burden, the end of existence itself insofar as care is its essence. One way of understanding Nirvana would be to take it as sheer annihilation. It could be, however, that the care for beings is extinguished not so much by death and annihilation as by another care, the care for Being. This second way of understanding the extinction would make much more sense of the Bodhisattva's vow. The Bodhisattva cares for all beings and yet he is carefree. He cares and he is carefree in the light of the ultimate truth, in the anticipation of Nirvana. If Nirvana were sheer annihilation, it could make sense to be carefree but it would make no sense to care. If, on the contrary, Nirvana is the extinction of the ordinary care for beings in the care for Being, then it makes sense both to care and to be carefree. The Bodhisattva's secret, it seems, is this, to care in such a way that care is not a pain and a burden. Let us see if we cannot penetrate this secret. Let us see first what the interest in Being does to thinking, and then let us see what the care for Being does to living.

To take an interest in Being is to reflect upon what all beings share, upon what is common to all, upon what is most taken for granted. It gives one's thought a negative turn, for there is little to say about Being except that it is no particular being. It is not the earth, not the sky, not a man, not a god. It is no thing, no-thing, nothing. Perhaps this is what Hegel meant when he said "Being is Nothing."[9] One can spend one's time thinking and talking like this; it is the kind of thinking and talking that fills Buddhist wisdom books like the Diamond Sutra and the Heart Sutra. It is not the complete waste of time that it seems to be. Reflecting upon what is most taken for granted gives one a new frame of mind. It is when one turns in this frame of mind to particular beings, though, that one's thought begins to become evidently fruitful. In this frame of mind one tends to see particular beings as participating, each in its own way, in Being. One starts trying to discover and define the different modes of participation.[10] This leads, I have found, to a way of thinking in which one studies a manifold such as cultures or lives or religions and tries to discover what it is that is most taken for granted in each element of the manifold, in each culture or in each life or in each religion. What is most translucent, most pervading, most seemingly necessary in a culture or a life or a religion, what is like the air one breathes there; this is what one seeks to discover.[11]

Say one is studying cultures. What is most fundamental in a culture, I think, is the culture's solution to the problem of death.[12] The question of Being in a culture, it seems, is the problem of death in that culture. What I mean by "the problem of death" is not so much the question of what happens to man after death as the question of what to do in the face of man's mortality. If a man must die someday, what can he do to satisfy his desire to live? The question is seldom posed this explicitly. We can find, nevertheless, what amounts to an answer to this question in the way of life characteristic of the culture, in the life story as it is told in the epic and dramatic poetry and in the historical and biographical prose of the culture. In some cultures the life story is a story of deeds; in some it is a story of experience; in some of the more modern ones it is a story of self-realization. Each of these types of life story goes with a way of life, and each story or each way of life is an answer to death. By doing deeds that will live on after his death, by running the gamut of experience before he dies, by realizing himself during life, man defeats death and overcomes his own mortality.

Each of these ways of overcoming death is a way of participating in Being, but only a particular way, a way which fails to exhaust Being and thus a way which ultimately fails to satisfy man. If one looks more closely at man, if one turns from man in the large as he appears in cultures to man in the small as he appears in individual lives, one finds further and more far-reaching possibilities. Many possibilities, although they exist in every man, fail to appear in man at large and are to be seen clearly only in the lives of individuals whose consciousness is unusually expanded. They appear when a man engages in a process of bringing time to mind, as he does when writing an autobiography. He has to recollect at least his own lifetime to write an autobiography, but he may go further and penetrate the greater time in which his lifetime is encompassed. Sometimes, in fact, the process of recollection is carried to great lengths, as in Augustine's *Confessions* where it is carried back beyond birth to the womb and beyond that to the nothingness preceding the beginning of life.[13] This nothingness, to Augustine, was the same as the nothingness preceding the beginning of time—he spends the last books of his autobiography talking about the beginning of time and the creation of the world from nothingness.

To confront the nothingness at the beginning of one's life is to become aware of one's existence in a new way; to see this nothingness as identical with the nothingness at the beginning of the world is to become aware of Being in a new way. It is as though one could remember the very beginning of time. Perhaps we could compare Augustine's recollection of the beginning of time with Gotama's recollection of his former lives. Augustine's recollection, it is true, was predicated on a denial of pre-existence, the kind of pre-existence he had once believed in as a Manichee and a Neoplatonist. Gotama's recollection, however, as Buddhist tradition emphasizes, was a recollection of *all* his former existences, not just of some of them.[14] To remember all one's former lives would bring one back to the beginning and the edge of nothingness. Maybe an expansion of consciousness like this, like Gotama's or like Augustine's, is the starting point of religions. The expansion, as it occurs in the religions, seems to take place in both directions, to the nothingness at the beginning, in the direction of birth, and to the nothingness at the end, in the direction of death, and it seems to transform not only thinking but also living.

A man goes from remembering to understanding, according to Augustine, and from understanding to willing.[15] This is how he verges over from thinking to living, we could say, from taking an interest in Being to caring for Being. The first thing he must do is remember. Or, since his consciousness must expand in both directions, towards the past and towards the future, perhaps we should use a more comprehensive terminology and say that he must "bring time to mind." He must reach backwards in memory to the nothingness of the beginning and he must reach forwards in anticipation to the nothingness of the end. How is he to go about doing this? The most practical way I have found of occasioning an expansion of consciousness like this is to sketch out an autobiography and compose a personal creed.[16] Sketching out one's autobiography will tend to bring consciousness at least to the confines of one's lifetime; composing a personal creed will tend to carry it into the greater time encompassing the lifetime, maybe even to the nothingness at the beginning and the end.

After remembering comes understanding. Once a man has brought his own life and times to mind, in the manner just suggested, he is able to improve his understanding of them by entering sympathetically into the lives and times of others, by passing over to the standpoints of others and coming back to his own standpoint enriched. Each time he comes back from passing over he sees his own existence in a new light. If he were able to pass over to all other lives and times, he would be able to see his own existence from all points of view and comprehend it fully. There is not time enough in a single lifetime, though, to pass over to all other lives one by one. There is, nevertheless, an overall understanding which can be achieved without having actually entered into all lives and times. The possibility of passing over seems to imply that each man is somehow all men, that each life is somehow all lives. If I can pass over to another man's standpoint and see things as he sees them, there must be something in me corresponding to what I find in him, something which awakens and resonates in me when I enter into his life. Even a limited experience with passing over can reveal this to me. If, therefore, I come to understand this, the basis of passing over which exists within myself, it is as though I had passed over to all lives and all times.

Of course I will not be able to comprehend fully the basis of passing over and to see distinctly in myself all the possibilities that would come to life in actually passing over, and so to that extent it will not be quite the same as having passed over to all lives and times. What I will understand, however, is that I have within myself in some manner everything that I will ever be able to discover in other men. This discovery by itself is enough to profoundly change my attitude towards other men. What happens is that I cease "wishing me like to one more rich in hope, featur'd like him, like him with friends possess'd, desiring this man's art, and that man's scope."[17] This is the willing that comes after understanding. Actually it is more like a cessation of willing; it is the cessation of envy, of the will to be what others are. At the same time, though, and for the same reason, it is the cessation of jealousy, of the unwillingness to let others be what I am. The cessation of envy is the cessation of a willing and thus leads to inactivity; the cessation of jealousy, on the contrary, is the cessation of an unwillingness and leads to a new kind of activity. It leads to a sharing with others of whatever one has and is—like the life which Gotama looked back upon when he lay dying, telling his disciples that he had concealed nothing, that he did not have the "closed fist of a teacher."[18]

The cessation of envy and jealousy means turning from the differences among human beings to what they share. What human beings share, though, is not merely a nature which sets them apart from other beings. The concept of man implicit in the process of passing over is that man is a microcosm, that he reflects the whole universe from a particular standpoint. He must indeed reflect the whole universe if he is to have the possibility of seeing the whole universe not only from his own standpoint but from every other standpoint as well. Leibniz conceived man in a fashion like this, as a microcosm reflecting the whole universe from a particular standpoint, but Leibniz's microcosms were monads "with no windows";[19] he meant by this that nothing could enter them from the outside, but he seems also to have had no thought of it being possible to pass over from one standpoint to another.

The very fact that a man reflects everything in the universe, it seems to me, implies that all possibilities, all standpoints, exist somehow within him, that he is able to adopt standpoints other than his own, and thus that his own standpoint, his selfhood, is much less constitutive of him than Leibniz supposed. Because man reflects the entire universe, to care for what human beings share is to care for what all beings share; it is to care not only for human nature but for Being.

Ordinarily a man's care locates him firmly and fixedly in his own standpoint, the autobiographical standpoint, the standpoint which he would take if he were telling the story of his own life. All other beings figure in this standpoint, but they figure only insofar as they play a role in his life. The world is simply the stage upon which the drama of his life is enacted. Other human beings are merely players in that drama. Some of them play major parts; some play minor parts; most are only extras. He himself plays the leading part. His care extends to others in proportion to the part they play. He cares very much about some persons, although they have little importance in the eyes of the general public, for they play essential roles in his life. He cares very little about others, although they may be famous and may be generally considered "very important persons," for they play little or no role in his life—he may have seen them at a public gathering or met them at a party or had some formal business with them. If he were to tell the story of his life, he would very rightly make little of these famous persons, probably not even mention them, for if he made much of them he would falsify the story, as though their casual presence in it lent it some kind of significance. He would make much, on the other hand, of the relatively unknown persons who played important roles in his life, and who formed the chief burden of his care.

All this is very proper and true to his life. If he were to engage in the practice of passing over, though, to the standpoints of other persons, not necessarily to the standpoints of famous persons but just to the standpoints of the persons closest to him, he would discover a different view of the world and of people and of himself. The world would appear in each instance as the stage for a drama, but always a different drama. Human beings would be players, but they would always have different parts. He himself might have a major part, if he were to pass over to the standpoint of someone close to him, but it would not be the leading part.

The practice of passing over like this would tend to have an effect on his care for others. As long as he remained in his own standpoint, he would care for others as belonging to him. By passing over, though, he would learn to care for others as belonging to themselves. This, it seems, would be considerably less burdensome. It would mean being willing to let others play the leading roles in the drama of their own lives as well as the subordinate and supporting roles which they play in his life, and on his part being willing to play the subordinate and supporting role which he has in their lives as well as the leading role in his own life.

This would already be a step towards caring for Being. It would become explicitly care for Being when he discovered what we have called the basis of passing over, the fact that man is a microcosm, that he reflects the entire universe from a particular standpoint. Once a man sees this and feels this within himself he feels a kinship with all beings, and he comes to care for all where before he had cared for few except those he considered closest to himself and belonging to himself. The cessation of envy and jealousy which occurs when he sees and feels this way makes it possible for him to dedicate his life to others. What he seeks for them is the very thing he has found for himself, that their possessive and burdensome care for beings be extinguished in or transformed into the care for Being. This, we suggested earlier, rather than sheer nothingness, is the meaning of Nirvana. Thus the Bodhisattva's vow to lead all beings to Nirvana. In this light, moreover, the nothingness at the end of life and time looks like a mask of Being, and the Nirvana spoken of in Buddhism seems very comparable to the Eternal Life spoken of in Christianity.

In this light too the nothingness at the beginning could be seen as a mask of Being; the whole universe of beings could be seen as owing its origin to the care for Being. This would be easy enough to say in the language of religions like Judaism, Christianity, and Islam where there is a doctrine of God and of creation. The care for Being would be the love or the consuming fire that God is, and would be the creative power that calls the world forth out of nothingness. In a religion like Buddhism, where there is no doctrine of God or of creation, but only a silence on such matters, this is not so easy to say. Perhaps we could say it nonetheless, at least without contradicting the teachings of Buddhism. The man who cares for Being, who is the shepherd of Being, we could say, is the shadow of a divine providence and a divine shepherd. The man who cares for beings as belonging to themselves rather than to him is the shadow of a God who, in spite of his love for the world, could permit all the suffering which exists in the world. How, we may now ask, would a man like this act? How would a God like this act?

2. *To Act Without Seeking the Fruits of Action*

"Whosoever would undertake some atrocious enterprise," Borges said in one of his stories, "should act as if it were already accomplished, should impose upon himself a future as irrevocable as the past."[20] Almost every one of the activities to which a man can devote his life can seem an atrocious enterprise. Consider these three: labor, work, and action.[21] To devote one's life to labor, to toiling with one's body, can seem like doing to oneself what a judge might do to a criminal, sentencing him to many years of hard labor. To devote one's life to a work of some kind, to an art or a craft, can seem tantamount to dwarfing oneself as a man, making oneself skilled but spiritually misshapen and ugly like the dwarves of legend who poured all their energies into their works. To devote one's life to action, to the use of power in public life, can seem like selling or losing or destroying one's soul, using other persons as means to an end, doing violence to them and becoming oneself a violent man. Even to devote one's life to sharing insight with others, as did Socrates or Gotama or Jesus, can seem an atrocious enterprise insofar as it can seem to be a life of giving without receiving, and thus an unbalanced and inhuman existence.

To act as if an atrocious enterprise were already accomplished, to impose upon oneself in undertaking it a future as irrevocable as the past, as Borges advised, has a liberating effect. It does not liberate one from the atrocious enterprise; it liberates one for it, it makes one free to carry it out. There are many things a man will find too difficult to do, many risks he cannot bring himself to take, many obstacles he does not trouble to overcome, as long as he still contemplates the possibility of abandoning the enterprise. Only when he has excluded that possibility will he be free to do those things, to take those risks, to overcome those obstacles. Gandhi speaks of the liberating effect which the vow of celibacy (*Brachmacharya*) had upon his life, how celibacy liberated him for public service and how the vow of celibacy liberated him for celibacy itself. "I realized," he says, "that a vow, far from closing the door to real freedom, opened it."[22] Perhaps we could compare his vow to the rather more transcendental vow of the Bodhisattva to lead all beings to Nirvana. The atrociousness of the enterprise in both instances, the reason a vow is needed, is that the life can sometimes seem one of giving without receiving. Such a life, however unbalanced it may appear, can yet seem well worth vowing. Would it be worthwhile, though, to dedicate oneself in this manner to the other activities we have named, to free oneself in this fashion for labor or for work or for action?

It could be, if freeing oneself for labor were to take the condemnation and punishment out of labor, if freeing onself for work were to prevent the dwarfing of manhood by work, if freeing oneself for action were to avert the selling of the soul in action. The message of the *Bhagavad-Gita* is that something like this can be done with action, and by implication also with work and labor. The Gita is a dialogue between a man and a God. The man, Arjuna, is a prince and a warrior and is about to join battle with his foes, but he sees his kin among them and this leads him to contemplate the possibility of giving up the battle. Killing his kin in battle seems to him indeed an atrocious enterprise. The God, Krishna, who is his charioteer, then exhorts him not to give up but to fight. Ultimately Krishna, who till then has appeared to Arjuna only in human guise, reveals his divine form. Arjuna sees a grim and terrible vision of the God; he sees his foes being devoured by flames in the God's blazing mouths. Krishna tells him to go ahead and fight, for his foes are already doomed. Arjuna is to act as though the atrocious enterprise were already accomplished; he is to impose upon himself a future as irrevocable as the past.

Prior to this Arjuna had been seeking what the Gita terms the "fruits of action." He had come to the battle attracted by the desirable fruit of battle, the "joys of kingship," the prize for which the battle was to be fought, but once he had arrived on the scene he was repelled by the undesirable fruit, the blood of his kinfolk which he would have to shed, the "sin of destroying a family" which he would have to incur. Krishna's teaching is that he should renounce the fruits of action, both the bitter and the sweet—that he should not let the sweet fruit cause his action nor let the bitter fruit deter it. To act in this way, without seeking the fruits of action, would be to act for the sake of the action itself. This is the way a man would have to act if he were to impose upon himself a future as irrevocable as the past, for he would have to be willing to carry through the action even if the bitter fruit were forthcoming, even if the sweet fruit were not forthcoming. This, Krishna reveals to Arjuna, is the way the God himself acts.

It may be possible for us to recapture something of this revelation, to catch a glimpse of this God, simply by considering what happens to labor, work, and action when their fruits are renounced. Consider, first of all, the fruits of labor and what it would be to renounce them. Renouncing the fruits of an activity, as this is understood in the Gita, does not mean giving up the activity: Arjuna is not to give up but to fight. It does not even mean giving up the fruits of the activity: Arjuna is to accept the bitter along with the sweet. Rather it means measuring the fruits by the activity instead of measuring the activity by the fruits. Renouncing the fruits of labor, for instance, would mean measuring the fruits of labor by the labor required to produce them instead of measuring labor by its fruitfulness or productivity. This sounds like the "labor theory of value," the theory that the quantity of labor in a product regulates its value. This was the theory Karl Marx utilized to vindicate for labor the sole rightful claim to production.

What we are speaking of here, though, is not a theory of value so much as an attitude which a man might take towards his own labor. He can define or construe his labor as "making a living"; he can construe it as "making a contribution" to society. The difference between the one fruit and the other, the excess of the contribution over the living, is what Marx called the "surplus value," and was the core of his theory of labor and his critique of capital. Now suppose instead of measuring his labor by its fruits, the living or the contribution, a man measures these by the time he puts into laboring. This, according to Marx, is the real value of labor and is what determines the exchange value of its products, the contribution and the living.[23] Let us suppose, though, that instead of adopting this as a theory and a program a man adopts it simply as an attitude. Suppose he measures the living he makes and the contribution he makes by the time, the portion of his life, which he puts into making them. In his own mind he will no longer be categorized by the living he makes as "low," "middle," or "high" income, nor will he be categorized by the contribution he makes as "important" or "average" or "insignificant." He will be in his own eyes not a poor man or a rich man, not an important man or an unimportant man, but simply a man.

Labor, we can say, is his activity considered as time. Now let us consider his activity under a different aspect, as activity in a space or in a place or in a world. Under this aspect his activity is the making or a part in the making of that space or place or world. Let us assume that his activity is creative in a very high degree. Say he is a poet—a "maker," as the name "poet" implies in its root meaning—and that he therefore creates "universes of discourse," worlds composed of words but also worlds composed of things insofar as his words bring things together in new relationships. Or say he is an engineer and that he creates spaces as an architectural engineer or places as a civil engineer or systems of power as a mechanical or electrical engineer. These worlds of discourse or space or place or power are the fruits of his activity as a maker. And yet, however creative he may be, once these worlds have been created they can be reproduced by automatic methods; and, what is more, his activity in creating them can be replaced to some degree by automatic machines or processes or systems.

"If I did not work," Krishna says in the Gita, "these worlds would perish."[24] Perhaps we could say the same of the man who is a maker. If he did not continue to work, but allowed his activity to be replaced by automation in order to multiply its fruits, then the worlds he creates by his work would perish. They would perish by losing their human significance. An example would be what is called "experimental music." There is one kind of experimental music which consists of creative experiments in the organization of sound and silence and time.[25] There is another kind, however, which consists merely in the production of conventional music by automatic procedures, such as an electronic computer.[26] Music of the latter kind is experimental in a direction opposite to that of the experiment we are now carrying out; it is an experiment in multiplying the fruits of an activity. A man will resort to automatic procedures of this sort only if he values the fruits rather than the activity of making. This has the effect of dwarfing him as a man. If, on the other hand, he is able to withstand the temptation of multiplying the fruits and to put his heart into the activity of making, he finds himself working according to a style or a principle rather than according to an automatic procedure. This, while enhancing his activity and the human significance of his works, has the effect of increasing his liability to failure.

A hard choice, therefore, may be imposed upon a man, between assured success and many works on the one hand and humanly significant activity and possible failure on the other. The choice may appear still harder if we consider his activity as action, as intercourse with other human beings. Under this aspect the choice between an assured existence and a possible failure is the choice between a private and a public life. Let us suppose that he has a public life of some kind, that his work is somehow an interaction with others, that he is in some way a man before others. He will have experienced considerable anxiety over this public life of his, we can assume, hoping for acceptance by others and fearing their rejection. The burden of anxiety will often have tempted him to withdraw from public life and retire into a purely private life. The temptation will have been reinforced by current views, both individualistic and collectivistic. There is the individualistic tendency to regard a man's public life as a kind of false front, a false position into which he has gotten himself and in which he is forced into playacting. Then there is the tendency of collectivistic thinking to regard an individual man as of no account up against the mass movements and massive forces involved in human affairs.

In the end he is bold enough, let us imagine, to flout both individualism and collectivism and to continue his public life. Instead of feeling that he is in a false position, he feels that others see right through him, no matter whether he is trying to playact or trying to be sincere. Instead of feeling impotent up against the mass movements and massive forces involved in human affairs, he feels that he has great influence upon others, though it is an influence which he cannot easily direct or control. The real problem, as he sees it, is the burden of anxiety, his hopes of acceptance and his fears of rejection. He begins to suspect that the disregard for public life in individualism and collectivism is really an attempt to escape its burdens. What he seeks for himself is a way of lifting the burden of anxiety without withdrawing into private life. To renounce the fruits of action, the way of the Gita, seems to be the very path he is seeking. If it is possible to renounce the hope of success and the fear of failure without losing all motive for engaging in public life, then the Gita's way is a possibility for him. Public life would have to be worthwhile to him in itself, apart from success or failure. Being a man before others would have to seem to him an integral part of being a man, like being a man before oneself and being a man before God.

Now if we compare the fruits of his public life with the fruits of his work and the fruits of his labor, we find that they are all ultimately one and the same thing. The living and the contribution which he makes by his labor is the world which he creates by his work, and this world is the sphere of influence and reputation which he achieves by his action. Similarly his labor, work, and action are ultimately one and the same activity. His activity considered as time or as a portion of his lifetime is his labor; considered as activity in a world or as the making of a world it is his work; considered as intercourse with other human beings or as activity before others it is his action. The Gita, to be sure, envisioned these as different activities proper to different castes of men: labor was the activity of the Sudras, work was that of the Vaisyas, and action was that of the Kshatriyas. And yet its doctrine of acting without seeking the fruits of the activity was supposed to apply to all, to Kshatriyas like Arjuna in the first place but also to Vaisyas and Sudras.[27] The experience of labor, work, and action in our own times reveals, it seems, that they are one and the same activity considered under different aspects.

They are different ways in which a man's activity can be construed. Thus it is possible for there to be a caste society like that of the Gita in which one man's activity is construed under one of these aspects and another's under another of them, and it is possible for there to be a uniform society like ours in which each man's activity is construed under all of them. The construing will make a profound difference in a man's experience, but the situation in the uniform society makes it seem that the differentiation even in the caste society is a matter of construing. To renounce the fruits of an activity without withdrawing from the activity is also a matter of construing, it seems, and it too makes a profound difference in experience no matter whether a man is living in a caste society or a uniform society. It does not change the caste society into a uniform society nor the uniform society into a caste society. What it does do is cause the man himself to emerge in both societies. He ceases to measure himself by the living or the contribution which he makes, by the world which he creates, by the sphere of influence and reputation which he achieves. Rather he measures these things by the labor, the work, the action that went into them.

This leaves him unmeasured. Formerly he measured himself by the fruits of his activity. Now that he measures the fruits by the activity that goes into them he is left without a measure of his own stature and being. Unless God is the measure. Arjuna, according to the Gita, is not to measure his activity by its fruits but by the divine activity of Krishna. But Krishna does not measure his own activity by its fruits; in fact, this is what Arjuna is to imitate in him. This leaves the God altogether unmeasured. And so he is intended to be in the Gita: the vision of God which occurs when Krishna reveals his divine form to Arjuna is the vision of a being that is literally "immense," "measureless." The practice of renouncing the fruits of one's activity does lead, it seems, to a new vision of things. Perhaps we could call it a vision of God and compare it with the vision recorded in the Gita. It consists like that vision in the sight of something immense, something at once fascinating and dreadful, and it is followed, as when Krishna shows Arjuna his human form once again, by relief at the sight of the human and the familiar.

At first the vision described in the Gita is fascinating and not yet dreadful. Arjuna is fascinated by the words of Krishna describing his divine form and begs to see it; and what he sees in the beginning is everything gathered into one. It is a vision of all beings, a vision of what all beings share, a vision of Being. "Behold now," Krishna tells him, "in my body, the whole universe, moving and unmoving, all in one, and whatever else you wish to see."[28] The experience of renouncing the fruits of one's activity is comparable to the experience of going over from the care for beings to the care for Being. When a man renounces the fruits of his labor, when he measures them by the labor that went into them rather than measuring his labor by its fruitfulness, his care about making a living and making a contribution changes into care about the time and the life that goes into making them. When this time no longer receives its significance from its fruits, it appears to bear significance in itself and to give significance *to* its fruits. Time bearing significance in itself, apart from all results, and giving results whatever significance they have, is much akin to Being. When a man is no longer gauging time by the results which he can produce or needs to produce in it, he no longer seems short of time; he seems to have plenty of time; time exists for him in a kind of fullness.

"I am Time," Krishna tells Arjuna, but the vision has changed from one of fascination to one of dread, for he is time the destroyer of all things, time that brings all men to death and decay, "world-destroying, waxed full and working here to compass the destruction of the worlds."[29] Earlier Krishna had said "If I did not work, these worlds would perish," but now he seems bent on destroying these worlds. A man, as we saw, can have the experience of creating worlds by his work. If he renounces the fruits of his work, however, he has simultaneously an experience of destroying the worlds that he creates. He destroys them, so to speak, by not putting his heart into them, by putting his heart rather into the activity of making. He is like an artist who does not keep his own paintings or sculptures but sells them or gives them away, or like a child playing, building castles of sand and then destroying them. It can seem shocking to envision God this way too, to think that God would not put his heart into the worlds that he creates but rather into the creating of them. Yet the death and destruction that we see about us conjure up visions of such a God. It remains to be seen whether such visions are as far as man can go in understanding what God is doing.

If man were only one of the many worlds that God creates, he could hope for nothing better than destruction like the rest. Because he is somehow one with God, though, he not only is created and destroyed but somehow he does the creating and the destroying. Thus after the dread vision of destruction Krishna returns to his human form, as though he and Arjuna were one and as though they were going to accomplish together the destruction of the worlds. Both the destruction and the creation seem to take place, according to the implications of the Gita, in man's activity as action, as human intercourse. When a man enters public life, when he becomes a man before others, he inevitably has a destructive as well as a creative effect upon others. He is "set for the fall and rise of many . . . and for a sign which shall be spoken against . . . that the thoughts of many hearts may be revealed."[30] This happens, it seems, even if he comes unarmed and makes no appeal to force. Let us see now how far the man who does this is doing what God is doing and how far he and his God are motivated by anything more than benign indifference to the fate of mankind.

3. To Do What God Is Doing

Imagine a man standing upon the seashore just before dawn. There is darkness and mist, and the tide is at slack water time when the flood has ceased and the ebb has not yet begun. Suppose then, at the appropriate moment, the man says "Let the sun rise," and the sun begins to rise. Then, "Let the mist vanish," and the mist begins to vanish. Then, "Let the tide ebb and let the beach appear," and the tide begins to ebb and the beach to appear. Then, "Let the sun climb into the sky and let the moon and the stars give way to it," and the sun begins to climb and the moon to sink and the stars to fade. Then, "Let the fish leap in the water and let the sea gulls fly to and fro over the water," and the fish begin to leap up and the gulls to fly over. Then, "Let human beings come down to the shore and let ships appear on the horizon," and human beings begin to come and ships to appear. And then, seeing that everything is as he wishes, suppose he sits upon the shore and spends the morning contemplating the world he has evoked.

He has been thinking about the creation scene in Genesis and has been re-enacting it in an imaginative way. He has been doing what God is doing, doing it in imagination. The events he has evoked, the sun rising, the mist vanishing, the tide ebbing, are all very real, but he knows quite well that he must wait for the appropriate moment or they will not occur at his bidding, and he also knows that if he did not bid them occur at that moment they would occur anyway. What, then, has he done? He has entered into concord with what is actually occurring, and he has given imaginative expression to this concord by bidding what is occurring to occur. He has gone from feeling to imagining and expressing; he has turned the truth of the concord into poetry. Would it be possible for him to go further, though, and do what God is doing in some more substantial way? One hesitates to equate the two phrases "what is occurring" and "what God is doing." There is a problem for understanding here. What is occurring? What is God doing? Perhaps understanding will show the way to action. The man we have envisioned has gone from feeling to imagining. We could envision him going on from imagining to understanding and from understanding to acting.

To understand what God is doing and to do what he is doing are the functions of Jesus in the Gospel of John. "The Son can do nothing of himself," he says, "but only what he sees the Father doing."[31] As this statement is elaborated in the Gospel of John it becomes apparent that this is how Jesus reveals God to men, how he is the revelation of God, the "word" (*logos*) of God. He understands what God is doing and he does what God is doing. By doing humanly what God is doing, he makes God's doings understandable to men and he makes it possible for them to go and do likewise. "He who believes in me," he tells his disciples, "the things that I do shall he do also, and greater things than these shall he do, because I go to my Father."[32] These "greater things" suggest the possibility of further and further revelations of God, as man understands more and more of what God is doing and acts upon his understanding.

The difficulty, though, is to understand what God is doing at all. If we look at what is occurring in the world we see war, famine, sickness, and death.[33] If we look at what Jesus does in the Gospels we see the opposite: making peace, feeding the hungry, curing the sick, and raising the dead. Perhaps this is putting the difference too flatly. To be more accurate we could say that if we look at what is occurring in the world we see both war and peace, both famine and plenty, both sickness and health, both death and life. If, on the other hand, we look at what Jesus does in the Gospels, we see that he is not merely remedying the evils that plague mankind, for the peace he brings is not merely the end of war, the food and drink he brings are not merely the end of hunger and thirst, the wholeness he brings is not merely the end of sickness, and the life he brings is not merely the end of death. Still in all, if Jesus is doing what God is doing, then what God is doing and what is occurring in the world at large are not identical. If a man, therefore, were to understand what God is doing, let us ask, what would he see beyond what is occurring? If he were to do what God is doing, what would he do beyond concurring in what is occurring?

It would be easier to say, first of all, what he would see if he did not see beyond what is occurring. He might see that there are cycles of war and peace, cycles of famine and plenty, cycles of sickness and health, just as there are cycles of death and life as one generation of human beings succeeds another. He would be likely to take these cycles, the usual course of events, for the divine scheme of things.[34] To see beyond it he would have to realize that it is merely usual, not inevitable. To be sure, there are inevitable elements in it, particularly death; and yet the moment of death is not fully determined according to a cyclical scheme, but men die at different ages. This could lead him to surmise that it is much the same with war and famine and sickness. It may be, he would think, that each of these things is inevitable in the course of human events, but the actual time when they are to occur is not determined. If there is a scheme of things, he might conclude, it is not a simple scheme of cycles. It is rather a statistical scheme, like a mortality table, only dealing with sickness and famine and war as well as with death.

No sooner will he have thought of this second scheme, though, than he will begin to feel uneasy about it. Einstein, remarking on a similar scheme for the physical world, said "The theory gives much, but it scarcely brings us nearer to the secret of the Old Man. In any case I am convinced that He doesn't play dice."[35] A statistical scheme of things, if it is taken perhaps too seriously, if it is taken to be more than merely a way of organizing information, if it is taken to be a set of laws which reality must obey, does tend to imply a God who plays dice. No doubt, such a God would be conceivable. It would be possible, however, to envision a scheme of things in which the actual occurrence of war, famine, sickness, and death is not left to chance and the laws of chance. This scheme need not be only another set of cycles. It could be instead a scheme which concretely apportions the time of war and the time of peace, the time of famine and the time of plenty, the time of sickness and the time of health, the time of death and the time of life.

This third scheme of things, the concrete apportionment of times, makes God's doings seem similar to the work of the three Fates in Greek mythology, spinning the thread of life, measuring it out, and cutting it off. It would be like a pattern for weaving in which there would be a warp of cycles and a woof of statistics, but overall a serial design distinguishing the cycles from one another and giving each statistic a unique place in the whole fabric. A serial scheme of things would arrange all occurrences of good and evil in a single or manifold series of events, like a chronology, in which each occurrence would have a proper place and none would be merely an instance, merely an example of something common. For all its concreteness, though, a serial world could appear devoid of any profound meaning to a man attempting to understand the course of human events. The only meaning a serial scheme could assign to a given event would be a place in an orderly sequence. All the important questions would still go unanswered: Why is there war? Why famine? Why sickness? Why death? To answer questions like these a scheme would be needed which relates opposites to one another, which relates each evil to a corresponding good.

A pattern of correlated opposites like this would ordinarily be called "dialectical."[36] A dialectical scheme of things, if it is taken to be more than a method of thinking, if it is taken to be the ultimate law of reality, implies a God who brings about good through evil. He would bring about peace through war, plenty through famine, health through sickness, life through death. This begins to sound like the Gospels, especially the last part about bringing life through death. There is an important difference, though. In a dialectical scheme of the kind we are now envisioning good comes about through evil because good is understood to be nothing but the negation of evil: peace is the negation of war, plenty the negation of famine, health the negation of sickness, life the negation of death. Evil comes first in the dialectical scheme because a thing must be posited before it can be negated. In the Gospels, on the other hand, especially in the Gospel of John, good is conceived to be more than a negation of evil: the peace Jesus gives is "not as the world gives,"[37] and so also the food and the drink, the wholeness and the life he gives. What is going on according to the dialectical scheme—the transition from war to peace, from famine to plenty, from sickness to health, even the transition from death to life so far as it occurs—is only an image, it seems, of what is going on according to the Gospel of John. What is obviously occurring in the world, we could say, is only an image of what God is doing.

To do what God is doing, according to this, would not mean imposing order upon things nor would it mean playing a game of chance with things; it would not mean apportioning to things their time nor would it mean bringing their good about through their evil. It would mean bringing a peace, a sustenance, a wholeness, and a life that no scheme of things can give. Suppose now a man understands things this way. What would he do? Once we have discarded schemes it is not easy to give any answer to this question except to say that he would do what God is doing. Such an answer seems merely to beg the question. Let us see, nevertheless, where it leads. The peace, for instance, that Jesus brings is defined in the Gospel of John in his prayer "that they all may be one, as you Father in me and I in you, that they also may be one in us."[38] To do what God is doing, we could say, means being in harmony with reality at its deepest level. There might be discord with what appears to be occurring according to the various schemes of things that man devises, but there would be concord with what is really and ultimately occurring. This concord, to paraphrase the words of the prayer, would be a oneness with God and with Jesus and with all men who are acting in concert with God.

The sustenance that Jesus brings is similarly defined in the Gospel of John. "My meat," he says, "is to do the will of him who sent me, and to finish his work."[39] Jesus finds sustenance, this seems to say, in doing what God is doing. If a man could only discover what God is doing and do it himself, we could agree, surely he would find sustenance in it, for he would be living in accord with the fundamental movement of the universe. It would be like breathing; it would be nourishing and restoring instead of tiring and exhausting. How, though, is he to discover what God is doing? Perhaps the nourishing and sustaining effect itself would be the sign to look for. If what he is doing is debilitating and corrupting, then it seems he could be fairly sure that it is not what God is doing and that he must try something else. At any rate, if there were a man who did discover what God is doing and did find sustenance in doing it himself, he could show others how to do it and could thus become in his turn sustenance to them. This apparently is the basis of Jesus' saying "I am the bread of life: he who comes to me shall never hunger, and he who believes in me shall never thirst."[40]

The man who learns from Jesus to do what God is doing draws his sustenance from Jesus, we could say, but ultimately he draws it, like Jesus himself, from acting in harmony with God, and can in his turn too give sustenance to others, as is implied in the injunction "Feed my lambs," "Feed my sheep."[41] Before learning this, though, he will have been acting quite otherwise and his action, being out of harmony with what God is doing, will have had a debilitating and corrupting effect upon him. He will have been acting, most probably, in accord with one or another of the schemes we mentioned, but insofar as such schemes fail to get to the bottom of reality there will have been in his life a fatal discord with reality. This discord and the debilitating and corrupting effect which it has upon him is perhaps the malignant "sickness unto death" that is implied by contrast in Jesus' words about the more benign sickness of Lazarus, "This sickness is not unto death."[42] The wholeness which Jesus brings seems to be the healing of this sickness. It is the wholeness a man begins to experience when he turns from working at cross-purposes to working in unison with God.

He becomes capable, too, once he has made the change himself, of showing others how to make it and thus of healing them. To heal them, to sustain them, to give them peace, all come to the same thing, it seems, namely to show them how to do what God is doing. All three—the peace, the sustenance, the wholeness—are summed up in a fourth, the life that Jesus brings. This life, as he speaks of it in the Gospel of John, seems to consist of sharing the intimate life of God. "The Father loves the Son," he says, "and shows him everything that he does."[43] By showing Jesus everything that he does, the Father admits Jesus to the intimacy of his own life. Jesus then does what the Father is doing and shows everything that he himself does to other men. "I call you not servants," he tells his disciples, "for the servant does not know what his lord does, but I have called you friends, for everything that I have heard from my Father

I have made known to you."[44] And they, having been admitted to the life and the doings of Jesus and the Father, are able to bring life to other men by making these doings known to them.

Everything hinges, therefore, on what God is doing, on who knows what God is doing, and on doing what God is doing. Perhaps we could turn things around and say that the life, the wholeness, the sustenance, and the peace are themselves the signs by which a man can know whether he is concurring with God and whether what he has learned to do from someone else really amounts to working with God. "Believe me that I am in the Father and the Father in me," Jesus tells Philip, "or else believe me for the very works' sake."[45] The works are giving men life, making them whole, giving them sustenance, making peace among them. It is at this point that he goes on to say, "He who believes in me, the things that I do shall he do also, and greater things than these shall he do, because I go to the Father." If a man can experience life, wholeness, sustenance, and peace as Jesus describes them, and if he can experience the lack of them, then he can tell from this whether he himself is acting with God or acting against God and whether what he has learned from Jesus is actually to cooperate with God. It is not that he is able to judge Jesus—he may have misunderstood his teaching. What he is able to judge are his own doings and his own understanding of things.

A new understanding of God, we could even say a vision of God, comes about when a man has reached the point where, according to these signs, he is acting jointly with God. It is the vision of a God who gives peace and sustenance and wholeness to man, who admits man to his own life. When Philip asks, "Lord, show us the Father and it is enough for us," Jesus answers, "Have I been with you so long a time and yet you have not known me, Philip? He who has seen me has seen the Father."[46] This vision, clearly enough, is not a massive experience, but simply a new way of seeing things that goes with a new way of doing things. How does it compare, we may ask, with the vision of God recorded in the Gita? That vision too was a new way of seeing things that went with a new way of doing things. It was the vision of a God who acts without seeking the fruits of action. The God revealed in Krishna acts in the midst of the war, the famine, the sickness, the death we see around us in the world. The God revealed in Jesus, on the other hand, gives a peace, a sustenance, a wholeness, a life which seem to have nothing directly to do with the evils we see around us.

If God acts without seeking the fruits of action, this would explain his apparent indifference to the evils which man suffers. The vision in the Gita bridges the gap, it seems, between what God is doing and what is obviously going on in the world. It leaves us in the dark, though, as to why God acts at all. If God does not seek the fruits of action, why does he act? Evidently for the sake of the action itself. But what good is this to man? No good, one might say, unless man acts this way himself and thereby finds life and wholeness and sustenance and peace in it. This is where the vision in the Gospel of John seems to arise. The benign indifference of the God who acts without seeking the fruits of action changes into warm love for mankind if one assumes that he actually seeks these good things for mankind. But wouldn't this be seeking the fruits of action? Not if, as we have been saying, the very meaning of these things lies in the action itself, in God and man acting together.

If man finds peace in acting with God, being thus in concord with what is really and ultimately going on in the universe; if he draws sustenance from it, as if it were like breathing; if he gains wholeness through it, in that discord with the universe is a kind of sickness; if he obtains life by it, since it is an intimacy with ultimate reality; then the good for man lies in God's action itself rather than in the fruits of his action. The fruits of God's action are both creative and destructive, both peace and war, both plenty and famine, both health and sickness, both life and death. So also are the fruits of man's action, no matter how hard he tries to make them only creative and not destructive. "If I had not come and spoken to them," Jesus said of those who rejected him, "they would have had no sin, but now they have no excuse for their sin. . . . If I had not done among them things which no other has done, they would have had no sin, but now they have both seen and hated both me and my Father."[47] So even the coming of Jesus could be destructive in its fruits. If God genuinely loves man, though, he cannot simply ignore this, even if he renounces the fruits of his action, nor can the man who is trying to act in conjunction with God. What, then, would God do about it? What could a man do about it?

4. *To Know What Man Is Doing*

Let us imagine that God often comes among us in human guise. Tales to this effect were told in ancient times. The Greeks told of gods coming among men as strangers and asking them for hospitality. The Hebrews told of God coming with two angels, the three of them disguised as strangers, asking hospitality of Abraham and seeking to learn the truth about the doings of men in the cities of Sodom and Gomorrha. Such tales have even been told in modern times. One of Rilke's *Stories of God* is entitled "The Stranger." Rilke tells there how he once received a stranger who was "without rank, without office, without temporal honors, almost without a name."[48] Having some suspicion as to whom the stranger was, he asked him "Do you still remember God?" Reflecting for a time, the stranger answered "Yes." Then, to reveal his suspicions without directly stating them, Rilke told the stranger a story about God's hands. He told how God had never really finished making man and how as a consequence he had never seen a finished man, how he determined to send his right hand into the world to take human form, and how he was not fully satisfied with what he learned from this one hand. "I often think," Rilke concluded, "perhaps God's hand is on its way again."

His suspicion, clearly enough, was that the stranger who asked his hospitality was the left hand of God. Let us put this together, for our own purposes, with something that Lessing said about the hands of God. Lessing said that, if God held all truth in his right hand and in his left the lifelong pursuit of it, he would choose the left.[49] Let us suppose that the right hand of God, the one which God first sent into the world according to Rilke's story, does hold all truth, and let us suppose that the left hand, the stranger of whom Rilke speaks, does hold the lifelong pursuit of truth. If it were true that man is unfinished and that God has yet to see a finished man, then it would make sense for God to offer man in turn all truth and the lifelong pursuit of it. For man's unfinished character would consist primarily in his incomplete possession of the truth. The finished man would be the one who possesses truth in its fullness.

Each of the incarnations which we have considered so far seems analogous to God's right hand, the one which holds all truth. The Bodhisattva is one whose essence is enlightenment; the Avatar, when he reveals himself as Krishna did to Arjuna, is a revelation of all things gathered into one; and the Logos, doing humanly what God is doing, is a revelation of God to men. It may be that in spite of everything the enlightenment or the revelation which occurs in each of these instances is not enough by itself to bring man to completion, and that God still needs to hold out his other hand to man and offer him the lifelong pursuit of truth. Jesus promises in the Gospel of John to send his disciples "the Spirit of Truth" who will be "another Comforter" to them when he himself is no longer among them in the flesh.[50] Perhaps we could generalize this and say that in each instance of incarnation wherein all truth is embodied another comforter is needed wherein the lifelong pursuit of truth will be embodied. What Jesus promises, to be sure, is a spirit of truth, not a new human incarnation. We could say, nevertheless, that this spirit becomes manifest in one human being after another.

Here is how Gandhi describes the idea of incarnation in Hinduism:

In Hinduism, incarnation is ascribed to one who has performed some extraordinary service of mankind. All embodied life is in reality an incarnation of God, but it is not usual to consider every living being an incarnation. Future generations pay this homage to one who, in his own generation, has been extraordinarily religious in his conduct. I can see nothing wrong in this procedure; it takes nothing from God's greatness, and there is no violence done to Truth. There is an Urdu saying which means "Adam is not God but he is a spark of the Divine." And therefore he who is the most religiously behaved has most of the divine spark in him. It is in accordance with this train of thought that Krishna enjoys, in Hinduism, the status of the most perfect incarnation. This belief in incarnation is a testimony of man's lofty spiritual ambition. Man is not at peace with himself till he has become like unto God. The endeavour to reach this state is the supreme, the only ambition worth having. And this is self-realization.[51]

In the sense defined here we could call everyone in whom the spirit of truth becomes manifest an "incarnation." There is a difference, however, between the right and the left hand of God, between holding all truth and holding the lifelong pursuit of it. The reason the right hand alone is not sufficient, it seems, is that a man cannot receive what is in the right hand except by receiving what is in the left. He can accept wholeheartedly the Diamond Sutra or the Gita or the Gospel of John, it is true, but still he finds that he sees more in these scriptures at a later stage of his development than he did at an earlier stage. There seems to be no way of jumping stages and leaping to the end.

The ways of passing over to God which we have learned so far from the study of incarnations can leave large areas of human life untouched. To care for Being can mean to ignore beings; to renounce the fruits of action can mean to ignore results; to do what God is doing can mean to ignore what man is doing. It is not that Gotama ignored beings or that Krishna ignored results or that Jesus ignored what man is doing. It is only that a man who tries to receive what these saviors have to give finds that he never quite ends up having what they have or being what they are. Is there a way, let us ask first of all, of caring about Being without ignoring beings? Actually the likelihood in our times is not that a man will ignore beings but that he will ignore Being, that he will not see the whole for the parts. It has been said that we have forgotten Being, that we have turned from the pursuit of wisdom to the pursuit of science, that our age far surpasses previous ages in science, in the knowledge of particular beings, but shows no corresponding advance in wisdom.[52]

The reasons for this may lie partly in the shortcomings of the ancient pursuit of wisdom, in the large residues which it left. Maybe the modern pursuit of science set out to remedy these deficiencies, to explore the areas which had been left unexplored, and, beyond just knowing, to care for the things which had been neglected. Now after several centuries of this we may be in a position to take stock of our gains and losses. To turn again at this time to wisdom and the care of Being might lead to something much more comprehensive than the ancient pursuit of wisdom. If a man living in our time were to take up the pursuit of wisdom, not in ignorance or forgetfulness of these centuries of science but in the light of them, he might well find a way of caring for Being without ignoring beings. He might take an inductive approach to Being, seeking to find Being in beings rather than in itself. What Gandhi did throughout his life and what we are doing in this book, experimenting with truth, seems to be just such an approach. The term "experimenting" suggests the pursuit of science, but the whole phrase "experimenting with truth" suggests a pursuit of wisdom which follows upon the pursuit of science.

To be sure, if a man were to devote his life to experimenting with truth, as Gandhi did, he might be reproached with ignoring the consequences of his actions, for in experimenting he seems to be acting without foreknowledge of the results. Gandhi himself was aware of that danger and said, commenting on the Gita, "renunciation of fruit in no way means indifference to the result: in regard to every action one must know the result that is expected to follow, the means thereto, and the capacity for it."[53] Is there actually a way, let us ask, of renouncing the fruits of action without ignoring results? Here too the likelihood in our times is not that a man will ignore results but that he will ignore the action itself, that he will be more concerned about results than about the action that produces them. The pursuit of science uses experimental methods, but the upshot of experiment is knowledge of a kind which Kant called "technical,"[54] "If this is done, then that will happen" or "If that is desired, then this should be done." It is not what he called "practical" or "ethical" knowledge; "This should be done" or "Do this."

We can employ this distinction of Kant's to differentiate between a scientific experiment and an experiment with truth. The aim of a scientific experiment, we can say, is technical knowledge; it is to determine the results of a given action or to find the action that will produce given results. The aim of an experiment with truth, on the other hand, is practical or ethical knowledge; it is to determine whether an action is good or bad. The technical kind of knowledge comes first, it seems, at least in our times; one should know the results to be expected from an action before one determines whether it is a good action. The results alone, though, will not tell one this since even the most noble action, as we have seen, can have destructive as well as creative effects. The phrase in the Sermon on the Mount "By their fruits you shall know them"[55] probably does not refer to what the Gita calls the "fruits of action," nor does it mean that we can know the goodness or badness of actions from their fruits. It probably means instead that we can know persons by the actions they perform. Actions are the fruits and persons are the trees: the good person produces good actions and the bad person bad actions.

Or, if we drop for a moment the simple distinction between good and bad and consider the whole spectrum of human differences, we can say that actions reveal the person, and more ultimately the person's God. By experimenting with truth, by performing actions, one comes to self-knowledge and knowledge of God and thus to what Gandhi called "self-realization." Is this knowledge, let us ask, coming as it does from action, the same as knowing what one is doing? A rather strange and little-known saying of Jesus on this subject is recorded in one of the codices of the Gospel of Luke. Jesus sees a man working on the sabbath and says to him "Man, if you know what you are doing you are blessed, but if you know not you are cursed and a transgressor of the Law."[56] The sabbath rest was thought to commemorate God's rest after creating the world. Maybe Jesus' saying here is connected with his saying "My Father works still, and I work."[57] If the man working on the sabbath works with the knowledge that God works still, then he is doing what God is doing and he is blessed. But if he thinks God is resting and that he is acting contrary to God, then he is cursed.

According to this a man cannot really know what he is doing unless he knows what God is doing; he cannot know what part his action plays in the story of the universe unless he knows what is ultimately going on in the universe. Experimenting with truth, we could say, leads to practical or ethical knowledge, to knowing what man should do, only because it leads to wisdom, to knowing what God is doing. Does it work the other way around, though—does knowing what God is doing necessarily mean knowing what man is doing? Only if science is conjoined with wisdom, it seems, and technical knowledge is conjoined with practical or ethical knowledge. To know fully what one is doing would be to know the action, whether it accords with God's action, and also to know the consequences of the action, both the creative and the destructive effects which can be expected of it. Again, the likelihood in our times is that a man will be concerned mainly with knowing the consequences and thus with acting responsibly. If he were to conclude, however, that responsibility is not enough and were to seek for wisdom in action, then he might be led to experimenting with truth and trying to discover what God is doing.

Science of human action would be essentially knowledge of the consequences of actions. It would not be merely one among the many sciences which have developed in our times, for example a behavioral science or the circle of behavioral sciences. Rather it would be all of the sciences, both behavioral and natural. All scientific laws, it seems, can be put into the form which Kant described, "If this is done, then that will happen" or "If that is desired, then this should be done." A physical law, for example, might describe how a magnetic field can be generated by putting an electric charge in motion; a chemical law might describe how a salt can be produced by combining an acid and a base; a biological law might describe how a new strain can be created by combining other strains or by effecting a mutation in a given strain; a psychological law might describe how a new reflex can be caused in an organism by conditioning. Not only the psychological law but also the physical, the chemical, and the biological laws are concerned with human actions or rather with the consequences of human actions, and in the psychological law itself it is not the reflex that is the human action but the act of conditioning the reflex. What these laws describe are physical, chemical, biological, and psychological effects which can be brought about by human action.

The integral unity of all these sciences appears, it is true, not from the viewpoint of the pursuit of sciencc but from that of the pursuit of wisdom. Interest in the consequences of action diverges in all the different directions that the consequences themselves take. It is interest in action itself that causes this kind of knowledge to converge once more. The divergence is towards beings; the convergence is towards Being. To act upon scientific knowledge is to act responsibly, for it amounts to acting with a knowledge of the consequences of one's action. To act this way is to care for beings, to weigh the results of action, and to that extent to know what one is doing. It is to do all those things which we were afraid of neglecting and ignoring in our attempt to pass over to God. The divergence, however, prevents it from becoming an adequate way of life in itself. One cares for some beings but not for all; one knows some of the consequences of one's action but not all; one knows to some extent what one is doing but not fully. It is only in the moment of convergence, when a man turns from the pursuit of science to that of wisdom, that he discovers a way of life which is humanly adequate.

Starting from this moment of convergence, a man might interpret the sciences as knowledge of the consequences of human action. One circle of sciences, the natural sciences like physics and chemistry and biology, he might see as dealing with the circumstances of human life and describing how man can alter those circumstances. Another circle, the behavioral sciences like psychology and sociology and anthropology, he might see as dealing with the manner in which man is produced by his circumstances and describing how man can alter himself by altering his circumstances. The consequences of human action which he might see, therefore, are twofold: changes in the circumstances of human life and changes in man himself. Turning from science to wisdom, however, he would realize that science itself does not tell which of these possible changes are good and which are bad. With this he would have a vision of the enormity of man's effect upon himself and upon his world. He would realize that man at once knows and does not know what he is doing. Man knows, collectively at least in that one man knows one effect and another knows another, much about the consequences of his actions upon his world and upon himself, but he does not know whether what he is doing to himself and his world is good. Or better, he knows that what he is doing is both good and bad in that it has both constructive and destructive effects. This leaves him quite in the dark, though, as to what he should do.

If man generally is in the dark as to what he should be doing, a man who turns to the pursuit of wisdom is a light in the darkness. True, he would not be the kind of light that Jesus was in the Gospel of John or the kind that Krishna was in the Gita or the kind that Gotama was in the Diamond Sutra. He would be rather the kind that Socrates was in the Dialogues of Plato. His wisdom, like that of Socrates, would be a knowledge of ignorance. More accurately, it would be a knowledge of knowledge and ignorance. It would be simply the realization that man in our time at once knows and does not know what he is doing. This is a small bit of wisdom, and yet it is a wisdom. Consider, for instance, what it would be to lack even this. A man in our time might be so impressed with our knowledge of the consequences of our actions that he would not realize that we are ignorant of what we should do. A man like this who knows our knowledge but is ignorant of our ignorance would act quite differently, it seems, from one who is aware of our ignorance.

He might be so impressed with the "operations research"[58] that goes into an industrial or military or governmental decision that he does not realize the final ignorance in which such a decision is made. The operations research which precedes the decision is a scientific and mathematical analysis which exhibits the various possible courses of action and their consequences. Sometimes the analysis will be statistical and the different consequences which are possible will each be assigned a probability. Confronted with an elaborate study of this kind, a man is liable to believe that no further thought is necessary. He is liable to think that all anyone has to do after this is make the decision, for a man who decides with such knowledge, it seems to him, surely knows what he is doing. What eludes him is the distinction between the technical and the practical, between knowing the consequences of an action and knowing whether it should be done. Industrial and military and governmental decisions ordinarily are made in our times with great technical knowledge and great practical ignorance. The practical ignorance is buried and concealed beneath the massive bulk of the technical knowledge.

A man who is aware of our ignorance in these matters could make this very awareness of his a basis for action. One thing he could do, of course, is to bring our ignorance to light, to call our supposed knowledge of what we are doing into question. This is the sort of thing that Socrates did. Once ignorance is brought to light, though, there is the problem of what to do about it. To cease acting and making decisions, on the principle that one should not act in ignorance, is not necessarily a solution, for inaction has consequences too—and these consequences could also be calculated by our methods of operations research. To continue acting, on the other hand, when one knows that one doesn't know what one is doing, amounts to experimenting with truth. Action in the knowledge of ignorance is experimental; so also is inaction. It is not, however, irresponsible, for we are supposing that there is knowledge of the consequences of whatever action is taken. Experimental action is aimed at discovery, to discover what should be done. Some things, such as the middle path between luxury and asceticism, cannot be discovered, we have seen, except by trial and error and thus by experiment. Action pervaded by the knowledge of ignorance becomes, therefore, a pursuit of truth, a pursuit of the very kind of truth which Gotama and Krishna and Jesus were revealing.

The pursuit of such truth, though, is not the same as the possession of it. That is why the man who makes the experiments we have been describing in this chapter looks more like Socrates than like Jesus or Krishna or Gotama. There was an experimental period in the life of Gotama and also in the life of Jesus, namely the time spent in the wilderness, the time of withdrawal before returning to preach. The experimentation continues throughout the life of the man we are envisioning now, however, and he communicates his discoveries to others as they occur. He tries to learn from Gotama how to care for Being. He is concerned, though, in his care for Being not to lose sight of particular beings. Being, he realizes, is what all beings share, and to care genuinely for Being is therefore to care for all particular beings; but to actually do this, he knows too, is for him a lifelong task, since it means finding Being in beings rather than in itself. His approach to Being is inductive and, like inductive approaches which involve an infinite number of particular instances, never comes to an end. The God who is revealed in his life is thus a God who is to be found not merely at the beginning and the end of life and time, in the care for Being whence all things come and return, but in the very midst of time, caring for each and every particular being.

He tries to learn from Krishna how to act without seeking the fruits of action. He is concerned, however, in renouncing the fruits not to lose sight of them. To understand action itself, he realizes, would be to understand the fruits since action is their source, but the kind of knowledge that is primarily available in our times, he knows too, is knowledge rather of the consequences of action. To reach an understanding of action, accordingly, it is necessary for him to work his way back through the consequences to the action instead of forward through the action to the consequences. The great multiplicity of the consequences makes this a lifelong task. He has to start with multiplicity where our knowledge lies and work back towards unity where our ignorance lies. The God revealed in his life is thus one who carries the burden of responsibility for all the consequences of action, not one who is benignly indifferent to consequences, and yet the burden of his God is light like that of the one revealed in Krishna, for the God's heart is in the action itself rather than in the consequences.

He tries to learn from Jesus to do what God is doing. He is concerned, though, in doing this not to lose sight of what man is doing. To know what God is doing, he realizes, is not merely to know about "acts of God" as they are called, events like floods and earthquakes for which man is not responsible. These are at best consequences of God's action; to know of them is not yet to understand God's action in itself. To penetrate through the obvious consequences to the hidden action which lies behind them requires an understanding of the events for which man is responsible or where man's and God's responsibility overlap, like war and peace, famine and plenty, sickness and health, death and life. He has to determine man's responsibility here before he can determine God's, and then he has to discover what God is doing in order to discover what man should be doing. To really understand what Jesus was saying and doing, he finds, can therefore be a lifelong task. As he goes about this, nevertheless, his life reveals God; it reveals God's action not in itself so much as in its consequences, and especially in events like war and peace and the rest which are due jointly to God and man.

The God revealed in his life, we could say, is a God who comes often among men, who comes among us whenever we need him, concerned as he is about particular beings and the consequences of action. Appearing in the life of a man like this who is engaged in the lifelong pursuit of truth, God shows the ordinary man how to live. For the ordinary man is not in possession of the truth but has to spend his life pursuing it. Yet the man we are envisioning would himself be a disciple of the great teachers of mankind, since they embody the truth he pursues. He could be called an "incarnation" of God in the somewhat loose sense which Gandhi gave to that word, but he is really more like Arjuna than Krishna. He is like the man who stands beside the God in the chariot; the God is his charioteer; and, as in the Gita, they are about to enter into action together. His life is a journey in time and God is his companion on the way.

NOTES

1. R. M. Dawkins (ed. and tr.), *Forty-five Stories from the Dodekanese* (Cambridge at the University Press, 1950), p. 270.
2. Rainer Maria Rilke, *Stories of God,* tr. by M. D. Herter (New York, Norton, 1963), p. 32.
3. *Bhagavad-Gita, IV,* 7. Throughout this chapter I am using four different translations of the Gita more or less in combination: Mahadev Desai, *The Gita According to Gandhi* (Ahmedabad, Navajivan Publishing House, 1956); Franklin Edgerton, *The Bhagavad-Gita* (New York, Harper, 1964); S. Radhakrishnan, *The Bhagavad-Gita* (London, Allen & Unwin, 1958); and R. C. Zaehner, *The Bhagavad-Gita* (Oxford, Clarendon, 1969).
4. Romans 6:10 and Hebrews 7:27; 9:12, 28; 10:10.
5. Cf. Martin Heidegger, *Being and Time,* tr. by John Macquarrie and Edward Robinson (New York, Harper, 1962), pp. 235 ff.
6. Cf. Mircea Eliade, *Yoga* (New York, Pantheon, 1958), pp. 11 ff.
7. Martin Heidegger, *Über den Humanismus* (Frankfurt am Main, Vittorio Klostermann, 1947), p. 19.
8. Edward Conze (ed. and tr.), *Buddhist Wisdom Books* (London, Allen and Unwin, 1958), p. 25.
9. Hegel, *Science of Logic,* tr. by W. H. Johnston and L. G. Struthers (London, Allen & Unwin, 1961) vol. 1, p. 94.
10. Cf. my article "St. Thomas' Theology of Participation" in *Theological Studies,* XVIII (1957), pp. 475 ff.
11. Here I am echoing Whitehead's description of what he calls "the form of the forms of thought" in *Adventures of Ideas* (New York, Macmillan, 1937), p. 14.
12. This is the theme of my book *The City of the Gods.*
13. Cf. my book *A Search for God in Time and Memory,* pp. 55 ff.
14. Cf. Eliade, *Yoga,* pp. 183 ff.
15. Augustine, *De Trinitate,* X, 11.
16. Cf. the preface to *A Search for God in Time and Memory.*
17. Shakespeare, Sonnet XXIX, lines 5 ff.
18. *Digha-nikaya,* II, 99 in F. L. Woodward, *Some Sayings of the Buddha,* p. 339.
19. Leibniz, *Monadology,* 7.
20. Jorge Luis Borges, *Ficciones,* ed. by Anthony Kerrigan (New York, Grove, 1962), pp. 92 f.
21. Cf. Hannah Arendt, *The Human Condition* (New York, Doubleday, 1959), pp. 72 ff. This distinction, as Hannah Arendt makes it, seems basically Aristotelian: labor is activity in the realm of nature, work is activity in the realm of art ("making"), and action is activity in the realm of prudence ("doing"). My own use and understanding of it differs from hers in that instead of taking labor, work, and action to be three different activities, I end up taking them to be three ways of construing human activity.
22. Gandhi, *The Story of My Experiments with Truth,* p. 207.
23. Actually Marx is speaking of the "average" or "social" labor time, as he calls it, which is required to make the product. Cf. Marx, *Capital* tr. by Eden and Cedar Paul (New York, Dutton, 1932), Vol. 1, pp. 7 ff. I am thinking instead of the actual time an individual puts into laboring.

Thus the difference between the theory and the program which Marx is proposing and the personal attitude which I am proposing.

24. *Bhagavad-Gita,* III, 24.
25. Cf. John Cage, *Silence* (Cambridge, Mass., M.I.T. Press, 1966), pp. 7 ff.
26. Cf. Lejaren A. Hiller and Leonard M. Isaacson, *Experimental Music* (New York, McGraw, 1959).
27. Cf. *Bhagavad-Gita, XVIII,* 41 ff.
28. *Ibid., XI,* 7.
29. *Ibid., XI,* 32.
30. Luke 2:34 f.
31. John 5:19.
32. John 14:12.
33. I am alluding here to the *Four Horsemen of Apocalypse* 6:1 ff.
34. The cyclical, statistical, serial, and dialectical schemes which I touch on in these four paragraphs are roughly parallel to the four methods (classical, statistical, genetic, and dialectical) which Bernard Lonergan examines in *Insight* (New York, Philosophical Library, 1958), cf. index under "method(s)" p. 771, except that I apply them to the problems of war and peace, famine and plenty, sickness and health, life and death.
35. Quoted by Max Born, *Physics in My Generation* (New York, Springer-Verlag, 1969), p. 160.
36. I am thinking here of an Hegelian rather than a Platonic dialectic. The idea which occurs at the end of this paragraph, though, about what is obviously occurring in the world being only an image of what God is doing is closer to a Platonic dialectic where time is a changing image of eternity. Cf. the correlation of the two kinds of dialectic in *A Search for God in Time and Memory,* pp. 49 ff. Note also that good tends to be conceived as the negation of evil in an Hegelian dialectic, whereas evil tends to be conceived as the negation of good in a Platonic dialectic.
37. John 14:27.
38. John 17:21.
39. John 4:34.
40. John 6:35.
41. John 21:15 ff.
42. John 11:4. The idea of deriving by contrast from this passage a notion of "sickness unto death" was Kierkegaard's. Cf. his *Sickness unto Death* (with *Fear and Trembling*), tr. by Walter Lowrie (Princeton, N.J., Princeton University Press, 1968), pp. 144 f.
43. John 5:20.
44. John 15:15.
45. John 14:11. Cf. also 10:13.
46. John 14:8 f.
47. John 15:22 and 24.
48. Cf. note 2.
49. Lessing's actual words were "If God held enclosed in his right hand all truth and in his left simply the evermoving impulse towards truth, although with the condition that I should eternally wander, and said to me, 'Choose!,' I should humbly bow before his left hand, and say 'Father, give! Pure truth is for you alone.' " Cf. Kierkegaard on these words in *Concluding Unscientific Postscript,* tr. by David F. Swenson and Walter Lowrie (Princeton, N.J., Princeton University Press, 1941), pp. 97 ff.

50. John 14:16 f.
51. Desai, *The Gita According to Gandhi,* pp. 128 f.
52. Heidegger speaks of the "oblivion of Being" in our times. Cf. his essay "The Way back to the Ground of Metaphysics," tr. by Walter Kaufmann in *Existentialism from Dostoevsky to Sartre* (New York, Meridian, 1956), pp. 207 ff. Bertrand Russell has said "although our age far surpasses all previous ages in knowledge, there has been no correlative increase in wisdom," quoted by Edward Conze in his preface to *Buddhist Wisdom Books,* p. 9. Cf. also Conze's remarks *ibid.*
53. Desai, *op. cit.,* p. 131.
54. Here is what Kant actually said: "Propositions called 'practical' in mathematics or natural science should properly be called 'technical,' for in these fields it is not a question of determining the will; they only indicate the manifold of a possible action which is adequate to bring about a certain effect, and are therefore just as theoretical as any proposition which asserts a connection between cause and effect. Whoever chooses the latter must also choose the former." This is a footnote in the *Critique of Practical Reason,* tr. by Lewis White Beck (Indianapolis-New York, Bobbs-Merrill, 1956), p. 25, note.
55. Matthew 7:16 and 20.
56. The saying occurs at Luke 6:4 in the Codex Bezae.
57. John 5:17.
58. Operations research includes such disciplines as games theory and linear programming. To get an idea of the extensive work that has been done in such fields cf. *Index of Selected Publications of the Rand Corporation,* vol. 1, 1946–1962 (Santa Monica, Calif., the Rand Corporation, 1962).

Part Two

A JOURNEY WITH GOD

IV

A Journey in Time

A JOURNEY CAN BE the making of a religion. An American example would be the great journey of the Mormons led by Brigham Young to Salt Lake. The prime examples would be among the world religions, particularly the religions of prophecy, as we might call them, like Judaism and Islam, as distinct from the religions of salvation like Hinduism and Buddhism. The Exodus of the Israelites led by Moses from Egypt to Palestine and the Hegira of the Muslims led by Mohammed from Mecca to Medina were the foundations of the religions of prophecy. There are other examples which we might hesitate to classify under the heading "religion," but in which we can clearly see a people being created by the experience of a journey. Such would be the Long March of the Red Chinese led by Mao Tse-tung, a journey which covered over six thousand miles and which still pervades the popular imagination of China. Another would be the Salt March led by Gandhi, a journey to the sea which initiated the struggle for the independence of India.

When it is a religion that the journey creates, there is usually another and more individual journey which takes place before or during the migration of the people. This is the journey of the prophet who is to inspire or to lead the migration. A classic example would be the famous "night journey" of Mohammed, in which he traveled in spirit from the temple at Mecca to that at Jerusalem and thence to the throne of God. An even more ancient example would be the journey of Moses to the top of Mount Sinai to receive the revelation and the stone tablets of God's law. The pattern can be found, though, even aside from the world religions, wherever a religion is based essentially on prophecy. For instance, the journey of the Mormons to Salt Lake was preceded by the prophetic journey of Joseph Smith to the Hill Cumorah. In each of these examples the prophet receives from God a heavenly book of some kind which he communicates to the people,[1] and this is as instrumental as the migration itself in uniting them in spirit and making them a people.

Looking at these examples with the eye of a skeptic, one finds the journey of a whole people far more impressive than that of the prophet. Yet the doubt about the prophet and his book tends to cast doubt also upon the inspiration which enabled a people to tolerate the hardships of migration. Maybe it will be possible for us to discover some means of entering into both journeys and thus of experimenting with their truth. A clue may be the fact that life itself, even apart from journeys of these kinds, is already a journey in time. Let us see if we cannot take advantage of this fact somehow to find a counterpart in our own experience, both for the prophet's journey and for that of a people. If we may make bold to treat the Koran as an autobiographical document, we can use it here as our guide.

1. The Prophet's Journey

It is a remarkable fact about Mohammed that he did not begin to receive his revelations until the age of forty. All the most significant happenings and experiences of his career occurred in the second half of life. The main things we know about his life previous to his call as a prophet are that he was an orphan and that he married at the age of twenty-five. The call came at Mecca when he was forty, and he spent the next twelve years trying to persuade the Meccans to believe in God and the day of judgment.[2] Then at the age of fifty-two he fled with his followers to Medina—this became the Year 1 in the Muslim calendar. At Medina he was ruler and was able in the next ten years to spread Islam to all Arabia.[3] He died finally at the age of sixty-two. Thus Mohammed's life, if we take it as an example and a guide, may tell us more about the second half of life than do the lives of Jesus and Gotama. Jesus died in his thirties; Gotama lived to an advanced old age but, as we saw in Chapter Two, all he did after his experience of enlightenment at the age of thirty-six was share that original insight with others. Mohammed's life, we might say, contains two great turning points: the first, occurring at the age of forty, was his call to be a prophet; the second, occurring at the age of fifty-two when he fled from Mecca to Medina, was his call to be a statesman.

This second turning point, the call to be a statesman, appears also in the lives of Jesus and Gotama, but there it is rejected and is considered a temptation. Jesus rejects the idea of being an earthly king when he is tempted to it in the desert and afterwards when enthusiastic followers want to make him king. Gotama rejects the idea when at the age of twenty-nine he leaves the palace of his father and becomes a forest-dweller and gives up the prospect of succeeding to his father's throne. It would probably be a mistake, though, for us to conclude that Mohammed succumbed to a temptation that Gotama and Jesus overcame, or vice versa that they resisted a call which he followed. The thing for us to do, it seems, is to try to enter into all three lives as much as we can and understand what happens when a man goes like Gotama from rejecting statesmanship to attaining enlightenment, and what happens when he goes like Jesus from receiving revelation to refusing statesmanship, and what happens when he goes like Mohammed from receiving revelation to exercising statesmanship.

It is possible to trace, at least in general outline, the process which took place in Mohammed's life. The parts of the Koran which were revealed at Mecca show us what happened when he followed the call to be a prophet; those which were revealed afterwards at Medina show us what happened subsequently when he followed the call to be a statesman. For the moment let us concentrate on the first turning point. If we can find a way of entering into his experience of revelation and into his problem of communicating the revelation to others, we will put ourselves into a better position to understand what it meant for him to become a statesman. Actually it is the experience of revelation itself which appears offhand to be the element in his life most remote from our own experience. Generally two kinds of revelation seem to have occurred—one like the "night journey" in which he was carried in spirit from the temple at Mecca to the temple at Jerusalem,[4] and the other like the "night of power" or the "night of glory" in which the Koran was brought down to him from heaven.[5] In the night journey the prophet went to receive the revelation; in the night of power and glory the revelation was brought to him.[6]

A clue to the nature of these experiences is the fact, mentioned in the Koran, that Mohammed was accustomed to spending the night or a good portion of it in prayer.[7] He may have learned to pray in this fashion from Jews or Christians. At any rate we may gather from the Koran that during the Mecca period he was accustomed to praying facing in the direction of the temple at Jerusalem.[8] In the light of these indications we can surmise what the night journey from the temple at Mecca to that at Jerusalem may have been. We can imagine him praying at night in Mecca, facing towards Jerusalem, and being rapt in spirit and being carried imaginatively in this rapture to the very place towards which his spirit had been reaching out in prayer. Similarly we can imagine the night of power and glory to have been a night of prayer in which his seeking for light from God was answered with a flood of spiritual illumination, an enlightenment so transforming as to provide his whole life with a new basis. The revelations, in short, appear to have been the kind of experiences which occur along the path of prayer. Now let us see, by looking to our own more limited experience, whether we can get some idea of the prophet's journey along this path.

"The spiritual adventure of our time," Jung has said, "is the exposure of human consciousness to the undefined and the indefinable."[9] We can see this being carried on among us in many different ways. One way is by means of drugs; another, the way Jung himself took, is by a personal confrontation with the unconscious side of life; another is by methods of meditation and prayer adopted from the world religions. By experimenting with these ways, particularly the last, we might well come to an understanding of the experience of revelation. Besides all this, though, there is another spiritual adventure. It consists simply in taking each further stage of one's life as a new experience, containing latent within itself a new understanding of things. To expose one's consciousness to new experience and understanding would be exposing it to something undefined but nevertheless definable. This, as a consistent way of acting, would put a man on a voyage of discovery, a spiritual adventure in its own right but one in which each discovery would be finitary. It would compare with the first adventure somewhat as a journey on earth might compare with a journey into outer space. When one travels into space there is no limiting horizon; one looks forward, as one moves, into endless depths. When one travels on earth, however, there is always a horizon limiting one's vision, though the horizon constantly changes as one moves forward.

If we associate the undefined and the indefinable with God, then the exposure of consciousness to this in drugs or in psychic confrontation or in meditation and mystical prayer is a confrontation with God. It is like the space voyager's confrontation with the boundless universe. On the other hand, the constant exposure to what is undefined but definable which occurs as one goes through life, taking each new stage of life as a further experience and finding in it a further understanding of things, is rather a journey with God. It is like the earth traveler's journey: he can always pause and look directly up into the endless depths of the night sky, but ordinarily as he goes on he looks towards the ever-changing horizon. Instead of facing God, a man on this second and more earthly journey walks with God, side by side, both he and God facing forward. Revelations such as those underlying the Koran appear to be the kind of experiences which occur when one directly exposes human consciousness to God; when one is facing towards God rather than facing forward with him. Mohammed's night journey was a journey to the throne of God; his night of power and glory was a night in which something came down to him from God. The question for us is whether such experiences can be understood by a man who is taking the more earthly path, whether the man who confronts the endless depths like Mohammed can be understood by the man who confronts only the changing horizon.

Let us see, first of all, how far the earthly journey may enable us to understand a journey to God like the rapture in which Mohammed was carried in spirit from Mecca to Jerusalem. As a man goes through life from childhood to youth to manhood to age, there is at each stage a seeking and a finding. This is so if his life is a voyage of discovery and if he expects each new stage to bring a new understanding of things and not simply to conform to what he already understands. The seeking is the active and effortful side of his voyage; the finding is the passive and receptive side. We can observe these same two elements, seeking and finding, in the life of prayer. Mohammed's night journey appears to have been an extension of the element of seeking in his prayer. He prayed in Mecca, facing towards Jerusalem, reaching out in that direction, as it were, towards God. In the rapture or ecstasy, however, the active seeking and reaching out turned into a passive experience of being drawn out of himself or out of the place where he was towards God or towards the place where God was.

In the ordinary experience of seeking there is usually a great deal of frustration. It is a well-known experience that the pursuit of happiness in the form of contentment is self-defeating: the more intensely one seeks contentment the more discontent one becomes. As we saw earlier,[10] the same can be said of the pursuit of certainty: the more intensely one seeks certainty the more uncertain one becomes. Perhaps this is because what is sought in each of these instances is a state of repose, a repose of heart or of mind which is incompatible by its very nature with the restless state of seeking. One can find repose only by ceasing to seek for it. If, however, one is seeking for something other than repose, the seeking itself does not prevent one from finding it but can rather help one come upon it. If, instead of seeking for repose of mind, one seeks for illumination of mind—if, instead of seeking for repose of heart, one seeks for inspiration or movement of the heart—one is likely to find what one is looking for. As one changes the orientation of one's seeking in this manner, one goes from a purely active and very restless pursuit to an experience of being drawn and carried towards the object of the mind's and the heart's desire. This begins to approximate what happens in rapture or ecstasy where one goes from lifting the mind and heart to God to being lifted to God in mind and heart.

Now if we can compare the night journey to the experience of seeking when one goes from seeking to being drawn, we may be able to compare the night of power and glory to the experience of finding. Once seeking has been reoriented, finding becomes a much more frequent occurrence. The Koran, composed as it was in small pieces over a period of twenty-two years, must have been based on frequently occurring experiences of finding in Mohammed's nightly prayer. The night of power and glory, the "blessed night" as he also called it,[11] in which the Koran was sent down to him from heaven, must have been an extreme and overwhelming instance of this. If the Koran had been literally given to him whole and entire in a single night, it would be difficult to compare the experience with the finding that occurs along the more ordinary journey in time. What actually seems to have happened, though, was that the Koran was given to him that night only in principle. A thousand and one other nights were required, so to speak, for the revelation to be spelled out. This was considered an objection by Mohammed's opponents at Mecca. "Why," they asked, "has not the Koran been brought down to him all at once?"[12]

The common experience of man at prayer is certainly not one of finding everything at once. It is more usually one of seeking without finding at all. A man who prays feels often that there is no response on God's part. His prayer seems to him a soliloquy. It becomes a real conversation with God only when something is communicated to him during prayer, only when his mind is enlightened and his heart moved. Illumination of the mind, inspiration of the will, these are the kinds of experience which count with him for responses from God. Such experiences occur regularly in the course of a life if a man is on the voyage of discovery which we have been talking about. They tend to occur as he goes from one stage of life to another, from childhood to youth to manhood to age, or from one phase to another within each of these stages. Illumination of the mind occurs not so much through the acquisition of new information as through the discovery of a new standpoint from which the available information can be regarded. Each new life experience, as a man goes from age to age or from phase to phase, is the occasion for a new understanding of things. The new understanding he attains is in itself an illumination of the mind, but it becomes also an inspiration of the will if he finds in it a new basis for action, if the new standpoint becomes a new plane of existence.

It was just this, a new standpoint and a new plane of existence, which Mohammed seems to have discovered on the "blessed night" when the Koran came down to him from heaven. The many subsequent revelations which he experienced probably consisted in seeing in this new light the various things that he already knew and those that he afterwards learned; they were a matter of seeing information, old and new, in the light of the new standpoint. As he eventually came to formulate it, the essence of this new standpoint and this new plane of existence was "surrender" (*islam*) to the will of God.[13] That this should be the content of the revelation is not surprising if we consider the nature of the experiences themselves. The stages of mystical prayer as they are described by Saint Teresa of Avila, who incidentally began like Mohammed to receive revelations at the age of forty, are increasingly passive as the mystic becomes more and more absorbed with God. She compares them to the various ways of watering a garden: by water from a well, by a waterwheel, by a running stream, by a heavy rain.[14] Each successive way involves less effort and less activity. The highest forms of mystical prayer which she describes in her autobiography, union and rapture, are the most passive of all: union is like the heavy rain, rapture is like the moisture rising again into the sky.[15]

The passivity of such experiences is the thing that leads to the idea of surrender to the will of God. Union, as Teresa describes it, is the absorption of all man's faculties with God, memory, understanding, and will, but especially will.[16] Rapture, being drawn out of oneself by God, is an experience in which one learns, she says, that God is stronger.[17] We can find similar, though less sublime, experiences on the more earthly journey with God. The further one goes on the voyage of discovery in life the more of an orientation one's life acquires and the more one becomes absorbed, mind and heart, in the voyage and, if one construes it as a journey with God, the more one becomes absorbed with God. Also, as one becomes oriented towards the journey itself rather than towards repose of mind and heart, the frustrating search for certainty and contentment gives way to a much more passive experience of being carried in mind and heart along the path of the journey. If one goes through the motions of Muslim prayer, standing, bowing, kneeling, and placing one's hands and face to the ground, one can feel in the very movements of the body the meaning of surrender to the will of God. This is the way it feels when one is facing directly, as it were, towards God. When one is on the journey with God, facing with him towards the horizon, surrender feels rather like letting oneself be carried by a very rapid stream towards an unknown destination.

If one not only goes through the bodily movements of Muslim prayer, the standing position alternating with inclinations and prostrations, but actually attempts to pray while doing this, one finds that praying like this really implies a certain notion of God, a God like Allah. Consider the following prayer which is the opening chapter of the Koran and which plays a role in Islam similar to that of the Lord's Prayer in Christianity:

> Praise belongs to Allah, the Lord of the worlds,
> The Merciful, the Compassionate.
> Wielder of the Day of Judgment.
> Thee do we serve, and on Thee do we call for help;
> Guide us [to] the straight path,
> The path of those upon whom Thou hast bestowed good,
> Not of those upon whom anger falls, or those who go astray.[18]

This prayer is a summary of the Koran's message, at least of the message delivered at Mecca. It may have been put in these words only after the message had already been delivered. The likelihood is, though, that Mohammed prayed with sentiments like these from the beginning. He knew of Allah as the Lord of the temple at Mecca and would therefore have prayed to him before receiving any revelations. He could have learned from Jews and Christians about the day of judgment and the straight path. All three of these matters, nevertheless, the God, the day of judgment, and the straight path, would have appeared to him under a new aspect in the light of his experience of surrender to the will of God.

These three matters appear under yet another aspect if one is oriented towards the earthly journey in time. When a man confronts God, he surrenders to one who is boundless, encompassing, and fathomless as the night sky: this is the same one he would meet on the way of drugs or that of psychic confrontation or that of pure meditation but, meeting him on the way of prayer, he dares to speak to him. On the journey through time, however, one would never meet God head on, though one might well surrender to him, but if one does surrender this means letting oneself be led by a God who is wild, who will not abide in the houses men build for him, who will stay only a short while and then move on. Maybe this is really the same God, but certainly he appears under a different aspect. The same could be said of the day of judgment and the straight path. On the way of confrontation the day of judgment is the ultimate confrontation with God and the straight path is the path of prayer, the path of the man who lives by the illumination and inspiration he receives in confronting God. On the journey with God the day of judgment is journey's end or the end of one journey and the beginning of another occurring at death, and the straight path is the path a man must travel through the stages of life to keep up with God as he continues to move on through time.

The difference between the two ways, as it emerges from these images and metaphors, is relational. Being before God and being with God are not the same, and yet a man can be before and be with one and the same God. There is a parallel in human relations. One can confront a person across a table, for instance, and one can work or travel with the same person on some common undertaking. The dynamics of the two relationships are quite different, and yet it is possible to understand one from the viewpoint of the other. When a man is confronting God, he tends to believe that he has the definitive revelation; when he is on a journey with God, on the contrary, he tends to believe that no revelation is final. It is possible, nevertheless, when confronting God to realize that one is confronting endless depths, and thereby to understand how there could be a journey in which one would go from discovery to discovery. It is possible too, when on such a journey, to realize from the endlessness of discovery that God is inexhaustible, and thereby to understand how confronting him would be quite a different thing from confronting a changing horizon.

The kind of revelation which is embodied in the Koran does seem definitive in a way that no discovery which occurs on the more earthly journey in time can be. Yet there can be further revelation. A confrontation with God like Mohammed's is boundless and yet finite, like one's visual field when one looks up into the night sky: there is no horizon up there, no boundary, and so it is boundless, yet at the same time one does not see infinitely far and so it is finite.[19] The experience of confrontation combined with this double awareness that it is boundless and yet finite is probably what makes a prophet. One might confront God in mystical prayer and be aware only of the boundlessness—this would most likely lead one to conclude that the experience is ineffable and would therefore prevent one from trying to communicate its contents to others. If one were aware also of the finiteness, however, one would probably see that it is actually communicable, and one might take its communicability as a call to share it with others. Very likely this, rather than some kind of compulsion to speak, is what constitutes the call of a prophet.[20] Let us see now what happens when a man does communicate the contents of such an experience, what effect it has upon the course of events, what effect it has upon the man himself.

2. *The Journey of a People*

There is a double movement in the course of events, it has been said, like that of a moving vehicle and its wheels—the circular movement of the wheels and the forward movement of the whole vehicle.[21] Corresponding to the turning wheels, there is a cyclical movement in history, the rise and fall of civilizations. Corresponding to the forward moving vehicle there is a linear movement, the pilgrim's progress of the world religions like Buddhism, Christianity, and Islam which cross over from one civilization to another. The world religions, according to this, are the carriers of history. It would greatly affect the course of events to found a civilization; it would affect it still more to found a religion. If a man wished to plot the course of events like a navigator in time, he might plot the course of civilization. He would do better, though, to plot the course of religion. If he tried to plot a straight course of forward progress for civilization, he would probably find his calculations foiled by the forces in human affairs which compel civilizations to decline and fall. It would be like steering a sailing boat straight for the point one desires to reach, taking no account of wind and current, making no allowance for leeway and the set of the tide.

An example of this kind of thinking would be Kant's plan for perpetual peace.[22] This was an effort to plan the future course of civilization so that it would issue into a world without war. Kant drew up his plan in the form of a constitution for a league of nations. This was at the end of the eighteenth century. In subsequent history, especially in the twentieth century, such leagues have been formed, notably the League of Nations after the First World War and the United Nations after the Second World War, but they have not succeeded so far in putting an end to war. The defect in Kant's scheme, it seems, is that it does not take into account the forces which make for the decline and fall of civilizations and which will therefore disrupt any unity and peace based on a given civilization. These forces, we could say, are the residues left by the civilization, the elements in man which the civilization fails to engage, the resources in man which it fails to tap. From among these residues come the elements and the resources of the new civilization which rises to replace the one which declines and falls. If we wish to devise a plan for perpetual peace, we would do better to base it on religion, perhaps on a convergence of the religions, than to base it on civilization. The difference between a civilization and a religion is that a religion is capable of engaging the whole heart, the whole mind, and the whole soul of man,[23] while a civilization, as its decline and fall testifies, is not.

We can see this power in each of the world religions. A peculiar thing about Islam, though, is that it set out consciously to usc this power to unite tribes, to unite civilizations, even to unite the religions themselves. Mohammed, when he was at Medina, attempted to do all three of these things. He succeeded during his own lifetime in uniting the various tribes of Arabia.[24] He tried to unite civilizations, sending letters in one year both to the Persian empire in the east and the Byzantine empire in the west, inviting their rulers to accept Islam.[25] This union was not accomplished in his lifetime, but only after his death and by conquest. He tried also to unite the religions, to have his message accepted by Jews and Christians, but he appears to have realized before he died that this would never come about. The one thing that has the power to withstand a world religion, it seems, is another world religion. It was this failure, however, particularly his failure to win over the Jews at Medina,[26] that brought Mohammed to the realization that he was founding a religion. Before, when he was at Mecca, he had assumed that there was agreement among the Peoples of the Book, as he called Jews and Christians, and that there would be agreement on their part with his message. Now, after encountering the opposition of the Jews at Medina, he realized that no such agreement would be forthcoming.

The consciousness of founding a religion, of creating a distinct people, is a step beyond prophetic consciousness. The founders of the world religions, Gotama, Jesus, Mohammed, have affected the general course of human events, it seems, more than any other type of individual man. Gotama and Jesus did this without taking up the sword, but the question has been asked about both of them as to whether they thought of themselves as founding religions. Mohammed did take up the sword and did, it appears from the Koran, come to think of himself as founding a religion. The sword and the conscious founding of a religion may go together somehow. It remains to be seen how they do. One thing we can say already at this point, though, is that the convincing power of Islam is not merely the sword. It is rather the experience of surrender. When Mohammed had refined his message to this point, that the true religion consisted of surrender to the will of God, he had a religion which could sweep the world. Let us see now how a message like this can create a civilization, how it can span civilizations, and how it can nevertheless fail to unite religions. Maybe in its failure on this last score we will find a clue as to how the religions may be united and how a perpetual basis for peace may be established.

How could a message like Mohammed's create a civilization? At the heart of a civilization or a culture there is a way of life, an answer to death.[27] Mohammed's message of surrender to the will of God appears to have provided the Arabs with such a way and such an answer. We can gather from the Koran and from the Sunna, the Islamic traditions, that four principal matters in human life were generally considered beyond human control and were ascribed in Arab paganism to time or fate: a man's sustenance (*rizq*), the term of his life (*ajal*), the sex of the child, and happiness or misery.[28] They constituted what we might call "the problem of death" among the Arabs of that epoch. The sustenance was a matter of life and death; the term of the life was the problem of how long a man would live and when he would die; the sex of the child was a matter of his survival through offspring; and happiness or misery was the question of whether his life was worthwhile or whether he was better off dead. All together these issues defined man's mortality and his subjection to time and fate. To a man facing these concerns in his own life the message of surrender to the will of God meant a liberation from time and fate and a subjection instead to a personal and benevolent will. By surrendering to the will of God and doing all the things which surrender was thought to entail a man changed his relationship to his own mortality.

Among us all four of these matters are thought to be subject in some degree to human control. A man's sustenance is thought to depend on the economic system prevailing in the society and on his own labor; the term of his life is admittedly beyond control for the most part, but some control can be exercised by means of medical science and there is the belief that life expectancy will be extended in the future; the sex of the child has been beyond control until recently but tentative ways have now been found of determining it; happiness and misery are also largely beyond control, but their eventual mastery appears to be one of the ideals of behavioral science. A civilization has been in the making, it seems, a central concern of which is to extend human control over just such matters as these. We are experiencing many doubts about this undertaking at the present time: there is doubt as to how far such control is possible and how far it is desirable. These are the kinds of doubt which arise, I suspect, in the early stages of a new way of life. They are due in part to the fact that the new culture has not yet been able to prove itself, and in part to its contrast with the ideals of the old and dying culture. They are not the graver doubts which will arise someday, I would expect, after this new culture has reached its height and has had a fair chance to prove itself and, like all previous cultures, has been found wanting.

The doubts we are now experiencing could make surrender to the will of God in these matters look like a possible and desirable solution. In reality, though, it would not be the same thing for us that it was for Mohammed's contemporaries. For them it was a liberation from time and fate; for us it would be more like a liberation from responsibility. For them sustenance was very uncertain, dependent on rainfall and pasture, both of which were very undependable in desert conditions; life expectancy was low, for death could come very easily and unexpectedly in a nomadic existence; the sex of a child was very important and its uncontrollable character strongly felt, female infants often being exposed or buried alive; happiness and misery were seen as contingent on the vicissitudes of fortune which could be as great in a patriarchal society as in the story of Job. To surrender to the will of God under these circumstances was not to abdicate responsibility; it was to take a religious instead of a merely fatalistic attitude towards the facts of deprivation, death, birth, and misfortune. For us, on the contrary, there is something we can do about each one of these facts. Besides merely facing the facts we can determine to some extent what they shall be, or at least it seems to us that we can.

The graver doubts which will someday be experienced about the civilization we are now creating will also be doubts about the possibility and desirability of controlling these matters, most probably, like the doubts we presently experience. They are likely, however, to have a sharper focus. Let us imagine that someday a limiting principle, or perhaps a whole set of such principles, will be discovered in these matters of control. Its form or their form, let us suppose, will be like that of the "uncertainty principle"[29] in physics. According to that principle the more accurately the position of a particle is determined by measurement the less accurately its momentum can be ascertained, and vice versa. We can imagine that limiting principles of this kind, already discovered in the now highly developed field of physics, will be discovered someday in the presently less developed fields of human biology and human behavior. Perhaps it will be learned that the more one factor is controlled in matters of man's sustenance or life expectancy or birth or fortune the more uncontrolled some other factor will become. If this happens, then there will be a hard choice to make as to which factor should be controlled. The possibility of control will look different in this light, and so will the desirability.

Thus the horizon of man's mortality changes as history goes on; what was once a solution to the problem of death is so no longer but may become so once again. How is it then that a message like Mohammed's of surrender to the will of God is passed on from one epoch to another and from one civilization to another? The secret, most likely, is that a message like this is really more than an answer to a particular epoch's problem of death. Surrender to the will of God really goes beyond man's concerns with his sustenance, the term of his life, the sex of his children, and his good or bad fortune. It is a matter of the whole heart, the whole mind, and the whole soul. This is what makes it a religion. Mohammed could unite the Arab tribes and create an Arab civilization with it because it did indeed meet the problem of man's subjection to time and fate as that was felt in the Arabia of his day. His own surrender to the will of God, though, was a surrender of his whole heart and mind and soul, not merely of those things which would have to be surrendered otherwise to time and fate. As a result the message he left in the Koran could speak to hearts and minds and souls which faced time and fate in different ways than he did.

Surrendering the whole heart and mind and soul to God would mean surrendering not merely the realm of necessity in one's life, where time and fate are supreme, but also the realm of freedom, where one exercises control over one's own affairs. In fact, it would be possible for a man to be on the double project of extending the realm of freedom in his life and surrendering that realm, as he extended it, to the will of God. For Mohammed's contemporaries the realm of freedom was that of righteousness and unrighteousness; to surrender to the will of God in this realm was to follow the "straight path," to be "rightly guided." There was no thought of extending this realm into that of necessity and bringing matters like man's sustenance or his life expectancy or his offspring or his good or bad fortune under human control. For us the realm of freedom is that of choosing one's way of life, "choosing one's essence" as existentialists would say,[30] and surrender to the will of God would have to mean letting God's will somehow determine one's choice of essence, one's way of life. Living at a time when human control is being extended over more and more aspects of human life, however, we could envision extending the scope of the choice involved in choosing a way of life while nevertheless surrendering in that choice to the will of God.

As the realm of human control is extended, choosing a way of life becomes less a matter of adopting an attitude towards the facts of one's life and more one of actually determining what the facts shall be. One can control one's sustenance to some extent by choosing among more and less lucrative ways of life; one can control life expectancy to a degree by choosing among more and less dangerous and stressful ways of life; one can control progeny and perhaps even the sex of one's progeny by choosing among ways of living together; and one can control one's fortune and misfortune in some manner by choosing between ways of life which are like games of chance and those which are like games of skill and those which are like a mixture of the two. As we conceived it earlier, surrender to the will of God on these issues would have meant not making any of these choices, but giving up control over such matters. As we are conceiving it now, though, it would mean making these choices but making them in accordance with God's will. This introduces a new standard of choice. One might end up choosing the more dangerous and stressful way of life, for instance, if one were following the will of God, while if one were thinking merely in terms of life expectancy one would choose the more secure and peaceful way.

But how is one to know the will of God? This seems the obvious thing to ask. It may be possible, however, to know what surrender itself is as an orientation of life without knowing what God's will is in specific instances.[31] To learn God's will in specific instances one would have to recur to illumination and inspiration in prayer, or more simply to the discoveries which occur at the turning points in life. What one finds in such illuminations and inspirations or in such discoveries and turning points is understanding rather than certainty. On the other hand, the orientation along the path of prayer or along the voyage of discovery is in itself a surrender or the surrender to the will of God, and thus is a way of life in itself or a way of living any specific way of life. Choosing one's way of life in accordance with God's will, therefore, would mean turning whatever specific way of life one chooses into a path of prayer or a voyage of discovery. Beyond that it would mean living by the discoveries which one makes and the understanding which one obtains on that path or voyage.

The religion of surrender to the will of God, if it is uprooted in this fashion from its original culture and transplanted in our own, can look very simple and unexceptionable. The trouble is that it has to be uprooted and transplanted before it will appear simple and unexceptionable to us. It has to be integrated with our own emerging answer to death, the expansion of the realm of human freedom and control. Any concrete formulation of a religion, it seems, has to integrate it with a culture, at least to the extent of speaking to the culture's problem of death. Is this perhaps the reason why neither Islam nor any other world religion has succeeded in uniting the religions? Any scriptural formulation of a religion such as the Koran, if our surmise is right, speaks not only to the whole heart and mind and soul of man but also to a particular people with its particular way of seeing life and death. What enables a religion to make its journey through time, from epoch to epoch, is the appeal to man's whole heart and mind and soul, but what enables it to make its journey through space, conquering the world or a portion of the world, is the appeal to a particular people who will carry it.

The process by which a religion carries over from one cultural epoch to another, however, may contain a clue as to how a religion might carry over from one people to another in a given epoch. If we could formulate this process, we might obtain a formulation which is not bound in the same manner as scriptures mostly are to a particular people. In the Bible we have scriptures of different cultural epochs side by side, each characterized by a different philosophy of life and death and by a different name for God.[32] There is the patriarchal epoch when God was called El and men looked to him for posterity; then there is the subsequent era when he was called Yahweh and men looked to him for the land; and then there is the time when Jesus called him Abba and men looked to him for a kingdom. Posterity, the land, and the kingdom, one can see, are answers to death, answers that could be given without any reference to God. With the reliance upon God for these things the cultures are transfigured by religion. To the names for God we could compare the names which God has in the Koran, principally Allah and less frequently ar-Rahman,[33] and to the concern with posterity, the land, and the kingdom we could compare the concern with man's sustenance, the term of his life, the sex of the child, and happiness and misery.

Generalizing from this, we could formulate two principles: (1) if the religion of one cultural epoch or people is compared with that of another it is impossible to learn any more about God from this comparison than what he is to the one epoch or people and what he is to the other, and (2) the relationship to God in each instance is one involving man's whole heart, his whole mind, and his whole soul. The first principle says in effect that El, Yahweh, Abba, ar-Rahman, Allah, and the like are names which in their context signify what God is or was to a given epoch or people, and that it would be fallacious to single out one of these names and the relationship it signifies as the only true one to the exclusion of the others. The second principle does not hold for all epochs and peoples: men did not give their whole heart and mind and soul to Zeus or to Odin. As it stands, therefore, this principle makes it possible to speak of El, Yahweh, Abba, ar-Rahman, Allah, and the like as though they were all names for one and the same God. Together the two principles allow us to put such names into a manifold sequence as a kind of history of God in his relationships with man, each name telling us something of permanent significance about God. The two principles apply in a straightforward way to the epochs and peoples from which the scriptures of Judaism, Christianity, and Islam derive, but they would also apply to subsequent epochs in the history of those religions and to religions like Hinduism and Buddhism, provided we do not assume that God has always to have a proper name.

What we are getting at here is a way of understanding the convergence of the religions which is taking place or may be taking place in our time. The conjunction of scriptures from different epochs and peoples in the Bible did not succeed in joining Judaism and Christianity, it is true, any more than the recognition given to the Torah and the Gospel in the Koran succeeded in joining those two religions with Islam. That this much could have been done already, though, seems to imply that still more could be done in this direction. With both the Bible and the Koran as precedents, it seems that it should be possible to formulate religion in our times in such a way that cultural relativity is recognized without impairing the total involvement of heart and mind and soul. Cultural relativity itself is relative in that it is a notion characteristic of our time, and so it too has only a relative validity. There are parallel notions, nevertheless, in the Bible and the Koran, about God speaking at different times through different prophets to different peoples. So we may have something here which can carry on through still other parallels beyond the decline and fall of our present culture.

Conscious relativity is not necessarily a peaceful thing. Mohammed was very much aware of the relativity of what he was doing, that he was prophet only to a particular people, and yet he took up the sword. Does the convergence of the religions which we are envisioning lead towards perpetual peace by way of holy war? When the relativity of standpoints is conscious, war can arise only by deliberately choosing a standpoint. It is like drawing or painting in perspective: one can be highly aware of the multiplicity of possible perspectives, but one chooses a single perspective so as to introduce order. Thus Mohammed set out deliberately to found what he calls in the Constitution of Medina "a community (*ummah*) distinct from the people (*dun an-nas*)," *i.e.* distinct from other people or perhaps distinct from the People of the Book.[34] The convergence of the religions we are envisioning does not involve the deliberate choice of a single standpoint. It consists rather in a mutual understanding, a going over from one standpoint to another. The peace it would lead to, accordingly, is not a "tranquillity of order" as in the classical definition,[35] at least not a tranquillity of order arising from the establishment of a single perspective.

There is an inner peace in each of the great religions, a peace within man, which leads to an outer peace, a peace among men, but by different paths, reflecting the different lives of their founders. The inner peace is created by the whole-heartedness, the whole-mindedness, the whole-souledness of the religions. It is a single-heartedness, a single-mindedness, a single-souledness. It is the tranquillity of an inner order, and it leads to the tranquillity of an outer order, but by a way which reveals its possessor's own heart and mind and soul. Islam spread by teaching and holy war, reflecting the life of Mohammed who preached and fought. Christianity spread by teaching and martyrdom, reflecting the life of Jesus who preached and suffered. Buddhism spread by teaching alone, without war or martyrdom, reflecting the life of Gotama who preached without fighting or suffering. Now if one passes over from one religion to another, one is set upon an inner journey which looks less single-hearted, less single-minded, less single-souled than the inner peace which can be found in any one of the religions taken alone. And one is set upon an outer journey which leads towards peace among men by paths which look rather more devious than holy war or martyrdom or teaching.

The inner journey is that of a man in pursuit of wisdom who is willing to find wisdom not only in the Gospel, if he has been brought up as a Christian, but also in the Dharma and the Koran. Let us suppose that he pretends to no higher viewpoint, such as humanism or historical criticism, from which he might look down upon the religions, but that the highest viewpoints he recognizes are those of the religions themselves. In that case the nearest thing he has to a single overall standpoint is the standpoint he always comes back to. If he has been brought up as a Christian, this will be Christianity; if he has been brought up as a Buddhist, it will be Buddhism; if he has been brought up as a Muslim, it will be Islam. This standpoint to which he always returns from his excursions into other religions is analogous to the one to which he returns from excursions into other lives. It is like his autobiographical standpoint. Say he is a Christian. His purity of heart, his singleness of mind, his peace of soul, such as they are, will in the last analysis be those of the Gospel. And yet his understanding of the Gospel will be transformed by his understanding of the Dharma and the Koran.

There is a further step, nevertheless, in the process of coming back, and that is finally to come back to the autobiographical standpoint itself. When he passes over to the lives of Gotama, Jesus, and Mohammed, he must finally come back to his own life. This places him at a distance from all the religions, even the one to which his own life is most closely related. The outer journey which he travels, therefore, reflecting as it does his own heart and mind and soul, will not necessarily be the traditional path by which his religion was spread. It might be nearer the path Kant traced out in his plan for perpetual peace. An example would be Dag Hammarskjold, who on his outer journey was Secretary General of the United Nations, while on his inner journey, as his spiritual diary attests,[36] was a Christian. The Meditation Room which he designed at the United Nations Building and the short leaflet he wrote for visitors reveal the connection between the two journeys, the inner and the outer, as he saw it. "We all have within us," he begins, "a center of stillness surrounded by silence."[37] Then he goes on to reflect on the scene in the Meditation Room, a shaft of light striking a block of iron ore which looks like an empty altar "not because there is no God, not because it is an altar to an unknown God, but because it is dedicated to a God whom man worships under many names and in many forms. . . . There is an ancient saying," he concludes, "that the sense of a vessel is not in its shell but in the void. So it is with this room. It is for those who come here to fill the void with what they find in their center of stillness."

So it is, we could say, with leagues of nations and plans for perpetual peace. They are vessels and shells. It is for men like Hammarskjold to fill the void with what they find in their center of stillness. By reaching this center, it seems, an individual reaches the Archimedean point where the world can be moved; he becomes capable of affecting the course of human events. This is something we can see exemplified in the lives of Gotama and Jesus and Mohammed. Gotama reached this point by renouncing power, by leaving his father's palace and giving up the ideal of being a Chakravartin, a universal sovereign, in order to pursue the ideal of being a Buddha, an awakened or enlightened one. Jesus too reached this point in the desert by resisting the temptation to power and an earthly kingdom, and he maintained himself at this point afterwards in his public life by continuing to resist the desire of his followers to make him king. Mohammed reached this point at Mecca when he wielded no political power, but afterwards at Medina, when he became conscious of founding a new religion, he did begin to exercise power.

Even of Mohammed, though, we can probably say that he was able to move the world because he reached the center of stillness, that what carries through from age to age in history is not what he accomplished at Medina so much as what he discovered at Mecca. Men like Gotama and Jesus and Mohammed actually affect the course of events because they "fill the void with what they find in their center of stillness." Man's journey in time takes him through desert places. The life in these places is only that which he brings there, that which he has within himself. He may have enough within himself to keep alive and to hold off death, so to speak, to solve the problem of death in a given era and thus to bring civilization to that time. Or he may have more, more than enough to answer death, enough to fill his whole heart and mind and soul, and thus to bring religion to that time. The excess of life which he has within himself, if he brings religion, is disproportionate to the time in which he lives. It seems to point beyond that time to eternity. Or it points beyond that time to other times. Let us follow up this clue. This excess of life which we find in the religions may be able to tell us something about all times, something about the whole course of human events.

NOTES

1. Cf. Geo Widengren, *The Ascension of the Apostle and the Heavenly Book* (Uppsala, A.B. Lundequistska, 1950).
2. On the Mecca period cf. W. Montgomery Watt, *Muhammad at Mecca* (Oxford, Clarendon Press, 1953).
3. On the Medina period cf. Watt, *Muhammad at Medina* (Oxford, Clarendon Press, 1956).
4. The night journey is mentioned in the Koran, XVII, 1. Cf. Widengren, *Muhammad, the Apostle of God, and His Ascension* (Uppsala, A.B. Lundequistska, 1955), especially pp. 96 ff.
5. The night of power and glory is the subject of Surah XCVII in the Koran. The term there is *qadr,* which can mean "power" or "glory." I translate "power and glory" to keep both connotations.
6. Two visions are described in the Koran in Surah LIII, 1 ff., one in which Mohammed sees the revealer on the horizon and then sees him draw near to make the revelation, the other in which he sees him near the sidra-tree in paradise. (There is a brief allusion to the first vision also in Surah LXXXI, 19.) The first vision, where the revelation is brought to Mohammed, seems comparable to the night of power and

glory. The second, where he sees the revealer near a tree in paradise, seems comparable to the night journey, where he is carried in spirit to paradise.

On these two types of revelation as two distinct patterns in the religions of the Ancient Near East cf. Widengren, *Muhammad, the Apostle of God, and His Ascension,* pp. 206 ff.

7. Cf. Surah LXXIII, 1 ff.
8. Cf. Surah II, 136 ff. on the change of *qibla,* or direction of prayer, from Jerusalem to Mecca after Mohammed had met with the opposition of the Jews at Medina. But cf. Watt, *Muhammad at Medina,* pp. 198 f. and 202 for the uncertainties surrounding the question of Mohammed's *qibla* when he was at Mecca.
9. C. G. Jung, *Psychology and Religion: West and East,* tr. by R. F. C. Hull (New York, Pantheon, 1958), p. 105.
10. Cf. *supra,* Chapter Two, Section 2.
11. Surah XLIV, 2.
12. Surah XXV, 34. Cf. Widengren, *Muhammad, the Apostle of God, and His Ascension,* pp. 100 and 208.
13. Surah III, 17 ff. Mohammed formulated it this way after meeting with the opposition of the Jews at Medina and becoming aware that he was founding a new religion distinct from Judaism and Christianity. Cf. Richard Bell, *Introduction to the Qur'an* (Edinburgh, Edinburgh University Press, 1953), pp. 109 f. on dating the use of the terms *islam* ("surrender"), *muslim* ("one who surrenders"), and *aslama* ("to surrender") in the Koran.
14. Cf. her *Life,* tr. by E. Allison Peers, *The Complete Works of St. Teresa of Jesus,* vol. 1 (New York, Sheed and Ward, 1946), pp. 65 ff.
15. *Ibid.,* p. 119.
16. *Ibid.,* pp. 109 ff.
17. *Ibid.,* p. 121.
18. Surah I, tr. by Richard Bell, *The Qur'an,* vol. 1 (Edinburgh, T. & T. Clark, 1960), p. 1. Bell translates verse 5 literally "Guide us the straight path." The ambiguity could be resolved by the preposition "by" or by "to."
19. Here I am using a comparison Wittgenstein employed in his *Tractatus Logico-Philosophicus* (New York, Harcourt, 1922), 6.4311 to illustrate the endlessness of life in spite of the fact of death. On his use of the comparison cf. my *City of the Gods,* pp. 9 f.
20. This would be a way of accounting for what Gerhard von Rad calls "the prophet's freedom" in his *Old Testament Theology,* tr. by D. M. G. Stalker, vol. 2 (New York, Harper, 1965), pp. 70 ff.
21. Cf. Arnold Toynbee, *Civilization on Trial* (New York, Meridian, 1958), p. 25.
22. Cf. Kant, *Perpetual Peace,* tr. by Lewis White Beck (Indianapolis-New York, Bobbs-Merrill, 1957).
23. I am echoing here and in the following pages the formulation in Matthew 22:37 "Thou shalt love the Lord thy God with all thy heart, and with all thy soul, and with all thy mind." The original formulation in Deuteronomy 6:5 has "with all thine heart, and with all thy soul, and with all thy might." Mark 12:30 has "with all thy heart, and with all thy soul, and with all thy mind, and with all thy strength." Luke 10:27 has a similar combination, only it places "strength" before "mind."

24. Cf. Watt, *Muhammad at Medina,* pp. 78 ff.
25. *Ibid.,* 345 ff. Watt discusses this tradition but considers it doubtful, though it comes from what he considers an otherwise trustworthy source.
26. Cf. *ibid.,* pp. 192 ff. on Mohammed and the Jews.
27. Cf. *The City of the Gods* where I compare cultures in terms of their answers to death.
28. Cf. Watt, *Muhammad at Mecca,* 24 f. Cf. also his *Free Will and Predestination in Early Islam* (London, Luzac, 1948), pp. 18 ff.
29. Cf. Werner Heisenberg, *The Physical Principles of the Quantum Theory* (Chicago, University of Chicago Press, 1930), pp. 13 ff.
30. Cf. Sartre's discussion of this kind of freedom in *Being and Nothingness,* tr. by Hazel E. Barnes (New York, Washington Square Press, 1966), pp. 559 ff.
31. Cf. the classical discussion of this point by Thomas Aquinas, *Summa Theologiae,* I–II, q. 19, a. 10.
32. Cf. my article "The Metamorphoses of Faith," in *The Review of Politics,* XXIX (1967), 291 ff.
33. Surah XVII, 110 has it that both Allah and ar-Rahman are appropriate names of God. The name Allah may be a contraction for *al-ilah,* "the God." The name ar-Rahman is apparently related to the term *rahmah,* "mercy," and probably means "the Merciful." Noeldeke held that the use of this second name was limited to the middle Meccan period in the composition of the Koran. Cf. Bell, *Introduction to the Qur'an,* pp. 101 ff. and 143.
34. Cf. Watt, *Muhammad at Medina,* p. 201. Cf. his translation of the whole constitution *ibid.,* pp. 221 ff.
35. This is Augustine's definition of peace in *The City of God,* xix, 13.
36. Dag Hammarskjold, *Markings,* tr. by Leif Sjöberg and W. H. Auden (New York, Knopf, 1964).
37. The English text of the leaflet is reprinted in Hammarskjold, *Servant of Peace,* ed. by Wilder Foote (New York–Evanston, Harper, 1962), pp. 160 f.

V
A Map of Time

"THERE IS A HISTORY in all men's lives," Shakespeare has Warwick say, "figuring the nature of the times deceased; the which observed, a man may prophesy, with a near aim, of the main chance of things as yet not come to life, which in their seeds and weak beginnings lie intreasured."[1] Warwick is explaining to King Henry how King Richard, whom Henry had deposed, was able to prophesy from his own experience the troubles of Henry's reign. All men's lives, Warwick is saying, have inscribed in them the past and future of mankind. Every man's life is a map of time. It is a map of the past "figuring the nature of the times deceased." It is also a map of the future from which "a man may prophesy, with a near aim, of the main chance of things as yet not come to life."

A life appears this way, as a map of time, especially when it is considered as a series of events. There are two basic ways, we could say, in which a life may be considered: as a series of events and as the life of someone. When it is considered as the life of someone, then its story appears to be a tale which could be told of no one else, a unique tale from which no conclusions could be drawn about other lives or about time as a whole. When it is considered as a series of events, on the other hand, then its story appears to be a tale of things and situations which could occur in other lives too, a tale which could throw light on the entire course of human events. Historically the life story has been told in many different and characteristic ways, as a story of deeds, of experience, of self-realization. Each story, though, is at once a story of events and the story of someone. In the ancient story of deeds there was a doer of deeds, thus someone, and there were the deeds themselves, thus events; in the ancient and medieval story of experience there was the one who underwent the experiences, again someone, and there were the experiences themselves, again events; in the modern story of self-realization there is the self, again someone, and there is the process of realization, again a series of events.

Any life we wish, therefore, from any time in history can be considered, without anachronism, as a series of events, and if it is considered this way it will throw light upon other lives and upon time as a whole. Even lives as extraordinary as those of Gotama and Jesus and Mohammed can be treated this way; perhaps better than most others, for they reveal possibilities which are liable to remain latent in more ordinary lives. Kierkegaard, conceiving the life story as a story of self-realization, speaks of the "moment" in which the self is realized.[2] This mysterious moment is what we are calling an "event"; it is a decisive moment, a moment of decision, a moment of conversion; it is the moment when a man freely enacts his relationship to eternity, when he re-enacts in his own life the turning point which divides time into B.C. and A.D. We could generalize this notion and speak of the moments in which other turning points in time are re-enacted, not only the revelation which occurred in the life of Jesus but also the enlightenment which occurred in the life of Gotama and the revelation which occurred in the life of Mohammed. We could go still further and speak of the re-enactment of all the great turning points in time. We could regard life as a recapitulation of time.

Consider the following list of turning points in time: the beginning of time, the transition from prehistory to history, the enlightenment and revelation experiences giving rise to the world religions, the transition from history to world history, the end of time.[3] Each of these events can have a counterpart in the individual life. The beginning of time is recapitulated in the beginning of life. The transition from prehistory to history which occurred when writing was invented and men began to record the past is recapitulated when the individual, by growing from immediate through existential to historical consciousness, attains the kind of historical awareness that went into the invention of writing and the recording of the past. The enlightenment and revelation experiences giving rise to the world religions are recapitulated when the individual, perhaps by experimenting with truth as we have been doing in this book, comes to share in the enlightenment and the revelation. The transition from history to world history which has been taking place in our time as the different civilizations and religions of the world enter into communication with one another and their stories become one story is recapitulated when the individual enters by the process we have called "passing over" into a sympathetic understanding of civilizations and religions other than his own, and then comes back to a new understanding of his own. The end of time finally is recapitulated in the end of life, in the moment of death.

Now if each of these moments is a point in the inner life of a man when he freely enacts a relationship to eternity, then he has the possibility of reliving the entire story of mankind and of determining, while reliving it, what the moral of the story shall be. The first and last events, to be sure, the beginning and end of life, are beyond his control. Insofar as a relationship to eternity is enacted at these points, nevertheless, maybe he has some freedom even here. Eternity, as we are using the term, is implicitly defined in Plato's saying, time is "a changing image of eternity."[4] The real nature of eternity is revealed in the insights into the changing image which occur in the course of life and time. To act upon an insight into time, the changing image, is to enact a relationship to eternity. Insight into the beginning and end of time is possible at least in recollection and anticipation, after the beginning and before the end. The other events we mentioned, the transition from prehistory to history, the enlightenment and revelation giving rise to the world religions, and the transition from history to world history, are themselves moments of insight and do not fully occur if the insights do not occur. If a person fails to attain these insights, the events take place in his life only as occasions, occasions which pass by like stations at which a train does not stop.

Let us see what we can learn from mapping a life onto time and from the inverse process of mapping time onto a life. We can choose a life that is well known to us, our own or that of some friend. Mapping the life onto time will mean finding events in the life to correspond to events we know of in time as a whole; mapping time onto the life will mean finding events in time to correspond to events we know of in the life. Let us begin by mapping the life onto time. The great events of time, when we find their counterparts in a life, make the life look interesting and important. At least there will be the beginning and the end, corresponding to the beginning and end of time. What occurs at these two points in life is peculiar to the individual: it is this individual who is conceived and who comes to birth; it is this individual who dies. Comparing them to the beginning and end of time, however, brings to light something rather more universal in them. They are indeed the beginning and end of time for the individual. He is contemporary at these points with the beginning and end of time for the world. By thinking back to the beginning he thinks back to the nothingness, or to the Being from which the world comes and from which he comes; by thinking forward to the end he thinks forward to the nothingness, or to the Being to which the world goes and to which he goes.

This same nothingness or Being can come to light in the events which take place between the beginning and the end. The transition from prehistory to history, the enlightenment and the revelation inspiring the world religions, the transition from history to world history—these events may recur in his life only as occasions for insight, occasions in which the insight is never achieved. In that case what will come to light on these occasions will look more like sheer nothingness than Being. If the transition from prehistory to history fails, if he fails to grow from immediate to existential to historic awareness, his life is liable to look like a preparation for something that never happens. If the enlightenment and the revelation fail to occur, he is liable to look like one of those earnest searchers for whom the heavens never open. If the transition from history to world history fails, he is liable to look like a man who is incapable of transcending the limitations of his own background.

If the insights occur at these points but he fails to act upon them, then his life will seem a failure in these ways in his own eyes, and he will consciously encounter the nothingness. If, on the other hand, they occur and he acts upon them, then it will seem to him that he encounters Being and that he freely enacts at each point a relationship to eternity.

Mapping a life onto time can thus make the life appear to be something great, at the very worst a failure of some great enterprise, failure at which is perhaps more worthwhile than success at any lesser undertaking. Mapping time onto a life, however, the inverse process, can give an encouraging or discouraging impression of time, depending on the life one chooses. "All life weighed in the scales of my own life," Yeats concluded in one of his autobiographies, "seems to me a preparation for something that never happens."[5] This rather discouraging conclusion he drew at a time prior to the breakthrough he later experienced, the turning point in his life which he describes in *A Vision*. What he was discouraged about, it seems, was the possibility of really entering history. One can be equally discouraged about the possibility of attaining enlightenment or receiving revelation, or the possibility of rising above the particular history of one culture or one religion and entering world history. It can seem that the heavens never have opened and never will open for any man. It can seem that no man can surmount his own background, that no one can be anything more than a product of his circumstances. All this depends on the life one chooses to map time onto and the point within the life at which the correlation is made.

No matter what life one chooses, though, the beginning and end of time, when they are correlated with the beginning and end of a life, start to look like the beginning and end of an individual. The world, that is, appears in this light to be an individual. Hegel called the earth "the universal individual" and he said that it does violence to all universal forms and classes.[6] It is as though general categories break and are shattered upon the rock of the earth's individuality. What Hegel had in mind was that our general classifications, particularly biological genera and species, are not as general as they seem but only refer to this individual planet, to life forms on earth. We could extend what he says to our terminology about time, to terms like "prehistory," "history," "world history," "enlightenment," and "revelation." All of them refer to events in time on earth. The "beginning" and "end" that go with them are the beginning and end of time on earth, not of time in the universe at large. Time becomes in this light "our" time, the story of our earth. With this increased sense of its concreteness some of the disproportion between time and the individual life disappears. It becomes less astonishing that individual lives like those of Gotama and Jesus and Mohammed could make so much difference in history. It begins to become credible that even lesser individuals might be able to make a difference.

True, mapping a life onto time and mapping time onto the life, as we have been doing, effectively takes the life out of time and correlates time and life as wholes. Once we put the life back into its context in time, it will look like part of time—a very small part, with much else going on before it, after it, and alongside it. The mapping, nevertheless, can lead to a discovery which changes one's view of life and time. The discovery is that the life, in spite of being merely a part, has a relationship to the whole of time, that the entire drama of time is enacted or re-enacted in the life. What is more, it becomes possible, when one has seen what is actually taking place in the course of human events, when one sees the great turning points as consisting in an enactment of man's relationship to eternity, to further the process in one's own life. Nikos Kazantzakis describes a discovery like this in his personal creed.[7] "Finally one night I started up in great joy," he relates, "for I had seen the red ribbon left behind him in his ascent—within us and in all the universe—by a certain Combatant; I clearly saw his bloody footprints ascending from inorganic matter into life and from life into spirit." He is speaking of a God who emerges in the story of the earth and the evolution of man. "I now clearly saw the progress of the Invisible," he says, "and suddenly I knew what my duty was to be: to work in harmony together with that Combatant; to transmute, even I, in my own small capacity, matter into spirit, for only then might I try to reach the highest endeavor of man—a harmony with the universe."

He is enacting here a relationship to the Invisible, to the Combatant, as he calls his God. He sees his whole life, in fact, as the enactment of such a relationship, as a cooperation with the Combatant who struggles to ascend from inorganic matter to life and from life to spirit. Kazantzakis' own part in the struggle, as he sees it, is to transmute matter into spirit in his own way, the way of a poet, to transmute the truth of his life into poetry. He finds in this a solution to the problem of death. "I work and think now with certainty," he says, "for I know that my contribution, because it follows the profound depths of the universe, will not go lost. Even I, a mortal, may work with the One who is immortal, and my spirit —as much as is possible—may become more and more immortal." His solution is to transmute as much flesh as possible, to consume the flesh, to leave nothing for death to take but bones. His immortality is to be in the "contribution" he makes to the work of the One who is immortal, or better in the action itself rather than in the fruits of the action, in "working with" the One who is immortal.

The synchronizing of life and time in a personal vision like this turns life into a journey with God: life is man's journey and time is God's journey. We need not take God's journey as literally as Kazantzakis does and view God as emerging in a process of evolution. Plato's saying that time is "a changing image of eternity" points to a better way of understanding it. If I synchronize my life with time as a whole, I synchronize it also with eternity as it reveals itself in the course of time. Kierkegaard spoke of "becoming contemporary with Christ" by recollecting and repeating in one's own life the moment which divides time into B.C. and A.D.[8] We could speak of becoming contemporary with each one of the moments we have mentioned, the beginning and the end of time, the transition from prehistory to history and from history to world history, the enlightenment and revelation. With the idea, moreover, that time is a changing image of eternity and that eternity therefore is revealed at each of these moments, we could speak of becoming contemporary at each point with God.

Let us examine each of these moments now and see what it would be to enact them and to re-enact them, to recollect them and to repeat them, to become contemporary with God as he creates the world in the beginning of time, as he leads man out of prehistory into history, as he enlightens man and reveals himself to him, as he draws all men together and makes them one people, as he brings the world to its consummation at the end of time.

"Where were you when I laid the foundations of the earth?" God asks Job. "Declare, if you have understanding."[9] An answer for Job can be found in the Book of Proverbs. "When he appointed the foundations of the earth," Wisdom says, "then I was by him, as one brought up with him, and I was daily in his delight, rejoicing always before him, rejoicing in the habitable part of his earth, and my delights were with the sons of men."[10] It is God's wisdom that speaks, but man is clearly called upon in the Book of Proverbs to share it. By means of wisdom man can go back in spirit to the beginning of time. That wisdom consists, it seems, in seeing what God saw in the beginning. "And God saw that it was good,"[11] we are told in the Book of Genesis again and again after each act in the story of creation—after he created light, after he separated land and sea, after he made the earth fertile, after he fashioned the sun and the moon, after he filled the sea with fish and the air with birds, after he populated the earth with animals. And when he had made man and finished the whole work of creation "God saw everything that he had made," we are told, "and behold, it was very good."[12]

When a man sees what God saw in the beginning, when he sees that it is good, that it is very good, then he too stands at the beginning. The experience of seeing that it is good is like the experience of kissing the earth which Dostoevsky describes in *The Brothers Karamazov:* Alyosha runs out into the night and falls upon the earth and kisses it, weeping and vowing to love it forever. "It was as though some idea had seized the sovereignty of his mind," Dostoevsky says, "and it was for all his life and for ever and ever: he had fallen on the earth a weak boy, but he rose up a resolute fighter, and he knew and felt it suddenly at the very moment of his ecstasy."[13] In that moment, we could say, he enacted a relationship to eternity, and so does every man when he kisses the earth, when he sees that it is good, that it is very good. An idea seizes the sovereignty of his mind; it is an insight into the goodness of the earth, into the goodness of creation. He vows to love the earth forever, to live all his life by this insight. He falls upon the earth weak but he rises up from it resolute, in the power of this understanding and this decision. His whole life lies before him in a different light; all time lies before him in this light.

This vision of the goodness of creation comes only after a vision of evil, however, especially of the evil in life and in time. It was to Job that God spoke of the creation, to Job who had lost everything, his possessions, his children, his health. It was Dostoevsky who spoke of kissing the earth, Dostoevsky who is perhaps better known for his vision of evil and suffering than he is for his vision of good. To see what God saw in the beginning is not simply to be in the beginning; it is to go back to the beginning. When a man says of creation "it is good," "it is very good," or when he tells the story of creation and says "God saw that it was good," he is speaking by contrast. The thought that it is good, that it is very good, arises to contrast with a previous thought that it is not good, that it is evil. The thinker here stands, it seems, at the end of a long process in which his consciousness has been expanding from a simple awareness and concern about the here and now to an awareness and concern about his life as a whole with its past and future, and beyond that to an awareness and concern about time and the course of human events. In the process he has seen the evil and suffering there is in human life and in the course of human events, but in the end he is able to return deliberately to his starting point, the immediate, to become as a child again and to see things with the eyes of a child.

The return to the immediate level of awareness with its childlike vision of reality is thus a return at once to the beginning of life and to the beginning of time. Yet this recovered immediacy can never be simply equivalent to the original immediacy one had as a child, when one actually stood at the beginning of life. Then too, it is true, one saw that it was good, but that original vision of the good was inarticulate and there was no evil to contrast with it. Now, as one recaptures the child's vision, one sees again the goodness of all things, but this time the vision is articulate and there is the memory of evil to set it off. When man first emerged from subman in the process of evolution, we can guess, he saw things as a child does. The original man was truly an immediate man. The gradual transition from prehistory to history, if we can correlate it with the normal growth of awareness in the individual,[14] was probably an expansion of consciousness in which the immediate man, limited to the here and now, was followed by the existential man, conscious of his lifetime as a whole, and the existential man in turn was followed by the historic man, conscious of the course of human events.

The first step, the transition from the immediate man to the existential man, takes place in the individual life as the child becomes a youth. The child is protected from evil by his immediacy. If he is hurt, he will cry, but he can go quickly from tears to smiles and laughter, forgetting the hurt in the small span of his awareness, when something pleasurable is placed before him. Ordinarily the only things which leave a mark upon his mind are things which are done to him repeatedly or which happen to him repeatedly and which he comes to expect. It is not hard, therefore, to be happy in childhood. Something which happens only once will not ordinarily take the child's happiness away; only something which happens again and again or something which happens once but is brought home to him in its effects again and again. As the child becomes a youth, though, he begins to lose this protective immediacy and to become concerned about the future and the past. He can feel uncertain of his future, resentful of his past. An event which occurs only once can now become a turning point for good or for ill. It begins to be far more difficult for him to be happy; it can seem to him that he has lost happiness along with childhood.

We can imagine something similar happening in the evolution of mankind in prehistory. Probably there was a time when man was much closer to the other animals, when men and women were immediate and spontaneous like children. It would have been easier to be happy in those days than it is now. That would have been the golden age which is spoken of in the legends and traditions of many peoples. There came a time, though, if the general correlation between life and time holds, when men began to become more conscious of having a future and a past, not yet a history but a future and a past in their own lives. This would have been the end of the golden age. Perhaps it occurred when man ceased to live by hunting and food-gathering and began to domesticate animals and cultivate plants. Certainly the domestication of animals and the cultivation of plants requires much more foresight and hindsight than hunting and food-gathering do. From this point on in prehistory, as in life itself, happiness must have become a much more difficult thing to attain; it must have seemed to man that he had been excluded from the garden of paradise, that he must earn his bread in the sweat of his brow.

With foresight and hindsight of this calibre goes an awareness of mortality, that he must die someday, which can lead man to expand his interest and attention still further, beyond the confines of his lifetime into the region of time encompassing the human life. When this happens the existential man becomes an historic man. This comes about in the individual life, as we know it today, when the youth becomes a man. The second expansion of consciousness occurs, it seems, to cope with death, to find some way of passing the boundary which death sets to life, just as the first expansion occurred to cope with life, to deal with the otherwise unforeseen future and to profit from the otherwise forgotten past. Each expansion of his awareness, however, carries a man further from immediacy and spontaneity, further from the golden age and the garden of paradise, further from any kind of simple happiness. Each step is an expansion in the scope of feeling, imagination, thought, and action such that a man really comes to live in the existential world where before he had lived in the immediate, and then to live in the historic world where before he had lived in the existential.

The original transition from prehistory to history occurred some five thousand years ago, when writing was invented and cities were built and the first literate civilizations were founded in Egypt and Mesopotamia.[15] We can imagine that what happened then was similar to what happens now when an individual enters history, when the existential man becomes an historic man. Writing had to be invented; it could not be discovered like a natural process. The recording of history which began at this time must have gone with a consciousness of making history, and we can guess that this consciousness is what led to the invention of writing and to the recording of what was being done. Man was apparently beginning to live on a greater than human scale, doing deeds and founding institutions which were meant to outlast his own life. His consciousness of doing these deeds and founding these institutions must have made it seem necessary to him to have the deeds recorded. The greater-than-human scale of what he was doing, nevertheless, could also cause him some misgiving, could make him feel that he had overextended himself, make him wish to return once again to the scale of the human lifetime or even to that of the immediate moment.

We could imagine the immediate, the existential, and the historic realms of consciousness as concentric circles, the immediate being the inner circle, the existential the median circle, and the historic the outer circle. The danger, one can see from this image, is that in expanding one's consciousness one might die from within and live only in the outermost circle of one's being, like a tree which is alive only in the outer circles of sapwood and dead in the inner circles of heartwood. Let us suppose that a man has expanded his consciousness to the historic realm but that he has begun to have misgivings, that he begins to suspect he may be dying from within. The first move that he makes, let us say, is to return to the existential realm, the circle of the lifetime, and, without ceasing to be an historic man, to become once again an existential man. He begins to give time to the spirit, to the inner life, to meditation and to reflection upon the course of his life. Say he begins to keep a diary of his meditations. Here he uses writing, a medium which came into existence with historic consciousness, but he uses it rather as a medium for existential consciousness. He writes trying to find his way in being before others, in integrating flesh and spirit, in aloneness.

These are personal problems but the consciousness with which he considers them is one that has been extended beyond the personal to the historic circle and is now deliberately focused again upon the personal or existential realm. As a result he will tend to see his problems in terms that are more universal than those in which he saw them in his younger days, when his main concerns had never reached beyond the personal. Being before others, integrating flesh and spirit, aloneness, he will see each of these and others of their kind as his problems and he will seek a solution for himself, but he will see them as the problems also of other men and will seek a solution for himself which will be at the same time a solution for all men. The medium he uses, words, if he writes his meditations, is conducive to universality because it leads him implicitly to look for solutions which can be put into words, for solutions which are communicable. He will find, if he can, a way of coping with aloneness which is a way for all men and he will put it into such words, even if he never proclaims them, that other men can find it and follow it.

A return like this from time to life is perhaps what led to the experience of enlightenment or awakening which inspired the higher religions of India and to the comparable and almost contemporary experiences inspiring the higher religions and philosophies of China and the Socratic and Post-Socratic philosophies of Greece. It is noteworthy that both Gotama the founder of Buddhism and Mahavira the founder of Jainism, who were contemporaries in India, were originally members of the princely caste, the Kshatriyas, rather than the priestly caste, the Brahmins. They belonged to the caste most involved in the purposes and cross-purposes of history, the caste dedicated not to labor like the Sudras or to work like the Vaisyas, or to contemplation and sacrifice like the Brahmins, but to action. Both of them left their palaces and went into the forest. It is as though they took leave of history and went away to live their own lives. Both then returned after some years, not to their palaces and the activities of rulers, but to spend their lives sharing their discoveries with others. It is as though their previous condition as potential rulers made it impossible for them simply to remain in the forest as ascetics and made it necessary for them, having withdrawn from history into their own lives, to return once again to history and the affairs of mankind.

The great epics of India, the *Mahabharata* and the *Ramayana,* which are better known among the people of India than the Vedas and the Upanishads, are the stories of princes who went for some years into voluntary exile in the forest. The prince who leaves his prospective kingdom and lives the life of a forest-dweller is thus a hallowed figure also in orthodox Hinduism. In the epics, to be sure, the princes do not return to teach other men, but to rule them. Arjuna and his brothers come back after twelve years in the forest and a thirteenth year in disguise to fight with their rivals for the kingdom; Rama, after retiring to the forest, is forced to fight in order to rescue his wife, and in the end comes back to rule his kingdom. In the Gita, the dialogue of Krishna and Arjuna, the prince is advised to act without seeking the fruits of action, to remain a prince, that is, to fight and to rule, but to value the moral quality of his life above all the purposes and cross-purposes of history. The Gita's ideal, in the terms we are now using, is to be an existential man without ceasing to be an historic man.

Is it possible to go one step further and, without ceasing to be historic and existential, to become immediate like a child? A man, let us say, begins to have misgivings about planning his life, about living according to a plan. The danger in a plan, it seems to him, is not that it may fail but that it may succeed, that he will live out his entire life on the basis of a single insight, the one embodied in his plan. To abandon the plan would be to leave himself open to further insight. A plan of life requires at least existential and can entail historic awareness. It consists in fixing the horizon of one's awareness, in not allowing the horizon to change, and thus in causing all things within the horizon to align themselves in a definite and definable manner. It is a piece of dramaturgy in which, depending on the prevailing form which the life story takes in one's time, one tries like a playwright devising a plot to determine what deeds one shall do, what experiences one shall undergo, what self one shall realize, what events shall occur in one's life.

A plan of this sort can be abandoned without loss of historic or existential consciousness. To abandon it would mean living from moment to moment, doing the deed which the moment calls for, undergoing the experience which the moment brings, being true to the self which comes to light in the moment, acting upon the insight which the moment makes possible. This is a kind of immediacy, and to that extent it is a childlikeness. Yet it is a deliberate immediacy, an immediacy that is aware of the past and the future. A man who stands in this present stands with his past consciously behind him and his future consciously ahead of him. He recollects the past and anticipates the future, but in his recollection he is aware that there have been turning points in his past and that the insight of one period in his past life would not have been sufficient for another period which followed upon a turning point, and in his anticipation therefore he is aware that there will probably be turning points in his future and that his present insight will not be sufficient for the remainder of his life. His conclusion is that he must receive in each moment the insight that is given to him.

"Time," Bergson has said, "is invention or it is nothing at all."[16] If we were to change this to "time is discovery or it is nothing at all," we would have the experience of the man who abandons a plan of life in order to live by insight. We would also have, it seems, the experience of time which underlies the religions of revelation, Judaism, Christianity, and Islam. If time is discovery on man's part, it is revelation on God's; or vice versa, if it is revelation on God's part, it is discovery on man's. Abraham is called by God to leave his home and country, to leave all that is familiar, all that he already knows, and to go to a land which God will show him. His life is a journey of discovery in the literal sense, a journey in which new land is discovered. The pattern is repeated throughout the history of Israel to the present day and the journey of discovery becomes a journey of rediscovery. The Israelites are called to leave Egypt and go to the land which God will show them, the same one he had shown long before to Abraham; centuries later they leave

Babylon and return once more to that land; many centuries afterwards, in our own century, they leave the Diaspora and go to make their homes in that land once again.

The time of wandering in the wilderness between Egypt and the land of promise is re-enacted in the life of Jesus when he goes out into the desert. He spends forty days and forty nights there, probably to commemorate the forty years of Israel's wandering. His sojourn in the wilderness, though, is also like that of Gotama and Mahavira, thinking, fasting, and waiting in the forest. He comes back not to a new land but to a new life and a new time. His message, "Change your minds and hearts, for the kingdom of God is at hand,"[17] speaks of a turning point, a change of mind and heart, and calls Israel to a new life and a new time, the kingdom of God. The journey from the land of captivity to the land of promise had always meant leaving an old life and an old time behind and entering upon a new one. With Jesus that is all there is. There is no longer any land to be sought, only a realm of being, the kingdom of God. What is discovered by man, revealed by God, is no longer a land but a life, eternal life. With Mohammed, by contrast, the journey from place to place becomes important again. There is his flight from Mecca to Medina, and there is the pilgrimage to Mecca. Still the meaning of the journey, as in Mohammed's journey in spirit from the temple at Mecca to that at Jerusalem, is ultimately a journey of the spirit.

To go into the forest as Gotama did, to go into the desert as Jesus did, is enough to change one's entire life, just as what they did was enough to change the entire course of events. To try to reenact both of these events, though—to try to taste both of Gotama's enlightenment and Jesus' revelation, or to set out generally to relive as far as possible the experiences underlying each of the world religions—is something else again. It is something which would appropriately be attempted in an age when man is making the transition from history to world history. It leads to an odyssey of the human spirit which carries a man, if he starts with Christianity, both in the direction of Hinduism and Buddhism and in that of Judaism and Islam. He may end up being neither Christian nor

Hindu nor Buddhist nor Jew nor Muslim. He may end up, like Odysseus among the Cyclops, calling himself "No One." Or he may end like Kazantzakis, who said he went from Christ to Buddha to Lenin to Odysseus.[18] He may end up believing in the odyssey itself, that is, in the journey of the spirit, rather than in anyone he has encountered along the way.

If his spiritual journey takes the form of "passing over" and "coming back," however, then it will be indeed an odyssey like that of Odysseus, a journey which always leads back to home. He will travel like Odysseus through wonderland to homeland. He will pass over by sympathetic understanding into other ways of life and return to his own with new insight. He will travel through the wonderland of other religions, other cultures, other lives, only to come back to the homeland of his own religion, his own culture, his own life. Why pass over? Because he will come back with new understanding and his religion, his culture, his life will be enriched. Why come back? Because otherwise he will lose his own religion, his own culture, his own life.

Passing over and coming back, it seems, is what brings about the transition from history to world history. Since the transition is taking place in our own times, the individual who does this is not merely re-enacting it; he is enacting it. The world wars, it is true, are the most obvious signs that the transition to world history has been taking place in this century. They have arisen rather from a failure to pass over, and they are massive events beyond the influence of the individual. That the failure to pass over should be so deadly, though, seems to show that the time for passing over is ripe and overripe. As for the massiveness and inevitability of the events, it is perhaps only the massiveness and inevitability that always makes its appearance when a journey of the spirit is called for and does not occur. There are two ways of going through life, Jung has said. One is to walk through upright and the other is to be dragged through.[19] We could say the same thing of time and history. The transition from history to world history is something man can walk through upright on a journey of the spirit, or it is something he can be dragged through in a series of world wars.

Walking through life upright means turning the human life cycle, childhood, youth, manhood, and age, into a journey of the spirit in which each successive stage marks a new understanding of things, and with that new understanding a new way of doing things. It means welcoming the new insight which each new phase of life brings instead of being dragged from childhood into youth, from youth into manhood, and from manhood into age. Walking through time upright is somewhat similar. It is, in fact, the same thing insofar as a man's life is a recapitulation of time. It means turning the course of human events, prehistory, history, world history, into a journey of the spirit in which each successive stage marks a new way of understanding things and a new way of doing things. It means welcoming the expansion of consciousness from the immediate to the existential to the historic realm, instead of being dragged from prehistory into history. It means welcoming the enlightenment that comes from seeing time in terms of life and the revelation that comes from seeing time and life in terms of the moment instead of going through time blind to the significance of life and to that of the moment. It means welcoming the enrichment that comes from passing over by sympathetic understanding into other religions, other cultures, other lives, instead of being forced into the confrontations which make world history.

The end of life and time, when one is walking towards it, looks quite different from the way it does when one is being dragged towards it. Death, when one is being dragged from youth into manhood and from manhood into age, looks like nothing more than the loss of life, a loss comparable to the loss of youth in manhood and the loss of manhood in age. Life looks like a day which begins in the darkness of the womb, dawns at birth, comes to high noon when a man reaches the height of his powers, then declines into afternoon and evening as his powers wane, and ends in night at death.

Walking through life takes nothing away from this, but it does add something. Life, if we keep the image of the day, becomes a "journey" in the root meaning of the word, a day's travel. One begins the journey in darkness, walks past dawn into the morning, past noon into the afternoon and evening, and past sunset into the night. The fall of night means the end of the day and the end of the journey, and yet it does not mean only the failing of light and the coming of darkness. It means also the attainment of the goal towards which one has been traveling.

The direction in which one has been moving, if one's life has been an adventure of the spirit, is towards greater and greater understanding. Each stage of life has meant a new horizon of feeling, imagination, thought, and action. One's life has grown richer and richer as one has gone on from one horizon to another. Life in this light looks like a becoming that is headed towards being rather than nothingness. What this being will seem to be at any point in life before death will depend on where one is on the journey. Each turning point in life will foreshadow the end in its own way. The consciousness of mortality, that one must die someday, arises as one's awareness expands from the immediate to the existential and the historic realm, as the child becomes a youth and the youth becomes a man. The realization that death must be something more than the mere loss of life, that becoming is headed towards being rather than nothingness, comes through enlightenment and revelation, through the recovery of life and the moment in time, the recovery of youth and childhood in the midst of manhood. A further realization that the being towards which becoming is headed is not purely personal, that it is a shared being (the Being we were speaking of earlier), comes about as one passes over from one's own life and culture and religion to other lives, cultures, religions, and returns to a more comprehensive understanding of one's own.

This last insight, that the being in which becoming ends is somehow a shared being, throws light also upon the end of time. In an epoch like ours when the transition is being made from history to world history, when the spiritual task is that of passing over, the end of time tends to be envisioned as the end of a converging evolution in which mankind will attain some sort of collective consciousness. Teilhard de Chardin, for example, saw the earth developing by a process of "involution," as he called it, a process of growing inwardness, in which the first great climax is the emergence of man from subman, the emergence of mind; and the second great climax, the Omega point of human evolution, is the emergence of collective mind.[20] To the extent that man walks upright through time, to the extent that he welcomes the mutual understanding that comes about by passing over; to that extent it does seem, at this time, that he is headed towards some kind of collective consciousness.

What the collective mind would be like can be seen in the experience of passing over, in the experience of having entered by sympathy and understanding into the life and way of life of another. The other half of the process, nevertheless, the coming back to one's own life and one's own way of life, indicates that the individual returns to himself. In the moment of passing over there is "no self" (*anatta*), as in Buddhism, or a universal self (*atman*), as in Hinduism; in the moment of coming back, however, there is a self as in Judaism, Christianity, and Islam. The end of the process of becoming, therefore, the end of life and the end of time, is both self and no self, both an individual and a universal self. Or, as a Buddhist wisdom book might say, it is neither self nor no self, neither an individual nor a universal self.

If life were not a recapitulation of time, if it were rather a game against time, then the end would be simply death, and the end of time would be collective death. "Time," Heraclitus said, "is a child playing, moving pieces on a board: the kingdom is the child's."[21] Time, he seems to be saying, is a child playing at draughts; a man can play against the child. but the child will win, the kingdom is his. One can play against time in one's life, one can race against death, trying to accomplish some lifework, trying to complete some life experience, but eventually time will triumph, and one will be conquered by age and death. If our general approach has been right, though, if life is a recapitulation of time, then one need not play against time. One can have time on one's side. In fact, if life is a recapitulation of time, then one is oneself the child playing. Or, to put it another way, if one is able to recapitulate time in one's life, then one is able to become the child, one is called to become the child.

Becoming the child that time is, we could say, is what a man is doing at each of the turning points in the process of recapitulating time. Going back in spirit to the beginning of time means going back in spirit to the beginning of life, going back to where one was a child and where time was a child, becoming immediate like a child, seeing reality with a child's eyes, seeing what God saw in the beginning, "that it was good." Going from prehistory to history, withdrawing from history to life and returning from life to history again, withdrawing from history to the moment and returning from the moment to history again, going from history to world history—these are moves in the game which the child is playing. The moves are not all straightforward like going from prehistory to history. They are playful: there is withdrawing and returning, and there is passing over and coming back. If one makes these moves in one's time, then one's life becomes playful too. It becomes playful by comparison with what it would have been if one had spent it working against time, working against death.

A man comes to have plenty of time when he ceases to work against time. "I have only one life to live," he may think as long as he is working against it; he will hurry to accomplish what he wants to accomplish in life, to experience what he wants to experience, to reach the goals he has set his heart upon, before death overtakes him. When he allies himself with time, though, all this changes. When he sees his life as a recapitulation of time, he sees that he has enough time, that he has all time at his disposal. He becomes by recapitulation the child that time is, playing at draughts, and the kingdom is his. The question remains as to what he will do with his kingdom. As a recapitulation of time his life becomes a re-enactment of the entire story of mankind. The question remains as to what moral he will give the story.

NOTES

1. *King Henry IV,* Part II, Act III, scene 1, lines 81 ff.
2. Cf. Kierkegaard, *Philosophical Fragments,* pp. 16 ff.

3. This list is much influenced by the scheme which Karl Jaspers gives in his *Origin and Goal of History,* tr. by Michael Bullock (New Haven, Conn., Yale University Press, 1953). Jaspers divides time into prehistory, history, and world history, and he speaks of an "axial period" in history when the first philosophies and higher religions arose.
4. *Timaeus,* 37d.
5. William Butler Yeats, *Autobiographies* (London, Macmillan, 1956), p. 106. This is the last sentence in the autobiography called *Reveries over Childhood and Youth.*
6. Hegel, *Phenomenology of Mind,* tr. by J. B. Baillie (New York, Macmillan, 1961), p. 325.
7. It is translated by Kimon Friar in the introduction to his translation of Kazantzakis, *The Odyssey: A Modern Sequel* (New York, Simon & Schuster, 1966), pp. *xxiii* f.
8. Cf. Kierkegaard, *op. cit.,* pp. 111 ff.
9. Job 38:4.
10. Proverbs 8:29 ff.
11. Genesis 1:4, 1:10, 1:12, 1:17, 1:21, 1:25.
12. Genesis 1:31.
13. Feodor Dostoevsky, *The Brothers Karamazov,* tr. by Constance Garnett, rev. tr. by Avrahm Yarmolinsky (New York, The Heritage Press, 1949), p. 280.
14. On the individual's growth from immediate to existential to historic awareness cf. my book, *A Search for God in Time and Memory,* pp. 126 ff., especially 133 f. and 143 f. and 154.
15. For a discussion of these first two civilizations in terms of their answers to death cf. the first two chapters of my book, *The City of the Gods.*
16. Henri Bergson, *Creative Evolution,* tr. by Arthur Mitchell (New York, Random, 1944), p. 371.
17. Cf. Mark 2:15 and Matthew 4:17.
18. Cf. Kazantzakis, *Report to Grecò,* tr. by P. A. Bien (New York, Bantam, 1966), p. 9.
19. Cf. Jung, *Answer to Job,* tr. by R. F. C. Hull (New York, Meridian, 1960), p. 185.
20. Cf. Teilhard's summary of his view in the Postscript of *The Phenomenon of Man,* tr. by Bernard Wall (New York, Harper, 1959), pp. 300 ff.
21. Heraclitus, fragment 52 (Diels). The term which I am translating "time" here is *aion.* It could also be translated "eternity." The meaning, perhaps we could say, is time as it was understood before Plato made the distinction between time and eternity.

VI

Parallel Lives and Times

Machiavelli used to spend several hours every night conversing in spirit with the great men of former times. "I am not ashamed to speak with them," he writes in one of his letters, "and to ask them the reason for their actions; and they in their kindness answer me; four hours may pass and I do not feel boredom, I forget every trouble, I do not dread poverty, I am not frightened by death; I give myself over entirely to them."[1] He is describing here the process we have called "passing over." A lonely man like Machiavelli, by passing over to other lives and times, could very well escape boredom and forget trouble and overcome the fear of poverty and of death. More than that, he could gain from the past an understanding of the present and future. Machiavelli's nightly conversations with the great men of the past were the source of his most influential work, *The Prince*. His views there were founded, he says, on "knowledge of the actions of great men, acquired by long experience in contemporary affairs, and a continual study of antiquity."[2]

The great men whose lives Machiavelli studied were those of classical antiquity, illustrious Greeks and Romans, along with further parallels drawn from his own times and his own experience. The moral he derives from these stories is understandably a ruthless one, for these are all lives of men who struggled for power and glory. They are all examples of what we have called the "historic man," the man who thinks and speaks and acts on a scale greater than that of the human lifetime. They contrast vividly with what we have called the "immediate man," the person who lives in the moment, and the "existential man," the person who lives on the scale of the lifetime. We have come across historic men, though, who are not merely historic. There is the historic man who deliberately becomes an existential man, who turns from time to life, like Gotama, who renounced kingship and a purely historic role and set out to make his life final, to attain Nirvana and show others the way to it. Then there is the historic man who deliberately becomes an immediate man, who turns from time to the moment, like Jesus, who also renounced kingship and a purely historic role and who taught men to "become as little children" and to "take no thought for the morrow."

Each different type of man is a standard by which all lives and times can be measured, and each leads to a different view of life and of history. Ordinarily the historic man is taken to be the archetypal man in views of history, and the existential man and sometimes the immediate man is taken to be archetypal in views of life. Politics is for historic men; ethics is for existential men and perhaps for immediate men. Let us see what would happen if we were to broaden the basis of both by taking all these kinds of men into consideration. When it comes to ethics, to drawing the moral of the life story, let us take the historic man into consideration, the kind of man Machiavelli was concerned with, as well as the existential and the immediate man. When it comes to politics, to drawing the moral of history, let us re-enact Machiavelli's experience of communing with historic men, but let us also take into account the historic man who becomes existential like Gotama and the historic man who becomes immediate like Jesus.

1. The Moral of the Life Story

"There is no such thing as a grown-up person."[3] This is the thought with which Malraux begins his *Anti-Memoirs*. He is right, I think, in that the immediate man, the child, lives on in the existential man and the historic man. In Malraux's own life, for example, the adventurer lives on in the novelist and the statesman. If we separate the story of the adventurer from that of the novelist and the statesman, we find that it is little more than a series of episodes. At one time he is in France, at another the Near East, at another India, at another Indochina, at another China. It is instructive to recount one's own life story in this fashion, to outline the story of the immediate man in oneself. The simplest way of doing it is to put the story into the form of a diary, to write down each year of one's life and to write alongside the year the place where one lived and the places where one traveled. The impressions of those times and places come back to mind as one does this and one can remember the situations and one's reactions. The story inevitably turns out to be very episodic; it seems to lack any overall plot.

What is the moral of an episodic story? Each episode can be resolved into two elements, character and situation. A man cannot readily see his own character; he will see rather the characters of others. It is like seeing his own face; if he calls to mind the incidents of his past life the one face that will not appear will be his own. What he will see, if he goes over the episodes of his life, will be the situations in which he has been. The story of his life for him will be like a "comedy of situation" in which the comic effect depends on the predicament or the complex of circumstances in which the characters are involved. Or, if it does not seem particularly comic to him, it will be more generally a drama of situation and the effect for him, comic or otherwise, will depend on the successive combinations of circumstances in which the persons of the drama find themselves. The moral he will draw will be something about how a man should act in a situation. As he considers the episodes of his life and tries to define the situations in which he has been, beyond a mere list of times and places, he discovers that to understand a situation, even in retrospect, is very difficult. It is far more difficult to understand, he sees, when one is actually involved in it. The comedy of situation, it seems to him, is essentially a comedy of errors.

The moral he will draw will be something like, "Act upon insight into the situation in which you find yourself." He will reflect, on drawing this moral, that if he could have attained insight into the situations in which he found himself and acted upon it the situations would have been changed. But ignorance was an essential element in them. When he was a child, for instance, and was living at home, it was inevitable that he should not fully understand the home situation. If he could have understood it, the situation would have been different, he would have been more an adult than a child, and home would have had an entirely different effect upon him. So too when he began living away from home, say in his later school years, it was almost inevitable that he should not fully understand his new situation, simply because it was unfamiliar, because it was other than home. Certainly if he had understood it fully, its effect too would have been different. So again with all the subsequent changes of his life. Each new situation, on account of its newness and unfamiliarity, on account of his initial failure to comprehend it, will have had an effect upon him which it could not otherwise have had.

To adopt at this point in his life the policy of acting on insight into the situation in which he finds himself will not change any of this. His former life will remain what it was, and new situations will still be new and he will have to meet them with initial ignorance. The one situation that his effort to act on insight may change is the type that is recurrent, the kind that has occurred again and again in his past and that can be expected to recur in his future. Although he has failed to understand such situations before, he may come to understand them now and thus to meet them with knowledge when they recur. To understand them he must do more than simply recall his impressions of them. The impressions that he recalls, taken one at a time, are the experiences that make the immediate man. Simple remembrance of them leaves him still no more than immediate and may have no effect on the situations when they recur. To arrive at an insight upon which he can act he must put his memories together into a story. The first step is to recount the episodic story we have spoken of, to list the situations in which he has been involved; but a further step seems necessary before understanding will be achieved, and that is to group together the episodes in which the same situations are repeated.

The immediate man, the man who lives from moment to moment, is unable to tell his own story. The only one who can tell it is the existential man, the man who lives his past and future in the present. In Malraux's life, for example, where the adventurer is the immediate man and the novelist is the existential man, the novelist is the one who is able to tell the story of the adventurer. Malraux the novelist transposes scenes from the life of Malraux the adventurer into fiction. As the story takes shape, one can see by trying to tell the story of one's own life, the first thing that emerges is a series of episodes corresponding directly to the immediate man's impressions. The next thing that emerges, when episodes are grouped together in which the same situation recurs, is the pattern of the immediate man's responses. This pattern of response is what would ordinarily be called "character." Before the episodes have been grouped together the life story, as we saw, looks like a "comedy of situation." After they have been grouped together it looks rather like a "comedy of character," in which the effect depends more on the man's character than on the situations in which he finds himself. The character that emerges from Malraux's story is that of the *farfelu*[4], as he calls him, the crazy quixotic adventurer.

To give one's own character a name like this is not easy, even when one has before one's mind the recurrent situations of one's life. Situations in which one stands before others, performing before them, having charge of them, conversing with them, approaching them and being approached by them, are recurrent in one's life and tend to evoke characteristic responses. So also are situations in which one is by oneself, alone with one's feelings, one's imaginings, one's thoughts, one's pursuits. And yet it is very difficult to name the responses and say what is characteristic about them without anything to compare them with. It is like needing a mirror to see one's own face. A possible solution is to look to the person or persons before whom one stands. In situations in which one stands before others the others are the mirror. Their responses reflect one's own responses; their enthusiasm, their warmth, their boredom, their coldness, their trust, their suspicion, their intimacy, their distance reflect one's own. In situations in which one is by oneself or stands before oneself the mirror is oneself; a happy solitude reflects the richness of one's inner life, an unhappy loneliness reflects one's inner poverty.

There are moments of happy solitude, one finds, and moments of unhappy loneliness. Similarly in one's relationships with others there are moments of enthusiasm, warmth, trust, intimacy, and there are moments of boredom, coldness, suspicion, distance. One's character still does not emerge. The thing to do at this point, it seems, is to compare one's life with other lives. If I compare my life with that of another man whom I consider somewhat similar to myself, I may come upon an aspect of myself of which I was quite unaware. I may find, for instance, that a feature of my life which I had called "loneliness" appears also in his life, but that in his life it has to be called "self-pity." It may be that in his eyes man is not and cannot be isolated and thus he never speaks of loneliness, but he does experience a heavyheartedness like mine and in those moments he speaks in a way that shows he feels sorry for himself. It occurs to me that self-pity has been an integral part of the whole experience which I have been calling "loneliness." This insight gives me a new basis for action. Now I know that the heavyheartedness I experience on occasion is due not merely to a situation, to a lack of companionship, but also to a response to that situation, to self-pity.

The moral I might draw from this could be "to conquer myself rather than fortune,"[5] as Descartes said, to conquer my self-pity rather than the fortune or misfortune of being alone. Another way of putting it, parallel to the moral we drew from the story of situations, would be "Act upon insight into your character." The insight I have at this point, the discovery of my self-pity, is of course only a partial one. I still do not know why sometimes when I am alone I feel sorry for myself and other times, in moments of happy solitude, I do not. All I know is that my heavyheartedness is due not merely to being alone but to indulging in self-pity.

Each comparison of my life with other lives yields a further insight into my character, but no one comparison is enough to yield full comprehension. A man can act upon insight into his character, he can act upon insight into the situation, but he never acts with full comprehension of his character or full comprehension of the situation. He never fully succeeds, therefore, either in conquering himself or in conquering fortune.

To conquer himself is the goal of the existential man; to conquer fortune is the goal of the historic man. Machiavelli devotes a chapter of *The Prince* to the subject of "What Fortune can effect in human affairs, and how to withstand her."[6] Fortune is changeful, he explains, sometimes favoring the impetuous man, sometimes favoring the cautious man. Men, on the other hand, tend to be steadfast in their character, the impetuous man always impetuous, the cautious man always cautious, no matter what the situation. To conquer fortune, accordingly, a man must know when the situation favors impetuousity and when it favors caution, and he must adapt his behavior to the situation instead of always acting in character. If he fails to adapt, fortune will desert him. The story of such a man, one can see, would be neither a comedy of situation nor a comedy of character, for the drama resides in neither situation nor character taken alone but in their interplay. If it is the story of a man whom fortune deserts—and this is what it will be if our surmise is right that one never fully succeeds either in conquering oneself or in conquering fortune—it will not be a comedy at all; it will be a tragedy. The plot of a tragedy is typically a change of fortune, a sequence of situations in which the hero, by always acting in character and never out of character, comes to disaster.

Before one can see the ways of fortune in one's own life, it seems, one has to see them in the lives of others, as Machiavelli did conversing in spirit with the illustrious men of former times or as Malraux did in his capacity as statesman conversing in person with illustrious men of our times like De Gaulle and Nehru and Mao Tse-tung.[7] The character of De Gaulle, it is easy to see, was utterly steadfast while the situation in France was highly changeable, with the result that De Gaulle came to power twice and twice had to go into retirement. Nehru, once he had come to power, remained in power until his death seventeen years later; his character or at least his behavior changed along with the situation in India, from the single-mindedness of the revolutionary in the time of the struggle for independence to the broadmindedness of the arbitrator in the time of self-rule.[8] Mao too, after coming to power, remained in power, though he had to retire as head of state after ten years and continue simply as party chairman; his character was always that of the uncompromising revolutionary, but when the time of revolution had passed in China he succeeded by means of a "cultural revolution"[9] in restoring something of the situation to which his character was adapted.

Asking the illustrious men the reason for their actions, as Machiavelli said he used to do, carries one deeper into their lives and reveals that each of them was acting on a vision of his life and of his times. De Gaulle was acting on a vision of De Gaulle and a vision of France; Nehru was acting on a vision of Nehru and a vision of India; Mao was acting on a vision of Mao and a vision of China. Each one saw the relationship between his life and his times differently. Thus De Gaulle could not adapt his life to his times, Nehru could, and Mao could adapt the times to his life. If one examines one's own life and times in this light, one is likely to find that one has no particular vision of the relationship between one's life and one's times, that one is not that much of an historic man. Still, one can see that there undoubtedly is some kind of relationship. Before one knows what the relationship is one can already draw the moral, "Act upon insight into the relationship between your life and your times." To find out what the relationship is one can divide the years of one's life or of one's prospective life into generations. One can expect there to be significant changes in one's times every generation, because of the number of new persons who will have come upon the scene by then and who will not have shared the experiences of the previous group. One has, moreover, the possibility of living with as many as three generations before one's life is over, that of one's youth, that of one's manhood, and that of one's old age.

At one period of my life I may have been ahead of the times; at another I may find myself with the times; and at another which I can foresee I may have every reason to expect that I will be behind the times. What am I to do? Machiavelli's observation is true, "I believe he will be well-off who adapts his way of doing things to the characteristics of the times, and likewise he will be badly off with whose ways the times disagree."[10] Certainly this is the way to conquer fortune, to adapt one's way of doing things to the "characteristics of the times" (*le qualità de' tempi*). Seeing how times change, though, and how he must grow old, become incapacitated, and finally die, a man may realize, as Stalin said, that "in the long run, death is the only victor."[11] A greater vision is possible here, an insight into the relationship not merely between one's life and times but between one's life and all time. This is the kind of vision we find in the lives of men who founded world religions, Gotama, Jesus, and Mohammed. This vision could be simply a vision of some power greater than mere fortune at work in time, as it was for Mohammed, or it could be a vision of something that dissolves time into life, as it was for Gotama, or something that dissolves time into the moment, as it was for Jesus.

Mohammed remained essentially an historic man, became a statesman as well as a prophet, but Gotama and Jesus both renounced kingship, withdrew from history and returned to it in a new guise. The story of Gotama's withdrawal is most straightforward. He saw, according to tradition, an old man, then a sick man, then a dead man. This was enough to make him realize in effect that death is the only victor. Then he saw an ascetic. This was enough to make him think there was an alternative to conquering fortune. He left his father's palace and withdrew into the forest to seek enlightenment. Malraux tells the story twice in his *Anti-Memoirs,* discusses it with Nehru, dwelling especially on the sentence "Prince, that is what is called a dead man."[12] He speaks of Gotama as "this figure who touches so lightly upon history but who brews so many dreams."[13]

If the figure of the Buddha touches lightly upon history, it is not because he has little effect upon it. The truth seems to be that his life really is somehow independent of history. This is why he brews so many dreams; he shows how life can be made independent of time, how the historic man can become existential. According to the story of his enlightenment the withdrawal itself was not enough;

it was in fact a failure; he spent seven fruitless years in the forest. Enlightenment came only when the failure was evident to him, and when it came it consisted of insight into failure. Insight turned failure into success; by understanding why withdrawal failed to lead to wisdom and peace he attained wisdom and peace.

Why does withdrawal fail? Apparently because man is historic, because there are times that are his just as there is a life that is his. To withdraw from his times does not take him out of his times, but only changes his relationship to them. Why then does insight into failure succeed? Apparently because insight or understanding is itself a relationship with the times, distinct from both involvement and withdrawal. To act upon insight into the inadequacies of involvement and the failure of withdrawal is to rise above those inadequacies and that failure, and to that extent to transcend the times. To Gotama it seemed that both the worldlings and the recluses of his times lived in ignorance: the worldlings lived in ignorance of the inadequacies of involvement; the recluses lived in ignorance of the failure of withdrawal. He came to an insight into the inadequacies of involvement when he saw the old man, the sick man, and the dead man. Seven years later he came to an insight into the failure of withdrawal when he saw the futility of his life of asceticism in the forest. Another man might have concluded at this point that there is no way to wisdom and peace. Gotama, however, not only realized the inadequacy of involvement and the failure of withdrawal but also realized that he realized this, knew that he knew, and saw that he could act upon this insight, that he could base a whole life upon it.

The first intimation of the way came to him when he was at the end of his effort to be an ascetic. He remembered a moment of peace in his past life, a moment when he was sitting in the cool shade of a rose-apple tree, meditating while his father was plowing the adjoining field. "Is this," he asked himself, "the way to wisdom?" and "Why am I afraid of that state of ease, that ease which is apart from sensual desires and ill conditions?"[14] It was then that he arose, took some nourishment, found the fig tree that was to become the "bo" tree, the tree of "enlightenment," and sat down beneath it to attain his enlightenment. The famous scene under the bo tree was evidently a re-enactment of the earlier scene under the rose-apple tree. To obtain a concrete idea of his way to wisdom, it seems, one could recall and re-enact some such moment of peace in one's own past life. It would have to be a moment in which one was at peace with oneself and with the world, for Gotama's way was to abandon both the recluse's attempt to conquer himself and the worldling's attempt to conquer fortune. The moral of his story, we could say, is "Act upon insight into your failure to conquer fortune and your failure to conquer yourself."

I may well discover in my own life a scene like that under the rose-apple tree, a moment when I was at peace with the world and with myself. I may even find that such scenes are recurrent in my life. When I examine them more closely, though, I may find that the peace has been due not to abandoning my ambitions to conquer fortune and to conquer myself, but merely to quieting them. This is the difference between the scene under the rose-apple tree and the scene under the bo tree. Under the rose-apple tree Gotama's ambitions were merely quieted or suspended; under the bo tree they were renounced. The thought of seriously giving up one's ambitions is terrifying. It becomes possible to contemplate the prospect only when one considers the peace one has experienced in moments of quiet and suspension. It appears then that by giving up one's ambitions one will actually fulfill them. The peace with oneself is like successful conquest of oneself; the peace with the world is like successful conquest of fortune. The man who gives up his ambitions and finds peace can look like an existential man who has found a way of life. This is how Gotama appears. Or, since he gives up both the ambition of the historic man to conquer fortune and that of the existential man to conquer himself, he can look like an immediate man who lives from moment to moment. This is how Jesus appears.

The pattern of Jesus' life is similar to that of Gotama's. It is the pattern of withdrawal and return, withdrawal into the wilderness and return to a life of teaching. The difference is in the short compass of Jesus' life, his short stay in the wilderness and his short public career. The shortness of his life made his death seem more imminent, his message more urgent. Malraux speaks of reading the life of Jesus, the Gospel of John, at a time when he himself was facing death. "I had sometimes wondered," he explains, "what the Gospel would mean to one in the face of death."[15] If one does this oneself, reads the Gospel at a time when one is very conscious of mortality, one is likely to feel, as Malraux did, that "all faith dissolves life into the eternal"[16] and, on the other hand, that life never seems so real as it does in the face of death. Actually, the story of Jesus, pervaded as it is by the imminence of death, does not dissolve life into the eternal but into the moment, the moment in which man enacts his relationship to eternity. At the prospect of death both the historic man's prospect of conquering fortune and the existential man's prospect of conquering self disappear, both time and life disappear, and all that is left is the moment.

Everything depends then on what one can find in the moment. One could find in it as little as the immediate man ordinarily finds, "Eat, drink, and be merry." Or one could find in it all the existential man hopes to find in life and all the historic man hopes to find in time. Insight takes place in the moment and so does action, though both of them reach beyond the moment in their scope. The crucial moment in the life of Gotama, the scene under the bo tree, is a moment of insight, a moment of contemplation; he had the whole remainder of a long life to act upon it. The crucial moment in the life of Jesus (whence the word "crucial"), the scene upon the cross, the violent end of a short life, is a moment of suffering and, insofar as he was willingly laying down his life, a moment of action. Giving, receiving, and related acts, the basic moments of action, seem to be the essential moments of his life, particularly as the story is told in the Gospel of John. He gives to men what God has given to him ("I have given them the words you gave me" and "the glory you gave me I have given them"); he does not receive from men ("I receive not testimony from man" and "I receive not honor from men"); but receives the men whom God gives him ("All that the Father gives me shall come to me, and him who comes to me I will in no wise cast out").[17] No one can take his life from him, but he gives it freely ("No man takes it from me, but I lay it down of myself"); and no one can take from him those whom God has given him ("Neither shall any man pluck them out of my hand").[18] Many do not receive him ("He came unto his own and his own received him not"); but he gives to those who do receive him ("But as many as received him, to them he gave power to become sons of God"); and these receive from him ("And from his fullness we have all received").[19]

Giving and receiving and the like have some role in every life. Together they constitute what could be called "love" in a life, if we understand love in terms of action more than in terms of feeling. The moral of the life of Jesus, in his own words, would be "Love one another as I have loved you."[20] Loving as he loved would mean giving to others whatever one has from God, not receiving testimony or honor from others, and yet receiving the others who are given to one by God. It would mean not abandoning those with whom one has been entrusted but being willing to lay down one's life for them. It would mean not being received by many, being received by a few, and giving what one has to those few. Understanding it this way, in terms of action, we could put it in terms parallel to those of the previous morals we have drawn, "Act upon insight into your action." Examining one's life in these terms, one is liable to find that one's life is not as loveless and actionless as one had supposed it to be. I may discover, for instance, that I have been thinking of love as something more intimate and action as something more spectacular than this, and have lacked insight into the giving and receiving that has been actually going on in my life. This will have had the effect of creating in me an unfulfilled longing for love, intimate love, and an unfulfilled longing for action, spectacular action. My mind will not have been on the giving and receiving that has actually been going on, and my heart will not have been in it.

There can be a giving and a receiving in intimate love and spectacular action too, to be sure, not because the love is intimate but because it is love, not because the action is spectacular but because it is action. The giving and receiving can exist apart from intimate love and spectacular action, however, in lives like those of Gotama and Socrates and Jesus devoted to the sharing of insight. Jesus, as he appears in the Gospel of John, saw a significance in this giving and receiving that overshadowed the intimate and the spectacular.

How is it possible, one asks oneself, to think as he did without delusions of grandeur? Perhaps the answer is just this, that he was thinking and speaking not of intimate love and spectacular action, the kind of thing about which one suffers delusions, but of simple giving and receiving. What he revealed to men was the profound significance of the basic moments of action, that in giving and receiving man is doing what God is doing. If in giving and receiving a man can see himself doing what God is doing, he can put his heart into it and can find in the moment what he might otherwise search for vainly in a whole life and time.

We end up, therefore, where we began, with the moment. Yet the first moral we drew, "Act upon insight into the situation in which you find yourself" and the last, "Act upon insight into your action," seem quite different. The situations of one's life are the occasions of one's behavior; the situation is the stimulus and the behavior is the response. Some situations may bring out the worst in one and others may bring out the best. To act upon insight into the situation may mean avoiding the ones which bring out the worst or, when they are unavoidable, trying to avoid one's usual behavior in them. Insight makes action possible. Behavior is mere response to the situation, response to stimulus. When insight intervenes, it becomes possible to act upon insight. Action, as we are using the term, means acting upon insight instead of merely responding to stimulus. The principle "Act upon insight into the situation in which you find yourself" means in short "Act instead of merely behaving"; it calls upon one to move from the realm of behavior to the realm of action, to make the moment a moment of action instead of a moment of behavior; and it tells one how to do this, namely by means of insight into the situation; but it does not tell one what to do once one has reached the realm of action.

The same is true of the second moral we drew, "Act upon insight into your character." Insight into character is insight into response, just as insight into situation is insight into stimulus. Both types of insight enable one to act instead of merely behaving. As a story of behavior my life is a comedy, a comedy of situation and a comedy of character. Insight, if I act upon my insight, transforms it into a story of action. I may find myself, for instance, making up in manhood for what I missed in childhood and youth. The story of what I did have, the story of what I missed, and the story of how I am making up for it is the story of my behavior. To realize that I am making up for what I missed is an insight. To act upon this insight would be to act my age, to be deliberately what I am, a person in his manhood. This, if I could do it, would have the effect of changing the story of behavior into a story of action. I would no longer be merely reacting, without knowing it, to the unfulfilled demands of childhood and youth. I would be free to act rather than merely react; I would not be merely undergoing my manhood, I would be enacting it. The question remains, though, as to what the story of action would be.

When a man begins to act, life no longer passes him by. What is more, time no longer passes him by. This last is implied in the third moral we drew, "Act upon insight into the relationship between your life and your times." The same question arises, though, as to what the story of action will be. The likelihood, when a man is concerned about life passing him by, is that the story of action will be the story of his attempt to conquer himself. When he is concerned about time passing him by, it will be the story of his attempt to conquer fortune. If I am concerned about life passing me by, if I see that I have been trying in manhood to make up for what I missed in childhood and youth, I may try to conquer myself, to renounce the desire to relive childhood and youth and devote myself to manhood. If I am concerned about time passing me by, if I see my way of doing things eventually falling behind the times, I may try to conquer fortune, to make sure of always being with the times. Both attempts, to judge from the life of Gotama, will ultimately come to nothing. I will probably succeed in devoting myself to manhood, and to that extent life will no longer pass me by, but I will fail to still my longing for fulfillment, for the things I missed in childhood and youth. I will probably succeed also in being with the times, and to that extent time will no longer pass me by, but I will be overtaken finally by death.

The attempt to conquer fortune is defeated by time, by death; the attempt to conquer self is defeated by life; and both attempts seem to arise from a lack of adequate insight. Thus the moral we drew from the life of Gotama was, "Act upon insight into your failure to conquer fortune and your failure to conquer yourself." This would amount to saying, "Act upon insight into the failure of action," if it were not for the fact that communicating insight is also action and is what Gotama spent the rest of his life doing. An insight into the possibilities of action is still possible, therefore, and is what we actually find in the life of Jesus. "Act upon insight into your action," the moral we drew from the life of Jesus, is the most reflexive moral we have drawn. "Act upon insight," the phrase with which we have begun the statement of each moral, has been our implicit definition of action as distinct from mere behavior. Insight into action means realizing the difference between action and behavior, seeing the failure of action as conquest, as taking what is not given, and seeing the possibilities of giving and receiving. Let us consider now what it would be like to see all history as a story of behavior and what it would be like to see it as a story of action.

2. *The Moral of History*

As a story of behavior it is conceivable that the future could be predicted. An example of such prediction would be Alexis de Tocqueville's surmises about the future of democracy in America. Writing in the 1830s, he examined the physical circumstances, the laws, and the customs of Americans, and was able to predict the expansion of the United States, its rise as a world power and its rivalry with Russia, and also its internal problems arising from the "tyranny of the majority."[21] The story of behavior, taken over any considerable period of time, is the story of the interplay between man and circumstances. Each generation responds to its circumstances, and in responding changes them. Tocqueville saw the circumstances of Americans as consisting essentially in an "equality of condition."[22] The response of each successive generation to this condition, he thought, was to further it, to seek an ever more complete equality. Answering questions such as "Why Americans are so restless in the midst of their prosperity" and "Why so many ambitious men and so little lofty ambition are to be found in the United States,"[23] he pointed to the equality of condition and how this affected the basic human condition of mortality. If men have only a limited time to live and are filled with the desire for equality with others, they will be afraid of missing out on something which others have, will brood on the advantages which they do not possess.

Reflecting on one's own life in these terms, one may find that one's response to "equality of condition" has been different at different times. I may have entertained lofty ambitions in the first half of my life, for example, ambitions to greatness and holiness, while I may be tempted in the second half of my life to brood over common advantages which I do not possess and to fear that I may miss something in life which men commonly seem to enjoy. Yet the lofty ambitions of the first half of life may have been enough to give me a permanent taste for greatness and holiness. "What interests me in any man is the human condition," Malraux said, "in a great man the form and essence of his greatness, in a saint the character of his saintliness, and in all of them certain characteristics which express not so much an individual personality as a particular relationship with the world."[24] Both greatness and holiness consist in a relationship with the world, greatness in an ascendancy, holiness in a transcendence over the world. Individual personality, on the other hand, appears to be defined with reference to an ideally complete personality. Concern about man's relationship with the world seems to go with an ideal of perfection and lofty ambitions of greatness or holiness. Concern about individual personality, on the other hand, seems to go with an ideal of completeness and fears about missing out and not having.

The lofty ambitions of the first half of life, if they leave a permanent taste for greatness and holiness, can be an antidote to the fears of the second half. They are perhaps a reaction against equality of condition, while the fears are a response in favor of it. The moral of the story of behavior, considered in this light, would be to act upon insight into one's historical condition. One's historical condition would be a modification of the basic human condition of mortality, in this instance Tocqueville's "equality of condition." Insight into it would amount to understanding how it can both provoke such a reaction as lofty ambition and evoke such a response as fear of incompleteness. This insight would enable one to predict the future like Tocqueville; and it would also enable one to act. Seeing the conflict between the ideal of perfection and that of completeness, one would try to find some way of joining them, some way of working towards them without being at cross-purposes with oneself. At first the conflict appears insoluble. Greatness and holiness seem to come to a man only at the cost of great personal deprivation, only by the sacrifice of personal completeness. The only way I see of pursuing greatness or holiness may be to resume in the second half of life the lofty ambitions of the first half and to cast aside, as much as I can, my fears of incompleteness.

The deliberate pursuit of greatness or holiness would place me outside the anticipated pattern of behavior, would translate me from the realm of behavior to the realm of action. Is the pursuit of greatness, though, the way to greatness? Is the pursuit of holiness the way to holiness? Now that I am trying to act upon insight such questions arise. Greatness and holiness, we were saying, are relationships with the world. It may be that a man's relationship with the world depends upon his relationship with himself. It may be necessary for him to take account of his individual personality and its incompleteness after all. If he seeks a certain relationship with the world without bothering about his relationship with himself, he may find it an unattainable ideal. His relationship with the world will be dictated by circumstances, it seems, unless there is some other relationship, not to his circumstances but to himself, on which the relationship with the world can be based. Let us examine in this light first the pursuit of greatness and then the pursuit of holiness.

The pursuit of greatness is the theme of Machiavelli's *The*

Prince. He tries to draw the moral of the lives of illustrious men; the moral, we might say, of history as a story of action. The moral he draws is quite similar to that which Plutarch draws in a work *On the Fortune or Virtue of Alexander.*[25] The two terms *virtù* and *fortuna* are central ones in Machiavelli's vocabulary.[26] Plutarch's thesis is that the greatness of Alexander the Great was due not to fortune alone, but to a combination of virtue and fortune. Machiavelli's thesis is more general, that the greatness of any great man consists essentially in *virtù* and that *fortuna* is something a man can bring at least partially into subjection, as we saw earlier, by synchronizing his life with his times. The meaning of the term "virtue" (*areté*) for Plutarch is courage, wisdom, justice, and temperance. Machiavelli's term *virtù* can usually be translated "ability," especially when he contrasts it with *fortuna* or "luck," but it also has something of the connotation of Plutarch's term when he contrasts it with *scelleratezza* or "wickedness."[27] The great man is a man of action, we could say, understanding "action" as we have been using the term in contrast with mere "behavior." Or, to take into account both virtue and fortune, we could say that he is a man of action whom circumstances provide with large scope for action.

As a story of action history is not merely the story of great men. There are many who without having large scope for action do nevertheless act. With the increasing numbers of human beings in the world, one might think, history must become more and more a story of behavior and less and less a story of action. This would be on account of the "law of large numbers," according to which the larger the numbers the less random the behavior. What this actually means, though, is that with increasing numbers there will be relatively less random behavior, not relatively less action. As long as insight can still occur action can still be based upon it. The only effect that increasingly uniform behavior could have upon action would be to widen or narrow its scope. When a man is acting with the trend of behavior his scope would be widened; when he is acting against the trend it would be narrowed. Moreover, there would still be a way of countering the trend of behavior, and that would be to communicate the insight upon which his action is based. This would have the effect of increasing the number of men who are acting instead of merely behaving.

Suppose I do share with others the insights on which I am acting. Suppose I see myself doing this for the rest of my life. "Am I to spend the rest of my life," I may ask myself, "doing what I am doing?" The thought may be somewhat appalling. Doing what I am doing would be a relationship with the world; giving my life to doing it would be a relationship with myself. Each relationship would have its story. What I am doing, although my whole life is spent in doing what I am now doing, would make a story, and so would giving myself to it, although I continue to give myself to it and never abandon it. The appalling thing would be the prospect of a storyless life, a completely uneventful life. As it is, the life has the possibility of being rich both in outer and in inner happenings. Greatness, if that were visible in it, would make the prospect still more attractive. The element of virtue is there, in the doing and in the giving of self. The element of fortune, however, the largeness of scope, is not assured. Sharing the insights on which one is acting widens one's scope by drawing others into concert with one's action, but it does not assure large scope as would acting in accord with the trend of behavior.

A man might do both; might act with the trend and communicate insight. Gandhi, for instance, both led a movement for national liberation and tried to communicate to the people he was leading the insight on which he was acting. He succeeded in the one, and failed, or at least thought he failed, in the other. "I have failed to convince India," he told Nehru. "Violence reigns all around us; I am a spent bullet."[28] He said this towards the end of his life at the time of the rioting and killing in the partition of India into India and Pakistan. Gandhi calling himself "a spent bullet" is not unlike Gotama, at the end of a life of trying to communicate the insight he had attained under the bo tree, calling himself "a worn-out cart."[29] A life spent in communicating insight is likely to be an arduous failure; men are more likely to behave than to act. Such a life seems worthwhile, nonetheless, especially if a man is seeking, like Gandhi, to act for the sake of the action itself, because of its inherent nobility, rather than for the sake of the fruits of action. "Even at the time of the Chowri murders I had never really had to face despair," he said to Nehru, but "now I know that I have failed to convince India."

When a man has to face despair in a life of communicating insight, what does he fall back on? On the richness of the insight itself? On the nobility of the act of sharing it? Whatever it is, it must be a kind of holiness. For if it could sustain him it would be a transcendence with respect to success and failure even in the highest cause, a real transcendence over the world. Gandhi seems to have fallen back on his sense of God as truth. He had said earlier, in his autobiography, "I worship God as Truth only" and "my uniform experience has convinced me that there is no other God than Truth."[30] At this later time, in his moment of despair, he said "without living Truth God is nowhere";[31] Hindus and Muslims were killing one another in the name of God but they could not do so, he believed, in the name of Truth. One can see here a vision of history as a story of truth and untruth. Such a vision must be characteristic of the holy man. The thing that sustains him and gives him his transcendence he envisions as truth; the things that he transcends, that he rises above, he envisions as untruth. History to him is the story of both. To Gandhi it was the story of *Ahimsa* ("non-injury") and the story of violence, just as to Augustine it was the story of the city of God and the story of the earthly city. To a man who is trying to share the insights on which he is acting it could be, as we have been saying, the story of action and the story of behavior.

"Without living Truth," Gandhi said at the time of his despair, "God is nowhere." This was the cause of despair for him, that in the reign of violence God appeared to be absent, and yet he could face the despair by falling back on God. If one asks oneself "What do I actually fall back on?" one can see how this might be. Suppose again that I am acting and communicating to others the insights on which I act. I may find that I am depending on being warmly received by others. What if I were to cease being well received? Or what if, while being well received, I were to see suddenly and finally that I had not really succeeded in giving what I was trying to give to others? My existence would no longer be the fulfilling life of giving and receiving that I had envisioned. I might find it difficult to fall back on the truth and richness of the insights I have been trying to communicate. The fact that others do not share them, that they have not been received when I have tried to impart them, may undermine my own confidence in them. The conviction that Gandhi fell back on, that "God is Truth" or, as he put it later on, "Truth is God," seems to mean something more far-reaching than the parallel statement on which Malraux and Nehru found they could agree in spite of their agnosticism, "Truth is the supreme value."[32]

In the face of despair a man cannot fall back, it seems, on truth as a value. If he falls back on truth, it is truth seen not as a value but as a power like that ascribed to God. I may see my life as a journey in time and God as my companion on the way. It is this that I would have to fall back on if I saw my life of giving and receiving as a failure. To be sure, this could be taken as a mere conviction, and taken this way it could be shaken like any other. It may occur to me, for example, that just as a child may play with an imaginary playmate so I may walk through life with an imaginary companion. In spite of this thought I can go ahead and walk with God. The journey with God is not merely something to tell myself; it is something to do, something to undertake, something to carry through. It is not merely a belief; it is an adventure; it is a whole life. Clearly, though, if it is to differ from playing with an imaginary playmate, the life must be more than a voyage of imagination; it must be a voyage of discovery. The crucial events in it must be discoveries rather than inventions. To fall back on the journey with God, accordingly, would mean not merely telling myself that my life is such a journey, but doing the things that are necessary to make my life a voyage of discovery.

This would take me back again to the life of giving and receiving. Among the things necessary to make my life a voyage of discovery is to let myself be influenced by others. This leads to a changing of my horizons and is a receiving. Another thing is to give articulate expression to my experience, to turn the truth of my life into poetry. This is a communication of the truth of my life to others and is a giving. Thus there is a receiving and a giving that comes before insight or discovery and makes it possible. When discovery does take place, then there is a new and higher giving, the sharing of insight with others, and a new and higher receiving, my receiving of the others who receive from me. It is the failure of this higher giving and receiving that drives a man back upon the underlying life of discovery, but the life of discovery brings him back again, in spite of failure, to this higher giving and receiving since it is the natural outflow of discovery. The greater giving, the sharing of insight, is simply a transformation of the lesser giving, the turning of the truth of one's life into poetry, and the greater receiving, the receiving of others, is simply a transformation of the lesser receiving, being influenced by others. The story of action, we could say more generally, is simply a transformation of the story of behavior.

Instead of transforming the story of behavior into a story of action a man may attempt to suppress behavior and replace it by action. This is likely to divide him and make his own life, like history, a twofold story of action and behavior. The behavior which he tries to suppress is likely to continue on in a hidden way, side by side with action. He could be very great and very holy, like Gandhi, and still be very incomplete as a human being. Gandhi's incompleteness appears especially in his human relations, his relations with his wife Kasturbai and with his sons, particularly with his eldest son Harilal.[33] His renunciation of sex and violence and his replacement of them by celibacy and nonviolent action apparently left pent-up feelings of sex and violence which emerged in various ways in his human relations. No doubt a single look at one's own life is enough to convince one that, if Gandhi was very incomplete while being very great and very holy, it is also possible to be very incomplete without being either very great or very holy. Is there a way, one may nevertheless ask oneself, to greatness and holiness which also leads to completeness?

The "middle way" of the Buddha seems to have been middle between the pursuit of greatness and the pursuit of holiness. The first twenty-nine years of Gotama's life were years in which he was educated in the pursuit of greatness, to succeed to his father's throne. The next seven years were spent in the forest in pursuit of holiness. The enlightenment which he experienced at the age of thirty-six was the discovery of a middle way between the two ways he had followed up till then, apparently therefore a middle way between the pursuit of greatness and the pursuit of holiness. Was it then a way leading to both greatness and holiness? Was it, since it led him to great inner peace and harmony, a way leading to completeness? The most surprising thing that Gotama taught, at least for us who have been brought up in the tradition of Western philosophy, is the doctrine of "no-self" (*anatta*), the doctrine that "I am" is an illusion. At the same time it is interesting to observe that the Western philosophy in which mind and body are most radically separated from one another is that of Descartes, in which "I am" is the starting point. Does the negation of "I am" by the Buddha go with some kind of integration of mind and body? If it does, then the way of the Buddha may be the way to completeness we are seeking.

The "no-self," we observed earlier,[34] is a condition which appears to exist only in the moment of passing over to other lives and times. When a man comes back to his own life and times the self, the "I am," reappears. This is not the teaching of the Buddha, of course, but an observation based on the experience of passing over and coming back. If it is a valid observation, then Gotama's own experience of "no-self" probably went with his experience of compassion for others and the passing over to others which this involved. Passing over, therefore, entering sympathetically into other lives and times, if we are on the right track, is the way to completeness. This is not an unlikely hypothesis. For whenever a man passes over to other lives or other times, he finds on coming back some neglected aspect of his own life or times which corresponds to what he saw in the others. Passing over has the effect of activating these otherwise dormant aspects of himself. If he were to stay fixed in himself, fixed in his own standpoint, never passing over but using the self as a vantage point from which to survey all things, as Descartes did, he would never experience his own wholeness.

The incompleteness of a great and holy man like Gandhi, appearing as it does in the inadequacies of his human relations, is probably due to a certain fixity in his own standpoint and a failure to pass over to the standpoints of others, especially those nearest to him. One's own incompleteness, the pent-up feelings of sex and violence which one finds within oneself, can probably be traced to a similar cause. I may have realized that I am not fully integrated, that I have urges towards sex and violence which run counter to my ideals and my way of life, without having seen any connection between this and the problem of passing over to other persons. I may discover, if I examine my relations with others, that I am unwilling to receive from others, that I try to maintain as complete an autonomy as possible. This in turn causes a reaction within me, an urge not only to receive but to take from others. Passing over would mean willingly receiving from others. The willingness to receive from others, it seems, along with the willingness to give to others, is what effectively transforms behavior into action. It transforms behavioral influencing and being influenced into active giving and receiving.

Willingness to receive from others, to be sure, is not a very evident trait in the lives of Gotama and Jesus as we know them, although willingness to give is quite evident. Perhaps this is inevitably the way the master appears to his disciples. They are conscious of receiving from him, not of giving to him; in their eyes, consequently, he is one who gives, not one who receives. The one element of receiving which we find in the life of Jesus as recounted by his disciples is his willingness to receive and welcome those who come to him, the men and women who walk with him. This receiving may well have been more important to him than it appeared to be from the standpoint of his disciples. The pattern of his life suggests, moreover, that there was a receiving not only from God but from man which was a source of his giving. The major turning points of his public life appear to have been points where his life intersected with that of John the Baptist: there was first his baptism by John the Baptist, followed by his withdrawal into the desert from which John had come; then there was the imprisonment and silencing of John, which was the signal for the beginning of his own preaching; and finally there was the execution of John, which was the sign to him of his own impending fate.[35] This pattern of turning points suggests that Jesus was deeply and willingly influenced by John, that he willingly received from him.

The life of Jesus, if we may understand it in this manner, can be seen as a rich and full life of giving and receiving. His saying that "it is more blessed to give than to receive"[36] could be supplemented by another that "it is more blessed to receive than not to receive." A life of giving without receiving, one can see from experience, has the effect of dividing a man against himself. If I try to live a life of giving without receiving, communicating my insights to others but unwilling to allow others to have an influence on me or to give me anything, I find myself becoming a troubled man before others, anxious to be well received by them, a troubled man by himself, keenly aware of the lack of intimacy in his life, a man with a troubled body, troubled by urges of sexuality and violence to take what he does not receive. The willingness to receive tends to change all this. It breaks down the unwillingness which keeps others at a distance; it opens the way to receiving; and the receiving itself diminishes the need to be received by others and the urge to take from others what is not given.

Giving and receiving as they figure in the story of behavior are apparently the root of the problem. On the level of mere behavior giving is influencing, receiving is being influenced; on the level of action, on the contrary, giving is sharing insight, receiving is passing over. What a man fears when he is unwilling to receive is being influenced, being controlled. He does not fear passing over; he knows little or nothing of it, or else he knows it only as an intellectual exercise, not as a movement of the whole heart and mind and soul. Influencing and being influenced mean stimulating and responding, but since there can be "choice among stimuli" and "choice among responses,"[37] they can mean controlling and being controlled. The "control" of behavior of which behavioral scientists speak[38] is exercised by determining stimuli and responses, by choosing among stimuli and among responses. A man can control his own behavior by choosing which stimuli shall affect him and which responses he shall make to them; he can control the behavior of another by choosing what stimuli the other person shall be subjected to and, by training or educating the other, choosing what responses the other shall normally make to stimuli. This situation, especially where history becomes largely a story of behavior, can give rise to intense desires to control and intense fears of being controlled.

These desires and fears, it seems, are what lead a man in the contemporary historical situation to attempt to live a life of giving without receiving. He wants to have control over himself and others, but he wants no person or institution to have control over him. The willingness to receive of which we have been speaking is a willingness to be influenced by others. When one is willingly influenced by others, however, one is not controlled by them. Rather one actively passes over to them and comes back to oneself. Similarly when one shares insight with others, one does not merely determine what stimulus they shall be subjected to or what response they shall normally make. Rather one gives them insight into the stimuli to which they are subjected and into the responses which they normally make, thus giving them a basis for action on their own. Behavior as stimulus and response, therefore, does not disappear in the transition to action. Neither does choice among stimuli and choice among responses. What disappears is controlling and being controlled, a choice among stimuli and responses exercised apart from insight and willingness.

History as a story of behavior is a story of increasing numbers and increasingly uniform behavior. Trends become more and more massive and more and more evident. This gives rise to fears of deviating and desires to conform and then to the desire for others to conform and the fear of those who deviate. Behavior becomes less and less random, not only by the sheer mathematics of increasing numbers but also because of the fears and desires which the rising mathematical uniformity causes. Meanwhile the possibility of controlling behavior by choosing among stimuli and responses leads to desires and fears, the desire to control and the fear of being controlled. There rises simultaneously an Apollonian ideal of control and a Dionysian ideal of freedom from control. The Apollonian and the Dionysian, instead of being two divergent characters as Nietzsche conceived them,[39] are one and the same man torn between his desire and his fear of control. There is a semblance of greatness in control over the behavior of others and a semblance of holiness in control of one's own behavior, while there is a semblance of completeness in freedom from all control. And yet these are only semblances; real greatness, real holiness, real completeness, we may conclude from all that we have seen, are to be found in action, not in mere behavior.

The difference between behavior and action is insight. Behavior is simply activity; action is activity based on insight. As a story of behavior the future is predictable; it is unpredictable as a story of action, except to the extent that one is already in possession of the insights on which action will be based. Control over the behavior of others, we were saying, is not greatness. A man can control the behavior of others without insight, simply by being in sympathy with their feelings and appealing instinctively to their hopes and fears. If he attains insight into the situation in which he and they find themselves and comes to an understanding of the stimuli and the responses which are at work, he may see for example that "the only thing we have to fear is fear itself,"[40] that the dangerous thing in the situation is not the thing feared but the fear itself and the responses to which it may lead. If he then begins to act on this insight and to communicate it to others, he is no longer controlling their behavior as he was, playing on their fears, but is making it possible for them to act, to resist their fears. A truly great man is a man who acts on insight and communicates the insight on which he is acting to others.

A holy man is like a great man; he acts on insight and shares his insight with others. The difference is that a holy man is able to fail in this without being shattered by his failure. He is able to fall back like Gotama on the insight he has been attempting to communicate and find peace in it in spite of any failure on the part of others to accept it. Or he is able to fall back on the nobility of his action, acting, as Krishna taught Arjuna to do, without seeking the fruits of action. Or he is able to fall back on his companionship with God, seeing himself, like Jesus in the Gospel of John, as doing what God is doing. Both the great man and the holy man are men of action, but the great man depends for his greatness on some measure of success in his action. The holy man is finally independent of success and failure. What gives the holy man his independence is the transcendence of the insight on which he is acting and which he is trying to communicate, or the transcendence of the action in which he is engaged. A man can be both great and holy, succeeding and yet transcending his own success or like Gandhi succeeding and yet failing and transcending his own failure.

A great and holy man, again like Gandhi, can still be incomplete as a human being. The full life of action consists in giving and receiving, but a great and holy man can attempt to live a life of giving without receiving and if he does he will suffer a division and conflict within himself, a conflict between his desire to receive and his unwillingness to receive. The danger is that under these circumstances his desire to receive will degenerate into a desire to take. The willingness to receive from others leads to a kind of completeness, a completeness that is compatible with greatness and holiness. The life of giving and receiving, giving what one has to others and receiving what is given, is thus at once a life of greatness and holiness and a life of completeness. This can make things sound easier than they really are. A life of pure giving and receiving means giving up persons and things when having them means taking what is not given. And that can cause a drastic feeling of incompleteness. There may be a person, for example, whom I love but whom I cannot have without wronging others, without taking what is not and cannot be given. To give up this person creates in me a sense of loss and incompleteness which is not compensated by a life of giving and receiving, however full.

There is a completeness, therefore, which truly is incompatible with greatness and holiness, and that is the completeness which comes from taking. And there is a completeness which is compatible, and that is the completeness which comes from giving and receiving. With this qualification we can conclude that the story of behavior can be transformed into a story of action. If completeness were utterly incompatible with greatness and holiness, then man's life and history would be hopelessly divided into a story of behavior and a story of action. The story of behavior would be the story of his striving for completeness, and the story of action would be the story of his striving for greatness and holiness. As it is, completeness, greatness, and holiness are one in the life of giving and receiving. This then is the moral we can derive both from the life story and from history, the ideal of transforming the story of behavior into a story of action. There remains the other completeness, the completeness that comes from taking and is never attained in the life of giving and receiving, the lack of which man must always feel along with the blessedness he finds in giving and receiving.

NOTES

1. Machiavelli, Letter to Francesco Vettori (December 10, 1513), tr. by Allan Gilbert, *Machiavelli,* vol. 2 (Durham, North Carolina, Duke University Press, 1965), p. 929. I have modified the translation slightly—cf. the original text in Machiavelli, *Opere,* ed. by Mario Bonfantini (Milan and Naples, Ricciardi, 1954), p. 1111.
2. Machiavelli, *The Prince,* tr. by W. K. Marriot (London and New York, J. M. Dent and E. P. Dutton, 1908), dedication.
3. Malraux, *Anti-Memoirs,* tr. by Terence Kilmartin (New York, Bantam, 1970), p. 1.
4. *Ibid.,* p. 11.
5. Descartes, *Discourse on Method,* Chapter 3, third maxim.
6. *The Prince,* Chapter 25.
7. Cf. Malraux, *op. cit.,* pp. 98 ff. and 118 ff. on De Gaulle, pp. 157 ff. and 278 ff. on Nehru, and pp. 405 ff. on Mao.
8. *Ibid.,* p. 300.
9. On Mao and the "cultural revolution" cf. Robert Jay Lifton, *Revolutionary Immortality* (New York, Vintage, 1968).

10. *The Prince,* Chapter 25 (my own translation).
11. Malraux, *op. cit.,* p. 126.
12. *Ibid.,* pp. 285 and 306. The story told pp. 221 ff. and 285 f.
13. *Ibid.,* 221 f.
14. *Majjhima-nikaya,* I, 242 ff., tr. by F. L. Woodward, *Some Sayings of the Buddha* (London, Oxford University Press, 1960), pp. 24 f.
15. Malraux, *op. cit.,* p. 193.
16. *Ibid.,* p. 194.
17. John 17:8 and 22; 5:34 and 41; 6:37.
18. John 10:18 and 28.
19. John 1:11 and 12 and 16.
20. John 15:12.
21. Tocqueville, *Democracy in America,* ed. by Phillips Bradley, 2 vols. (New York, Vintage, 1959). Cf. the conclusion to vol. 1 on the expansion of the U.S., its rise as a power, and its rivalry with Russia. Cf. Chapters 15 and 16 of vol. 1 on the tyranny of the majority.
22. *Ibid.,* introduction to vol. 1.
23. *Ibid.,* vol. 2, pp. 144 ff. and 256 ff. Cf. my book *The City of the Gods,* p. 164 on the difference in the attitude towards death in an hierarchical and an equalitarian society.
24. Malraux, *op. cit.,* p. 10.
25. Plutarch, *Moralia,* 326d ff.
26. Cf. *The Prince,* especially Chapters 6, 7, 8, and 25.
27. *Ibid.,* Chapter 8.
28. Malraux, *op. cit.,* p. 301.
29. *Digha-nikaya,* II, 99, tr. by Woodward, *op. cit.,* p. 340.
30. Gandhi, *The Story of My Experiments with Truth,* pp. *xiv* and 503.
31. Gandhi, "The Task Ahead" in *The Gandhi Reader,* ed. by Homer A. Jack (Bloomington, Indiana, Indiana University Press, 1956), p. 463.
32. Malraux, *op. cit.,* p. 285.
33. Cf. Erik Erikson, *Gandhi's Truth,* pp. 235 and 243 f.
34. Cf. Chapter Two, Section 3.
35. On the turning points in the life of Jesus cf. my book *A Search for God in Time and Memory,* pp. 8 ff.
36. Acts 20:35.
37. For these terms cf. R. Duncan Luce, *Individual Choice Behavior* (New York, John Wiley & Sons, 1959), pp. 1 f.
38. Cf. the discussion of "control" in B. F. Skinner, *Science and Human Behavior* (New York, Macmillan, 1965), pp. 227 ff., 313 ff., 333 ff. and 415 ff.
39. Cf. Nietzsche's *Birth of Tragedy* in *The Complete Works of Friedrich Nietzsche,* ed. by Oscar Levy (New York, Russell, 1964), vol. 1, pp. 22 ff.
40. Franklin Delano Roosevelt, First Inaugural Address, March 4, 1933. Roosevelt is speaking of the fear at the time of the Great Depression. Yet his diagnosis seems valid also for the contemporary situation in America.

VII

The God in Time

"EVERYTHING HAPPENS," Sartre says, "as if the world, man, and man-in-the-world succeeded in realizing only a missing God."[1] This is how things tend to look to a man when he experiences his own incompleteness and sees no way of ever becoming complete. Say he is devoting his life to attaining and sharing insight, but has a desire for intimate love and also a desire for spectacular action which are going unfulfilled. There is love and action in what he is doing but it is not intimate love, not spectacular action. Whatever value he sees in what he is doing, he feels incomplete, lacking intimacy, lacking power and glory. So it would be, whatever way of life he chose. By going one way he necessarily excludes all other ways, unless he can somehow find on this one way everything that he would have found on the others. Not finding everything on his way, he seems not to find God; he seems to realize only a missing God.

"Even the enlightened person remains what he is," Jung says, "and is never more than his own limited ego before the One who dwells within him, whose form has no knowable boundaries, who encompasses him on all sides, fathomless as the abysms of the earth and vast as the sky."[2] A man's failure to attain completeness is his failure to become God. Still there is a God, dwelling within him, encompassing him, deep as the earth, vast as the sky. This is also an experience, as real as the experience of incompleteness. It is the experience, however, of a man with a rich inner life. It is, in fact, an experience of completeness, a sense that "everything which belongs to an individual's life shall enter into it."[3] Man experiences incompleteness in choosing his path, choosing one and excluding all others, but his life is not merely a doing—It is an undergoing, and in this undergoing everything which belongs to his life does indeed seem to enter into it. For instance, he may not be going the way of intimate love, but if intimate love belongs to his life it will enter into it, according to this, in spite of the path he chooses; he may not be going the way of spectacular action, but if power and action of this kind belong to his life they will enter into it in spite of his plans.

Is it really true, though, that everything which belongs to an individual's life shall enter into it? Let us examine this proposition. As it stands it is a proposition about the lifetime. Let us consider also the corresponding propositions about time and the moment. Let us start with time and move from there to the lifetime and from there to the moment. First let us examine the proposition "everything which belongs to the story of mankind shall enter into it," then the proposition "everything which belongs to an individual's life shall enter into it," and finally the proposition "everything which belongs to the moment shall enter into it."

1. The God in History

Man is on earth, it has been said, "to kindle a light in the darkness of mere being."[4] This would accord well with the story of mankind as we have been telling it. The main turning points in the story, besides the beginning and the end, are the transition from prehistory to history, the enlightenment and revelation experiences giving rise to the world religions, and the transition from history to world history. Each of these events is indeed a kindling of light, the light of consciousness, in the darkness of mere being. We could see the story of mankind as the story of an awakening, the story of man's own awakening, but more than that, the story of being's awakening through man. Without man being is "mere being," according to this; with him it is conscious being. The earth and the sky, the living and the dead, everything and everyone belong to man's story and they enter into it when they pass from the darkness of mere being into the light of consciousness. The proposition "everything which belongs to the story of mankind shall enter into it" would mean that everything which lies in darkness shall come to light.

The phrase "the darkness of mere being" suggests, however, that there may be another and darker purpose at work in man's story, darker at least from the standpoint of man's consciousness. It suggests that besides consciousness there may be another and more fundamental goal, namely being. The noun "darkness" and the adjective "mere" make it sound like an inferior goal, but it may be in fact the more important and more ultimate goal. Man may be on earth for the same reason that every other creature is, simply to be. This is a dark purpose to man, for without full knowledge of what he is he does not know what it is for him to be. First he would have to gain knowledge, become fully conscious, if that were possible, and only then would he be able to judge being. As it is, he lacks full consciousness and self-knowledge. He is on a voyage of exploration. Until he has circumnavigated the world he will not know what there is in it. So in the meantime his goal can only be to explore the world, to gain knowledge. If there were a mind for which consciousness was not a problem, a mind which already had full knowledge, such a mind might be more interested in being than in consciousness.

The two goals, being and consciousness, do appear to be the goals of two different minds, of two different agencies in human history, God and man. Consciousness is man's aim; being is God's. Man brings things into the light of consciousness; God brings them into being. The two goals are compatible with one another, even include one another since conscious being is a mode of being and being comes into consciousness. All the same a God who seeks to bring things into being and a man who seeks to bring them into consciousness might find themselves sometimes at cross-purposes. Man might find himself sometimes wrestling with God like Jacob. The life of an idiot, for example, has to seem meaningless from man's standpoint; it can only seem better that the idiot had never been born. From the standpoint of consciousness the idiot's life is senseless, but from that of being it may yet be worthwhile. We cannot tell, for we do not fully understand what man is and what the idiot is. Man, seeking to promote consciousness, strives to prevent the existence of the idiot; God, on the other hand, seeking to promote being, may nevertheless bring the idiot into existence.

The idiot is a parable of the difference between God and man at every point in the course of human events. The beauty there is in the idiot's existence is the beauty that can exist in "the darkness of mere being." Much that has come to be in the course of human events seems to have no beauty other than this. The story of mankind is largely a story of behavior rather than a story of action. Man, that is, lives and has lived mostly in darkness. The term "mere behavior" could be compared to the term "mere being." Yet there may be a beauty in mere behavior that the terms "behavior," "response to stimulus," do not suggest. To see this beauty, if it exists, would require a more profound understanding of human activity than analysis in terms of stimulus and response can yield. Man's ideal must be to transform the story of behavior into a story of action, to act in the light of consciousness rather than in the darkness of mere being. Yet the expansion of consciousness, the growing light, can reveal beauty that was hidden in the darkness, beauty that man did not suspect when he was busy trying to escape from the darkness and to rise above mere behavior.

While man is on his voyage of discovery, therefore, he may discover that there is something more important than discovery itself, that there is a purpose at work greater than his own of kindling light in the darkness. What difference would such a discovery make in the voyage and in his own purpose? One thing is that the stages in the evolution of mankind would no longer seem to be merely stages. As long as the story of man is seen only as a story of consciousness and its development, then the lower stages of consciousnes appear to be only a preparation for the higher stages: prehistory seems merely a preparation for history and history a preparation for world history; prehistoric man seems merely the precursor of historic man and historic man the precursor of world-historic man. Once we reckon with the possibility that man is on earth simply to be, however, the relationships of man with man across time look quite different. No epoch seems merely a stage on the way to another epoch, no man merely the forerunner of another man.

Most of man's time on earth, some hundreds of thousands of years, has been prehistory; only the last five thousand years are recorded history. Those immense ages of prehistory, if we look rather to being than consciousness, were much more than a mere preparation for the historic era. The men and women of prehistory had their own labors and their own sorrows. Great migrations of peoples took place in their times. Their concerns may not have reached beyond their own lifetimes, but these were enough to fill their lives. The expanded consciousness of historic man, his concerns reaching beyond his own life to the past and future of mankind, is an advance in human development which brings to light many new problems and dangers that prehistoric man did not yet have to face. Future centuries may well bring further advances, further problems, and further dangers. The men and women of history too have their own sorrows and their own joys; they do not live merely to prepare the way for these future centuries, though they do think of the future and though what they do, whether they are thinking of future centuries or not, does prepare the way for them.

Yet the significance of all these lives and times, apart from the degree of consciousness that appears in them, is dark to us, for the only light we have to see by is that of consciousness. If we reflect on prehistoric lives and times, we find ourselves reflecting on what significance there can be in immediate and existential awareness, in consciousness of the moment and of the lifetime. Likewise if we reflect on historic lives and times, we find ourselves reflecting on what significance there can be in historic awareness and in action based upon it, in consciousness that reaches beyond the confines of the lifetime. We fail to see what significance there may be in the unconscious side, the dark side of all these lives and times.

What we need is some way of seeing in the dark. The question is posed in the Upanishads, "How can the knower be known?[5] Man is always more than he knows about himself; his being is always greater in compass than his consciousness. If there were some way of seeing in the dark, of knowing without the light of consciousness, then the knower could be known, man could know what man is.

As it is posed in the Upanishads, the question "How can the knower be known?" is meant to be unanswerable. The very posing of the question, though, shows a kind of wisdom, a realization that man never knows what he is. There is a way of seeing in the dark, it seems, but it consists more in seeing the darkness than in seeing the things that are hidden in the dark. "How can the knower be known?" means "How can man know what he is?" There is a word in the Upanishads for what man is, Atman, but it is like an algebraic symbol for an unknown quantity. The word signifies what we would know if we knew what man is. There is also a word for what God is, Brahman, and there is a tendency in the later Upanishads to equate Atman and Brahman.[6] Actually the two words stand for two questions, "What is man?" and "What is God?" To know the answer to the one would be to know the answer to the other. This, perhaps we could say, rather than simple identity is the meaning of the equation between the two. If we knew what man is, then we would know God's purpose in the story of man and to that extent we would know what God is.

If we knew what man is, then we would know why the things that have happened to man in the course of time have occurred. Suffering, guilt, strife, chance, death, all these things seem to belong to the story of mankind and to enter into it. So do their opposites, joy, innocence, love, purpose, life. If a man were the playwright, he would probably try to eliminate suffering, guilt, strife, chance, and death from the plot of the human drama. God, according to Hinduism and Christianity, instead of eliminating the ills of human existence, becomes a man and shares in them. Asked why he did not prevent the war and the destruction of the Kuru family described in the great war epic of India, Krishna replied

"Since I am now born in the order of men, I appealed to the Kurus as a human being."[7] When God becomes man, he must act as a human being, as a participant in the human drama rather than as its author. He can attempt to persuade other human beings, to dissuade them from seeking to destroy one another, from seeking the fruits of action, but he cannot compel them.

The story of God among men as a man, persuading and dissuading yet not compelling, is perhaps our best clue to what God is and what man is. The Gita comes after the Upanishads; the Gospel comes after the Prophets. The question of what man is and what God is had already been raised when the story was told of God becoming man. The story does not directly answer the questions "What is man?" and "What is God?" but it tells us much about both man and God. It tells us that man is a being that God could become, that God is a being that would become man. It tells us, moreover, that God among men acts as a man, that he persuades and dissuades but does not force others to his will. This is a surprise. Man would dearly love to have the kind of power he imagines God to wield. All through his history he has tried to acquire it by way of magic, by way of science. Or in lieu of having such power for his own he has tried through religion to borrow some of God's. The prospect of doing without such power altogether, of being unable to prevent evil or to enforce good, is hard to contemplate. That God himself should do without it is amazing.

The power that man has sought to acquire through magic and science, that he invokes through religion, can seem to him indispensable. In *The Golden Bough* Frazer likened the story of mankind to "a web woven of three different threads—the black thread of magic, the red thread of religion, and the white thread of science."[8] All three, we could say, belong to the story of mankind and have entered into it. The possibility of doing without the power that is sought through them, nevertheless, exists too. Besides spells, prayers, and formulas there is the discourse of one human being with another. It is this, simple human discourse, that has been the vehicle of revelation and enlightenment. Consider, for instance, the words of Jesus or Gotama or Socrates. It is through teaching such as theirs, more than anything else, that light has been kindled in the darkness, that God and man have come to light. Perhaps this tells us something about what still lies hidden in the darkness. It is through magic, religion, and science that man has attempted to dispel the darkness, to acquire knowledge and power. Yet the transition from prehistory to history, the enlightenment and the revelation, the transition from history to world history, the great turning points in the development of man's consciousness, do not seem to have come about through these efforts.

Magic, religion, and science as endeavors to acquire knowledge and power are efforts which man makes in the light of the consciousness he has. The answers he obtains depend on the questions he asks. The questions are not addressed to human beings, however, but to nonhuman powers, to God, to nature. Spells, prayers, and formulas have this in common that although they are composed of words the words are not addressed to human beings as in ordinary discourse. The questions are not addressed to human consciousness so much as to being.[9] Now the questions man poses to being in magic, religion, science are always posed in the light of his actual consciousness and are therefore limited by his degree of consciousness. An increase of consciousness brings new questions, questions he had never thought of before. When there is a transition to a new realm of consciousness, new realms of magic and religion and science are opened up to him, but the transition itself is the work neither of magic nor of religion nor of science. A real increase in consciousness is rather a passive occurrence than a result of man's endeavors. The most a man can do when it occurs is to share it with other men, to speak with them of it, to act in the new light and to tell others how he sees things in it.

An increase in the scope of consciousness is occasioned ordinarily, it seems, by the failure rather than the success of man's endeavors; by the failure of his magic, his religion, his science. The new consciousness takes the form of an insight into failure. The paradigm of this is the enlightenment of the Buddha, his insight into the failure of known ways to wisdom and bliss. Perhaps each of the great turning points in time is like this. Historic consciousness may have arisen by insight into the failure of the magic, the religion, the science of prehistoric man. Insight into the failure of historic man's religion may have been at the origin of the enlightenment and the revelation which led to the world religions, and insight into the failure of historic man's culture may be at the origin of the transition from history to world history which appears to be taking place in our times. The failure in each instance arises from the disproportion between consciousness and being, the inadequacy of a given form of consciousness, historic or prehistoric, its inability to encompass man's being. The insight into failure, to be sure, is a human act of understanding, but the understanding is not the one which man sought, not even the kind of understanding which he expected.

Suppose, for instance, we say that contemporary man has been living in a future-oriented culture, a culture which dreams of planning the future. Suppose, moreover, the attempt to plan the future is doomed to failure for the very reason we have been speaking of, that man does not know what he is. He would have to fully understand himself in order to plan his future, or else things would come to light which he did not anticipate and his plan would be overturned by them. Suppose, however, it is not generally realized in the culture that man is necessarily an enigma to himself. Suppose, on the contrary, the prevailing view is that "a man, viewed as a behaving system, is quite simple: the apparent complexity of his behavior over time is largely a reflection of the complexity of the environment in which he finds himself."[10] An ant's path over a very rough and irregular surface such as that of a seashore looks very complex, but the ant is a very simple being—the complexity of his path is due to the numerous obstacles he encounters. Thinking of man in similar terms, a planner might project his future, reckoning on simplicity in man himself and complexity only in his environment. Now if the plan were to be actually worked out and its failure actually perceived—that man's problems had all been merely displaced from inside him to outside him—then we would have the occasion for an insight into failure and an increase in the scope of consciousness.

The understanding that would come of this would not be the understanding of the future that was sought and expected. It would be rather a new understanding of our ignorance of what man is, new because such a plan had not been attempted before. Each insight into failure in the story of mankind has the same root, that man does not know what he is, and yet each is different because the failure is always specific. In each instance consciousness comes up against being and is found wanting, and yet the outcome is an increase in the scope of consciousness. Each time man wrestles with God, and like Jacob he is lamed and yet blessed. As the story is told in Genesis, Jacob wrestled with God all through the night. God lamed him at dawn but Jacob would not let him go until he blessed him; so God blessed him and changed his name from Jacob to Israel.[11] The night, we could fancy, is the darkness of being; the dawn is the kindling of the new light of consciousness. The laming is the defeat of man's consciousness, its failure to encompass his being. The blessing is the new scope which consciousness attains. The old name expresses man's old understanding of himself, the new name his new understanding.

Man comes out of the encounter with God lamed, blessed, and newly named. He walks in the light where before he walked in darkness, but he walks with a limp. Mere behavior and control of behavior give way to action, but the insight upon which action is based is an insight into failure. The failure of planning, if that were to occur and be perceived as in our supposition, would be a laming experience, the dashing of an important hope. The future would seem richer for it, though, less dreary, more mysterious, more fascinating and dreadful. A future that could be successfully planned would be a grey prospect of predictable behavior. Walking into a knowingly unknown future, man would have only the confidence that what belongs to his future shall enter into it. What belongs to his future is what pertains to his being. It has entered into his story all along, but under cover of darkness. In the future it will come into the light.

2. *The God in the Lifetime*

"Everything that from eternity has happened in heaven and earth, the life of God and all the deeds of time," Hegel said, "are simply the struggles of mind to know itself."[12] So it seems, at any rate, from man's point of view as he struggles to grow in consciousness. If what we have been saying is true, though, he wrestles with a God who has a darker purpose in creating him and his world, a purpose man could never understand without already knowing himself, without already having grown to full awareness. We could look upon the individual life story in the same way, as a story of an awakening and, to some extent, the story of a failure to awaken. Without knowing in advance what we are awakening to, though, we do not really know the darker purpose at work in our lives. The immediate awareness of the child is followed by the existential awareness of the youth and the historic awareness of the man, we have seen, much as prehistory is followed by history. Beyond this there is the possibility of a return from time to the lifetime, from historic to a new existential awareness, and from time to the moment, from historic to a new immediate awareness, as in the enlightenment and revelation experiences. Then there is the possibility of passing over from one's own life and culture and religion to other lives and cultures and religions, and coming back to a new understanding of one's own.

The process, it seems, can go on indefinitely, especially the process of passing over and coming back. No matter how conscious a man is, therefore, he is never fully conscious; no matter how much he knows, he never knows everything a man can know. If he circumnavigates his world, he sails around it in a rhumb line, a spiral that coils around the world again and again without ever touching the poles. So on each voyage around his world his path is a different turn on the spiral and he makes new discoveries. Always making new discoveries, he never reaches the point where he knows everything about his world. The proposition of Jung's we originally set out to consider, "everything which belongs to an individual's life shall enter into it," would have to be understood with this proviso, that the individual never reaches the point where he knows everything which belongs to his life.

Comparing life stories to see how the world enters human lives, we find that it enters some mainly as an outer world and others mainly as an inner world. The autobiographies of Malraux and

Jung make a good example of the contrast. Malraux's *Anti-Memoirs* aim to tell only the outer story, the story of a man's relationship with the outer world; hence the *Anti* in the title.[13] Jung's *Memories, Dreams, Reflections,* on the contrary, aim to tell only the inner story, the story of a man's relationship with himself. "My life has been singularly poor in outward happenings," Jung says in his prologue. "I cannot tell much about them, for it would strike me as hollow and insubstantial; I can understand myself only in the light of inner happenings; it is these that make up the singularity of my life, and with these my autobiography deals."[14] Malraux's life was rich in outward happenings, adventures involving the risk of death, scenes that could be transposed into fiction, conversations with famous men. Jung's life was rich in inner happenings, adventures of the mind involving the risk of insanity, feelings from which archetypal images could be elicited, conversations with the strange figures that appear in dreams and myths.

Both lives, however rich, were also poor. Malraux's was poor in inner happenings, Jung's in outer happenings. Only the outer world entered fully and richly into Malraux's consciousness, only the inner world into Jung's. Yet both worlds belonged to both lives and entered into them. In both lives, we can see, the reach of being was much greater than the reach of consciousness. In the end Jung experienced a kind of reversal in which the outer world became clear and the inner world clouded. "It seems to me as if that alienation which so long separated me from the world has become transferred into my own inner world," he said, "and has revealed to me an unexpected unfamiliarity with myself."[15] This is the concluding sentence of his autobiography. A man ultimately comes up against the disproportion between his being and his consciousness. What once seemed clear to him begins to seem dark. A moment will come when he will realize that his clarity was like an optical illusion in which a clear pond seems more shallow than it really is.

When this moment comes, when a man sees through his own clarity, then his life can begin again. If he is old like Jung when he sees this, he can count it as his final wisdom, but if he is young, his life can become an adventure. The stage of life at which clarity becomes a temptation is in manhood when a man attains historic awareness, when his consciousness reaches its full expansion over time and he sees all time in a kind of panorama. In childhood when he is living in the moment the world is full of wonder, and in youth when he is trying to find his way in life it is full of darkness, but in manhood when his consciousness extends not only to the confines of his own life but beyond to the greater past and future the world can seem clear. He may believe at this point that he has reached a summit from which he can survey the world. He can live out of this consciousness, act on it, make plans in the light of it. The trouble is that there is nowhere for him to go, as far as he can see; there is apparently no further degree of awareness; nothing can happen, it seems to him, except within the scope that he has already attained. He is already dead somehow before death.

A new awareness does eventually come to him, nevertheless, the almost timeless awareness of old age. When old age fails, so to speak, it is "second childhood" in the usual sense, the loss of all a man has gained in youth and manhood. When it succeeds, then too it is a return to childhood, to the simplicity of childhood, but a childhood enhanced by all the experience of a lifetime.[16] This enhanced childhood, it seems, is the condition of the sage. According to the scheme of ages traditional in India a man is first a student, then a householder, then a forest-dweller, and finally a sage.[17] The consciousness of the sage looks timeless because it is a step beyond historic awareness, beyond the time of history. It is a return, however, to the time of life or to the time of the moment, a return to youth or to childhood. Actually, as we can see from the lives of Gotama and Jesus, it is not necessary to wait for old age to attain this kind of consciousness. A man is in a position to attain it as soon as he has reached manhood and historic awareness. As soon as he has seen the panorama of time, as soon as he has reached clarity, he is ready to see beyond it and to realize that his clarity is only an illusion of shallowness.

One way of seeing beyond history is to realize that historic awareness is only a stage of life or, to put it more strongly, that history is a stage of life, the stage namely of manhood. This has the effect of causing a man to return from the time of history to the time of life. When a man reaches historic awareness and does not yet see beyond it, he is liable to see the whole world as a kind of museum. Something like this seems to have happened in the lives of Malraux and Jung. The outer world was a kind of museum to Malraux, a museum of cultures. The past existed in the present but it existed as past; thus the museum, he believed, was the perfect embodiment of the civilization of the present—a place where statues and other objects which were once sacred have become objects of art. The process by which things become historical, lose their sacredness and become things of the past, he called "the metamorphosis of the gods."[18] The inner world was a kind of museum to Jung, a museum containing all the archetypes of human experience. But for Jung the archetypes, the images of the gods, were still alive in the unconscious; they were dead only in consciousness. For both Malraux and Jung, to explore the world was to tour the museum, the museum without or the museum within.

When Jung discovered an "unexpected unfamiliarity" with himself at the end of his life, however, it seems that he was seeing beyond the museum. The museum of the inner world was familiar to him; he had toured it many times. Each time he toured it he made new discoveries, though the discoveries were all of a similar sort, but now he makes a discovery of an entirely different sort. The seeming familiarity gives way to a profound sense of the unknown. It is as if he has asked himself the question of the Upanishads, "How can the knower be known?" "All are clear," he quotes Lao-tzu. "I alone am clouded."[19] It is the knower that is unknown, not many things he knows. These many things are clear, he alone is clouded. When he realizes that his historic awareness, in spite of its clarity and seeming completeness, is really only a stage on life's way, then he realizes that he must outgrow his own historic vision and that he is not included within his own vision. "The world, brethren, has been fully understood by the Tathagata," Gotama told his disciples. "From the world the Tathagata is set free."[20] The Tathagata, the "thus come" or the "thus gone," we could say, is the sage who has seen beyond the historic panorama. By seeing beyond it, by seeing that he himself is not contained within its clarity, he is set free of it.

The world from which the sage is set free is the panorama of history. The Tathagata in the passage we quoted knows the "world" and is freed of it; he knows the "arising of the world," the "ceasing of the world," and the "way to the ceasing of the world." He realizes that the panorama of history is something a man sees in the course of his development. It is the householder's view of things, and the forest-dweller's. The householder sees like Malraux the panorama of the outer world; the forest-dweller, fleeing this, sees like Jung the panorama of the inner world; the sage sees beyond the panorama. What he sees is the overriding significance of life, how historic awareness is merely a stage of life and how it is followed by another, that of his own almost timeless awareness. His own awareness is like that of an old man who is taking leave of the world at the end of his life. Thus his view of the world appears negative; he appears to deny rather than to affirm the world. He leaves behind him all the things which fill the active years of a human life, the intimacy of a private life with wife and children and the power and glory of a public life. All he has remaining to him is the life of insight and the sharing of insight with others. The life of insight is his only private life, the sharing of insight with others his only public life.

When an old man becomes a sage, his life is already behind him. When a young man devotes himself to the life of insight and the sharing of insight with others, he is likely to feel more keenly the lack of intimacy and the lack of power and glory. Suppose I am trying to live a life of celibacy and dedication to teaching, to give myself entirely to the life of insight and the sharing of insight with others. I may find that in spite of my ideal I do get involved in intimate relationships and in struggles for power and glory. Maybe I am experiencing the truth of Jung's saying, "everything which belongs to an individual's life shall enter into it." The part which intimacy and power and glory have in my life may be a measure of my distance from the enlightenment of the sage. On the other hand, the part they have may be in accord with a higher purpose at work in my life which reaches beyond the horizons of my own striving. Wisdom for me may consist in seconding this purpose, in seeing it as God's purpose, in trusting God that whatever belongs to my life shall enter into it and whatever enters into it shall belong to it.

Is there a wisdom which overreaches the wisdom of the sage, which can begin before a man has attained the sage's renunciation, which can lead him to the sage's enlightenment, which can perhaps carry him beyond the sage? If there is, it is this trust in God. Consider the founders of the world religions, Gotama and Jesus and Mohammed. Gotama embodies the wisdom of the sage; Jesus and Mohammed embody the wisdom of trusting in God. Trust in God never led Mohammed to the sage's renunciation of intimacy and of power and glory, but it did lead Jesus to something like that. The sage's wisdom appears to be a particular stage in human development, the last stage according to the scheme traditional in India. Gotama attained it in his thirties, but he went through the previous stages, those of the student, the householder, and the forest-dweller, however quickly. The wisdom of trusting in God, by contrast, does not seem to belong to any particular stage in human development. A man could attain it in old age, in manhood, in youth, even in childhood. His coming to this kind of wisdom could never be premature because it always puts him into accord with his life, whether he attains it as a child or a youth or a man or an old man, and once he has reached it he can live by it through the remaining stages of his life.

It can lead him to something like the sage's renunciation of intimacy and of power and glory. This we can see in the life of Jesus. We can surmise that Jesus too went through the previous stages, that in the first thirty years of his life he came like a householder to see the panorama of the outer world, that he saw beyond it and went into the wilderness, that in the wilderness he came like a forest-dweller to see the panorama of the inner world, that he saw beyond this too and returned to share his insight with others. Throughout all the stages he will have been acting on the wisdom of trusting in God, of following God's lead. "And immediately," we read in Mark's Gospel, "the Spirit drives him into the wilderness.[21] The Spirit "drives him," or we can translate "leads him," from one stage to another. There are two kinds of wisdom in his life, therefore, the wisdom of seconding the higher purpose which appears to be at work in his life and the wisdom of seeing beyond the panorama of the outer and inner world. The renunciation seems to occur in his life as in Gotama's when he leaves the world and goes into the wilderness, when he sees beyond the panorama of the outer world. The strength to live the renunciation, to live without intimacy and without power and glory, seems to come when he overcomes the temptations in the wilderness, when he sees beyond the panorama of the inner world.

Thus he comes back from the wilderness with a wisdom like the sage's. Yet this is not the last great turning point in his life. There is still a further enlightenment which comes to him, it seems, as he faces death and darkness. At this point he is called upon to give up not merely intimacy, not merely power and glory, but his life itself. The sage's life devoted to insight and the sharing of insight with others is a revelation of what man can be and therefore of what man is. Living without intimacy, without power and glory, the sage reveals that man does not live by these things alone. When a man comes to this by following God's lead, as Jesus did, he reveals not only something about man but also something about God. When he goes on from sharing insight with others to laying down his life for others, he reveals something further and deeper. He reveals the kind of love man is capable of and he reveals, hidden within man's love, God's love. If God then raises him from the dead, as he is said to have done in the story of Jesus, then something still greater is revealed, something about man's destiny and about the dark purpose of God which is at work in human life. Man's life is revealed as a becoming headed towards being rather than nothingness.

All the stages together make a rather complex journey in time. First there is the immediate awareness of the child who lives in the here and now. Then there is the existential awareness of the youth who is trying to find his way in life. Then there is the historic awareness of the man who sees the panorama of the world and to whom his path seems clear. This historic awareness may go through two stages. First there is the consciousness of the man like Malraux, whose life is rich in outward happenings and whose vision is mainly of the outer world. This is the experience of the householder, who enjoys the intimacy of a private life and the power and glory of a public life. Then there is the consciousness of the man like Jung, who sees beyond the panorama of the outer world and whose vision is mainly of the inner world. This, according to the tradition of India, is the experience of the forest-dweller, who withdraws into the wilderness and whose life becomes poor in outward happenings and rich in inward happenings. Then there is the consciousness of the man like Jung at the end of his life, who sees beyond the panorama of the inner world and finds an "unexpected unfamiliarity" with himself. This is the experience of the sage, who asks himself the question of the Upanishads, "How can the knower be known?" and realizes that he transcends his own vision of the inner and outer world.

Beyond the sage and his life of insight and sharing insight with others there is the man who lays down his life for others, and who finds life in laying down life. This is the experience of a man who tries to follow God's lead, who trusts that what belongs to his life shall enter into it and what enters into it shall belong to it, including his death. Seconding God's purpose, though, if we are right, is something which can begin before this stage in a life. It can begin before the sage's enlightenment and before the forest-dweller's withdrawal too; it can begin when a man is not yet free to give up intimacy or to give up power and glory, much less to give up his life. This kind of wisdom appears, therefore, to be independent of the stages on life's way. It has much to do with the stages, to be sure, in that it can lead a man from one to another. Yet in itself it is not a stage. Certain other things, such as the intimacy of the private life, the power and glory of the public life, the renunciation of both, the life of insight, and the sharing of insight with others—all of which we would ordinarily consider to be alternative life styles—appear to be stages of life, phases in one and the same process of human development.

In fact, all the various forms of having and not having, intimacy and celibacy, power and glory and the renunciation of power and glory, life and the laying down of life, appear to be stages of life. So do the consciousness and the insight which go with each of them. As a man goes through life the having and the not having will enter into his life stage by stage. This, it seems, is what Jung meant when he said "everything which belongs to an individual's life shall enter into it." It shall enter the man's life, Jung added, "whether he consents or not, or is conscious of what is happening to him or not."[22] Consent and consciousness, according to this, may or may not be present, but the having and the not having will be present, at least unwillingly and unconsciously. On the other hand, there is something which may be present at any and every stage and if it is present will bring with it a consent and a consciousness, and that is the following of God's lead, the cooperation with his dark purpose at work in one's life and times. What happens, let us ask, if a man does become conscious of such a purpose and does consent to it? What does he discover? Where is he led?

3. The God in the Moment

"I don't know Who—or What—put the question, I don't know when it was put, I don't even remember answering," Dag Hammarskjold wrote in his diary, "but at some moment I did answer *Yes* to Someone—or Something—and from that hour I was certain that existence is meaningful and that therefore my life, in self-surrender, had a goal."[23] We can see in Hammarskjold's life the latter phases in the process of human development, the historic man and the historic man's return to life and to the moment. His public life was that of an historic man; his inner life, recorded in *Markings,* his diary, looks like a return to the lifetime and existential concerns; and the "moment" he speaks of, dividing his diary into two halves, a dark earlier half and a bright later half, looks like a return to the moment and to immediacy. The moment, as he describes it, is a unique moment in his life, a moment of consent, a moment in which he said "Yes" in answer to some ultimate question that was put to him. Yet his consent in that moment seems to have led him to live in the moment from then on. "From that moment," he goes on to say, "I have known what it means 'not to look back' and 'to take no thought for the morrow.' "[24]

Instead of the "immediate man," the "existential man," and the "historic man," we could speak of "immediate moments," "existential moments," and "historic moments." Speaking this way would mean realizing that there is no one immediate or existential or historic situation, but as many as there are turning points in a life. Realizing this would mean returning to the moment and thus to a kind of immediacy, but the moment to which one returns would not really be the immediate moment in which one lived as a child. It would be rather a moment that is at once immediate and existential and historic, a moment enhanced by all the awareness one has attained in the course of one's life. Hammarskjold, when he began to live in the moment, did not withdraw from public life, nor did he cease recording his inner life in his diary. He remained thus an historic and an existential man in the midst of his new immediacy. What brought him to the moment was apparently the consent he gave, the "Yes" he said to the question that was put to him. What was this question? "Who or What," we may ask in his own words, "put the question?" He says "I did answer *Yes* to Someone—or Something—and from that hour I was certain that existence is meaningful and that therefore my life, in self-surrender, had a goal."

This Someone or Something, we can surmise, is God. The uncertainty as to whether God is Someone or Something, it seems, is an uncertainty as to how to construe his experience of God. If a man were to live his life as a voyage of discovery, going from one immediate and existential and historic situation to another, he could see his life as the gradual discovery of Something and yet he could see himself being led all the while by Someone. The Something he is discovering is what God is. The question "What is God?" is an impersonal question; it asks for a "What," for "Something." If a man were to discover with the New Testament that "God is love,"[25] he would be discovering Something, but this would not be incompatible with God being Someone. What a man will actually discover in the course of a life, to be sure, is likely not to be as simple and unified as the insight conveyed in the sentence "God is love." The journey through life involves on one level a series of physical transformations, as the child grows and becomes a youth, as the youth matures and becomes a man, as the man ages and becomes an old man, as the old man decays and dies. These physical changes are transformations of the base of perception and feeling and imagination and thought and action. The world of the child thus will differ from that of the youth, the man, the old man. The God of the child likewise, the God of the youth, the God of the man, and the God of the old man will differ.

If there were to be a split, moreover, between the level of physical transformations and that of the inner and spiritual journey; that is, if a man were to see his spiritual journey as relatively independent of his bodily metamorphoses; then the two processes, the physical and the spiritual, might seem to point towards two different Gods. The physical changes by themselves might point towards a God who delights in the eternal play of formation and transformation which we see in the physical world, but who brings all his victims to an ugly end in death. The spiritual journey, on the other hand, might point towards a God who has no love for earthly beauty, but values only the pain and suffering that lead to spiritual growth and emancipation from the earth. All these splits—that between the physical and the spiritual process and those among the various stages in the process—are really splits in man, it seems, more than in God. To realize this, that the split is in man, and to act on this realization is to turn all the split features into phases and aspects of a single journey.

The "Yes" of which Hammarskjold speaks may be in effect a "Yes" to the journey itself. The question to which the "Yes" answers is apparently something like this: "Are you willing to go on a journey which leads to death?" The journey is life, but it leads to death. Let us imagine the question being put to us. At first the question seems pointless since we are already on such a journey whether we like it or not. On further thought it begins to seem important to determine whether we do like it or not, whether we are willing or not to go on such a journey. Just before he speaks of saying "Yes," Hammarskjold quotes in his diary the last lines of Ibsen's *Brand* where Brand, caught in an avalanche of snow, cries out to God as he sees death coming and is answered by a voice which is the roar of the avalanche itself, "God is love."[26] Man's striving, his life project, ordinarily does not include death, but death strikes him down from the outside, interrupts his project, comes upon him like an avalanche. Death has been seen this way, as an outside power rather than as part of life, more and more in Western civilization, ever since the fourteenth century when Europe was ravaged by the Black Death.[27] The journey a man is willingly traveling is thus usually a journey which is interrupted by death, rather than one which leads to death.

"We have, in fact, every chance of dying before we have accomplished our task," Sartre says, "or, on the other hand, of outliving it."[28] A man who is on a journey which has nothing to do with death may die before his journey is finished or, on the other hand, he may finish his journey and live on for a while without any further purpose in life. Here Sartre is speaking directly out of the mentality which has been developing in the West since the time of the Black Death. If death is thought to be something which strikes from the outside, then it makes no sense to journey towards it. Also it becomes very difficult to believe that it could be the gateway to any kind of further life. Examining our own purposes in life, we are likely to discover just such a "task" or "project" as Sartre envisions. We are likely to find that we are aiming at accomplishing something in our lifetime and that we could indeed be cut off by death before we have accomplished it; and on the other hand, that we could conceivably accomplish it and then live on for a while without any further purpose. Reflecting further, we are likely to find that the thought of living life as a journey towards death is very repugnant and that it is very difficult to take seriously the idea of a life beyond death.

To say "Yes," therefore, to a question like "Are you willing to go on a journey which leads to death?" would mean a change in our projects and purposes. It would mean seeing death as part of life rather than as something striking life from the outside. "Man is the desire to be God,"[29] Sartre has said. Perhaps this is the meaning of our projects and purposes in which death has no part. The project of becoming God has no place in it for mortality. A project of which mortality is a part would be a project of becoming human, a project of becoming man. Suppose that my aim in life has been to attain insight and to share it with others. One way of understanding and living this project would be, as Jung said, "to kindle a light in the darkness of mere being." If I saw my life this way and lived it this way, I would be struggling against the darkness of mere being, struggling to kindle the light of consciousness in myself and others. My project thus understood and lived would be interrupted by my death. On the other hand, if I were to become insane or senile and incapable anymore of kindling light in the darkness, I would outlive my project. Clearly my project, understood this way, does not include my mortality as a part of its inner meaning.

There is another way, however, of understanding it and living it. My aim, we are supposing, is to attain insight and to share it with others. Now instead of seeing myself kindling light in the darkness, suppose I were to see myself receiving light in the darkness. Suppose I were to count each insight a gift, a gift to be shared with others. Instead of kindling the light myself or perhaps stealing it from the gods like Prometheus, I could see myself receiving it from a God who is himself like Prometheus, a friend of man. Two gifts were said to have been given to man by Prometheus—fire, and man's ignorance of his fate.[30] The one was a light and the other was a darkness. In accord with this I could see both the light by which I live and the darkness in which I live, which conceals my fate from me, as a gift. I could communicate both gifts to others too, the insight that lights the way and the sense of adventure which goes with the darkness and the lack of foreknowledge. Both of these, the light and the darkness, are essential to the journey. Without the light a man would lose his way; without the darkness, if he already knew his fate, there would be no adventure.

To consent to the journey thus understood is to consent to both gifts, the light and the darkness. The relative proportions of light and darkness change with each stage of life. In childhood the light is a luminous point in a field of darkness; the immediate situation, the here and now, becomes luminous but the existential and the historic situation are dark. In youth there is a circle of light surrounded by darkness; the existential situation, the situation in life, becomes luminous, but the historic situation, the situation in time, remains dark. In manhood the light reaches all the way to the horizon, the historic situation becomes luminous, and there seems to be no more darkness, but the darkness still exists beyond the horizon. Afterwards in manhood or in old age a man may go to the borders of the darkness beyond, but then the light seems to become again a circle of light, or in the vast expanse a mere luminous point surrounded by darkness; the historic situation appears to be only the historic stage of life or merely an historic moment, and life and time appear to be still largely unexplored.

At every point on the journey there is both light and darkness. The light always reveals somehow man's situation; the darkness always conceals somehow his fate. The sun rises on his life, we could say, as he goes from immediate to existential to historic awareness. At the high noon of his life, when he has attained historic awareness and the light reaches all the way to the horizon and there seems to be no more darkness, a man might think he could say "Yes" to the light and to his life and death without saying "Yes" also to the darkness. Nietzsche spoke of the "great noon"[31] in which the higher man says "Yes" to his own life and death and wills to live his life and die his death again and again eternally. This, he believed, is the secret both of life and death, both of the "noon" and the "midnight," that time is a great circle and every life is lived again and again in eternal recurrence. "Midnight too is noon," he said.[32] He imagined the higher man lying on his deathbed and looking back on his life and saying "Was that life? Well then! Once more!"[33]

Both of these moments, the noon and the midnight of life, are points at which a man's fate can seem to be clear. The noon is the high point of life, when he has attained full manhood and full awareness and clear vision of life and time. The midnight is the end point, where he lies on his deathbed and looks back on a life already lived. "Yes" at either of these points can seem to be "Yes" to a known fate. In reality, though, it is not a man's fate that is known at these moments but his situation. At the noontide of life what is revealed in the full light of day is a man's historic situation. If he mistakes this situation for his fate, he may lose all hope. For instance, a man living in our times might see himself living under threat of nuclear war. The nuclear bomb is an embodiment, it seems, of the modern sense of death as a force outside ready to strike down life. If a man interprets this situation as his fate rather than his situation, he is likely to see his life heading towards a death which has nothing to do with his life, which makes his life a mockery. The same thing could happen at the midnight of life when he lies on his deathbed; it could seem to him that the death which approaches has nothing to do with the life he has lived.

Insight into the situation would be to realize, as Yeats said, that "Man has created death,"[34] that death as a force outside which strikes down life is something man has made of death. Man has created this by construing death this way and ultimately by constructing embodiments of it like the nuclear bomb. The construing and constructing create a situation, but they do not create a destiny. To realize that death as an external force is a human construct dissipates the illusion that death is supreme in the world, that death is a kind of power which man can use and which can be used against him; that death, as Hegel said, is the "sovereign master."[35] It leads to the very simple and sober realization that death is only man's mortality, his fragility, his weakness. At the same time the dissipation of the spectre of death's power makes it possible to see a power at work in human life other than death, a creative power drawing man out of nothingness and towards being. This creative power, it seems, is the "Someone—or Something" to which Hammarskjold said "Yes" at the turning point of his life.

"Yes" to the creative power at work in one's life means "Yes" to the dark purpose which has one's being as its aim. This being, it seems, is always something more than one's life project, something more than one's conscious purpose at any given time. To consent to it is to consent to something which one experiences but does not fully understand. The best one can do is know that one does not know, understand that one does not understand, see the darkness as well as the light. The experience is that one's life at any given time is richer than one's life project. For instance, in the example we have been using, if the project is one of attaining and sharing insight, there will be involvements in intimate relationships and in struggles for power and glory which have no apparent place in the project. Consent to this richer life could then mean letting these things enter the life project, letting them become matter for further insight and further sharing, coming to understand one's involvements in intimacy and in struggle and communicating this new understanding to others. The consent thus could lead to insight, to expansion of the realm of light.

Finally, though, it leads to the failure of the project. "Yes" to the creative power and its dark purpose is "Yes" finally to a destined being which, because it is richer than one's projected being, necessarily overturns one's life project. One can see this in the life of Jesus when he faces death and the prospect of failing to convert Israel to his God. The conversion of Israel, we could say, was his lifework; the failure of this and the darkness which he faced when he cried out "My God, my God, why have you forsaken me?" concealed a destiny that was greater than the one he had intended.[36] One can see something similar in other lives. Gandhi, when he saw his lifework, the liberation of India, going down in the partition of India and the riots between Hindus and Muslims in which half a million people were killed, spoke of having to "face despair,"[37] and soon afterwards was assassinated. Yet the significance of his life seems somehow richer and greater than the project of liberating India, or of being the one who liberated India. Hammarskjold, speaking of the "moment" when he said "Yes" to "Someone —or Something," went on to write, "I came to a time and place where I realized that the Way leads to a triumph which is a catastrophe, and to a catastrophe which is a triumph, that the price for committing one's life would be reproach, and that the only elevation possible to man lies in the depths of humiliation."[38] This was in 1961, the year of his death.

The paradigm here is the life of Jesus. "As I continued along the Way," Hammarskjold says after the words we just quoted, "I learned, step by step, word by word, that behind every saying in the Gospels stands one man and one man's experience."[39] Jesus taught his disciples to be on intimate and familiar terms with God, to call God "Abba," the informal term for "Father," like "Daddy" or "Papa." And yet he taught them also to pray "Lead us not into temptation" as though the God they trusted was quite capable of leading them into temptation. He himself was led into temptation when all had failed and he was in darkness on the cross, and it seems that everyone who consents to God and to God's dark purpose is ultimately led into temptation. For in consenting to this a man is consenting to a purpose which encompasses and surpasses his own. This does not mean that he should have no purpose of his own, no life project. Without a project, for example the one we mentioned of attaining and sharing insight, a man would have no way of walking along the road of the journey. Saying "Yes" to God, nevertheless, means being willing in the end to lay down not only his life but also his life project.

The journey to which this leads, a journey towards a death which conceals eternal life, towards "a triumph which is a catastrophe and a catastrophe which is a triumph," is a journey which a modern man cannot seriously undertake without a considerable change of mind and heart on death. A change would be required even if a man saw death more humanly as part of life, as nothing but man's mortality. For it would mean seeing a creative power at work in human life leading man through a process of becoming from nothingness to being. A much greater change is required when man sees death as an inhuman force outside which strikes down life. For then not only is the creative power not visible, but almost the opposite, a destructive power, seems to be visible. When a modern man does make the change, from a vision of destruction to a vision of creation, he has a feeling of great paradox. The message of Jesus when he first began preaching was "Change your minds and hearts, the reign of God is at hand." The parallel to that message in our times, it seems, would be something like "Take heart, the reign of death is at an end."[40]

The moment, therefore, the turning point in life and time, contains both light and darkness, a light which reveals man's situation and a darkness which conceals his destiny. Consent to all that belongs to the moment, the darkness as well as the light, leads to a hope and an adventure as in the message we have envisioned, "Take heart, the reign of death is at an end." The proposition about the moment which we originally set out to consider, "everything which belongs to the moment shall enter into it," would be true of the light and the darkness. Both the light and the darkness belong to the moment and enter into it. Whether the moment is the dawn, the noontide, the twilight, or the midnight of the life, it has its own light and its own darkness. At noon when the man is at the climax of historic awareness, the darkness lies over the horizon. At midnight when he is on his deathbed and his life is behind him, the light lies over the horizon. "Yes" to the light and the situation revealed in the light can be an affirmation of man's own will and purpose, as when Nietzsche's higher man, standing at the noontide of his life, wills to recur eternally or, lying on his deathbed, says to the life he has lived, "Once more." "Yes" to the darkness and the destiny concealed in the darkness is a human affirmation of God's will and God's dark purpose at work in the life.

"Yes" to both means wrestling with God, affirming both man's purpose and God's purpose, being lamed like Jacob, as man's consciousness proves to be inadequate, and yet blessed like him, as man's purpose is paradoxically fulfilled in its own defeat and the triumph of God's. The proposition about the lifetime which we set out to consider, "everything which belongs to an individual's life shall enter into it," speaks of the triumph of God's dark purpose. This triumph comes about again and again in the course of a man's lifetime. Each transition from one stage of life to another involves the defeat of a certain kind of human consciousness and of the purposes which were based upon it. The immediate awareness of the child proves inadequate to the demands of youth, the existential awareness of the youth inadequate to the demands of manhood, and the historic awareness of the man inadequate to the demands of further growth. The dark purpose which is triumphing at each of these turning points is one which seems to have man's being as its aim. It is a purpose which is dark but creative. Man's life proves richer at each point than man's purpose; each failure leads to the rise of a new and richer consciousness.

The same thing seems to happen at each of the great turning points in the story of mankind, the transition from prehistory to history, the enlightenment and the revelation inspiring the world religions, and the transition from history to world history. The proposition which we set out to consider about time, "everything which belongs to the story of mankind shall enter into it," speaks of the working of a dark and creative purpose in time like that which can be seen working in life. This purpose, while it always leads through failure to new and richer forms of consciousness, does not seem to have mere consciousness as its aim. On the contrary, its aim seems always to be man's being. It is accomplished at each epoch of man's story and shows in the fact that man's life in any epoch, prehistoric or historic, is always richer than his consciousness. If consciousness alone were the aim, then one epoch would be merely a preparation for another, the prehistoric for the historic and the historic for the world historic. The epoch of lesser consciousness would exist only to make way for the epoch of greater consciousness.

As it is, one epoch does prepare the way for another, one stage of consciousness does lead to another. The light is a gift, but so is the darkness. When a man regards the light alone as good, he feels his life to be very incomplete. He sees himself kindling a light in the darkness, attaining insight and sharing insight with others, but he sees well enough in the dark to realize that there is a large realm of darkness which lies outside the realm of light in his life. To see the darkness too as good, to receive it as a gift, to say "Yes" to both gifts, the light and the darkness, enriches the life and gives a man a sense of completeness. His life project is transformed. Before it was to attain insight and to share insight with others. Now it is to receive the two gifts, the light and the darkness, and to share both gifts, darkness as well as light, with others. To share the light is to share insight. To share the darkness is to share the sense of adventure which goes with the darkness and the journey into the night.

NOTES

1. Sartre, *Being and Nothingness,* tr. by Hazel E. Barnes (New York, Washington Square Press, 1966), p. 762.
2. Jung, *Answer to Job,* tr. by R. F. C. Hull (New York, Meridian, 1960), p. 203 (last sentence).
3. *Ibid.*, p. 184.
4. Jung, *Memories, Dreams, Reflections,* p. 326.
5. *Brihadaranyaka Upanishad,* II, 4, as tr. by Juan Mascaro, *The Upanishads* (Baltimore, Penguin Books, 1965), pp. 132 and 45. F. Max Müller translates "How should he know (himself), the Knower?" in *The Upanishads,* vol. 2 (Delhi, Motilal Banarsidas, 1969), p. 113.
6. Cf. S. Radhakrishnan, *The Principal Upanishads* (New York, Harper, 1953), pp. 77 ff.
7. *Asvamedha Parva,* LXXXVI, as tr. by C. V. Narasimhan in *The Mahabharata* (New York and London, Columbia University Press, 1965), pp. 195 f.
8. Sir James G. Frazer, *The Golden Bough,* Part VII (London, Macmillan, 1913), vol. 2, p. 308.
9. Kant, speaking of the science of his time, said "Reason must approach nature in order to be taught by it: but not in the character of a pupil, who agrees to everything the master likes, but as an appointed judge, who compels the witnesses to answer the questions which he himself proposes," in the preface to the second edition of *The Critique of Pure Reason,* tr. by F. Max Müller (New York, Doubleday, 1966), pp. *xxxi* f.
10. Herbert A. Simon, *The Sciences of the Artificial* (Cambridge, Mass., M.I.T. Press, 1969), p. 25. The parable of the ant is Simon's.
11. Genesis 32:24 ff.
12. Hegel, *Lectures on the History of Philosophy,* tr. by E. S. Haldane (New York, The Humanities Press, 1955), vol. 1, p. 23.
13. Cf. the prologue to Malraux, *Anti-Memoirs,* especially pp. 2 and 7 and 10.
14. Jung, *Memories, Dreams, Reflections,* p. 5.
15. *Ibid.,* p. 359.
16. Cf. my discussion of old age in *A Search for God in Time and Memory,* pp. 154 ff.
17. Cf. Heinrich Zimmer, *The Philosophies of India,* ed. by Joseph Campbell (New York, Pantheon, 1951), pp. 155 ff. Cf. my discussion of these stages above in Chapter Two, Section 2.
18. Malraux, *The Metamorphosis of the Gods,* tr. by Stuart Gilbert (New York, Doubleday, 1960).
19. Jung, *Memories, Dreams, Reflections,* p. 359. Cf. the *Tao Te Ching,* XX.
20. *Iti-vuttaka,* 112, tr. by F. L. Woodward in *Some Sayings of the Buddha,* p. 290.

21. Mark 1:12.
22. Jung, *Answer to Job*, p. 184.
23. Dag Hammarskjold, *Markings* tr. by Leif Sjöberg and W. H. Auden (New York, Knopf, 1964), p. 205.
24. *Loc. cit.*
25. I John 4:8 and 16.
26. Hammarskjold, *Markings*, p. 204. Cf. Ibsen, *Brand*, tr. by F. E. Garrett (New York, Dutton, 1951), p. 223.
27. Cf. *The City of the Gods*, pp. 191 ff., and *A Search for God in Time and Memory*, pp. 76 ff. and 120 ff.
28. Sartre, *Being and Nothingness*, p. 657.
29. *Ibid.*, p. 694.
30. Aeschylus, *Prometheus Bound*, 250–253. Note how Prometheus' name means "forethinker."
31. Nietzsche, *Thus Spoke Zarathustra*, tr. by Walter Kaufmann in *The Portable Nietzsche* (New York, Viking, 1960), p. 439 (the end of the book) and *passim* (cf. especially pp. 387 ff.).
32. *Ibid.*, p. 435. Cf. the "Midnight Song" on pp. 339 f. and 431–436.
33. *Ibid.*, pp. 269 and 430.
34. W. B. Yeats, *Collected Poems* (New York, Macmillan, 1934), p. 270.
35. Hegel, *The Phenomenology of Mind*, p. 237.
36. Cf. my discussion of the turning points in the life of Jesus in *A Search for God in Time and Memory*, pp. 8 ff.
37. As quoted by Malraux, *Anti-Memoirs*, p. 301. Cf. my discussion of this in Chapter Six, Section 2.
38. Hammarskjold, *Markings*, p. 205.
39. *Loc. cit.*
40. Cf. my essay in Bernard Murchland (ed.), *The Meaning of the Death of God* (New York, Random, 1967), p. 169. Cf. the phrase "death reigned" in Romans 5:14 and 17.

VIII
The Journey with God

IMAGINE TWO FIGURES on a road, walking together into the distance. As long as the daylight lasts the two can be seen walking side by side. As the night comes on, however, it becomes difficult to distinguish them any longer. As the darkness grows the two seem to merge into one.

Say the two figures are man and God. Say the day's journey is the course of man's life from birth to death. The merging of the two figures at nightfall, in man's death, suggests the famous sentence of the Upanishads, "You are that" (*tat tvam asi*).[1] The sentence means "You are what man is" if we take "that" to mean Atman, the essence of man. If we consider the tendency of the later Upanishads to equate Atman and Brahman, though, to equate what man is and what God is, the sentence could mean "You are what God is." The experience which leads to statements like these seems to be the one we have called "passing over," passing over to other men and passing over to God. Passing over to other men, entering into their lives by sympathetic understanding, is an experience of sympathy and resonance. It means finding within yourself something corresponding to what you see in another. It leads to the general discovery that you have within yourself everything that exists in every other man, that "You are what man is." The saying can seem a commonplace if we interpret it this way, something on the order of Terence's saying "I am a man; I consider nothing human alien to me."[2]

It is one thing, however, to believe that nothing human should be alien to you and quite another to actually find no human thing alien. A man may well consider himself a man and think therefore that nothing human should be foreign to him, but then find many features of human life foreign to his feelings and his way of thinking. He may find many human interests utterly uninteresting, many human attractions utterly repulsive, the ways of many men utterly strange.

The saying "You are what man is" would mean that these uninteresting interests, these repulsive attractions, these strange ways are really not alien to you. If a man were to pass over by sympathetic understanding into other lives and cultures and religions to the point where he could actually understand the interest in these interests, the attraction in these attractions, the sense in these ways, where he could find a resonance to them within himself, then he could truly say "I find nothing human alien to me" and he could say with full meaning "I am a man." The standpoint where he stands when he says this is one of universal compassion. It is really a divine standpoint. Think of the invocation with which each chapter of the Koran begins, "In the name of Allah, the compassionate, the merciful." The compassion of God extends beyond mankind to all living beings and all creatures. Passing over to God would mean going over into a bottomless abyss, entering by sympathetic understanding into the lives of all living beings and into the existences of all things. Yet entering into sympathy with all men already carries you into this abyss, and it seems when you are doing this that indeed "You are what God is."

This is the way things appear when you are passing over, "You are what man is" and "You are what God is." Besides passing over, nevertheless, there is an equal and opposite process which we have called "coming back." The coming back is the return to yourself. When you pass over to other lives, and by way of other lives to other cultures and other religions, you come back again with new insight to your own life, and by way of your own life to your own culture and your own religion. In the moment of passing over you see your oneness with other men and with God, but in the moment of coming back you see your own concreteness and individuality. In passing over the two figures, man and God, merge into one; in coming back they resolve again into two. In passing over it appears that man, as we put it in the first part of this book, is "God in disguise." In coming back it appears that man, as we put it in the second part, is on a "journey with God." The parable we are now proposing, two figures on the road, distinct as they walk in the daylight and indistinct as they go into the darkness, combines the two perspectives. It suggests that coming back reveals somehow the truth of life and passing over, though it takes place during life, reveals somehow the truth of death.

Passing over and coming back are ways of experimenting with the truth of life and death. In passing over to other lives one is led to turn the truth of one's own life into poetry.[3] This is especially clear when one comes to the point of saying to oneself "You are what man is" and "You are what God is." Still the poetry here is not a falsification of the truth; it embodies rather a deeper insight into the truth. Passing over to other lives changes one's understanding of what man is and what God is. Before passing over one is liable to think that man's troubles are due to his humanness and that well-being is to be found by rising above the human condition. Before one has discovered within oneself the realms of feeling and imagination and thought and action which correspond to those in the lives of others one is unaware of the richness of being man. One strives instead to escape somehow from the cares and concerns of a human existence. Thus in our Parable of the Mountain we envisioned a man climbing a mountain, endeavoring to escape from the valley of human cares and concerns and to reach the summit where he imagines God to dwell. We envisioned him reaching the top and finding nothing there but gravel, and then turning back and coming down the mountain again into the valley of human affairs.

When a man goes down into the valley, when he discovers by going over to other men that he is what man is, he discovers the richness he had sought at the summit; he discovers that God is to be found in the valley, that God goes down the mountain and comes among men. Coming back from all this to his own life, he is led to turn the poetry into truth, to live by the insight which he has found. He sees that the things which were missing from his life, the things he discovered in himself by discovering them in others, are actually a dark and unexplored realm in his life. They were there all along but he did not understand them. He saw them as dark forces at work in his life, dark tendencies of sexuality and violence which threaten to subvert his life. These were the very things he was fleeing when he climbed the mountain. Now he sees them as parts of his life which have yet to be understood and assimilated. Somehow the sexuality must be transformed into love and the violence into action. How this is to be done he does not yet know. He knows only that he must come to understand his sexuality and his violence and act on his understanding of them.

His withdrawal, the climbing of the mountain, proves to have had some value, though it was an experience of failure. He learns from it as one can learn only from failure. The pattern of withdrawal and return, going into the wilderness and then returning again among men, appears in the lives of the great teachers of mankind like Gotama and Jesus. The life which emerges from this pattern is what we have called "the simple life," the life of insight and sharing insight with others. It can seem completely disproportionate to the problem of transforming the dark forces in man, transforming sexuality into love and violence into action. Yet if we examine the lives of Gotama and Jesus and comparable figures like Socrates, we do see something which looks to be like this very transformation. The insight is attained, it seems, in the phase of withdrawal, and it is, as one would expect, an insight into failure. This is particularly clear in the life of Gotama: his stay in the wilderness was much more protracted than that of Jesus and he spent it trying to conquer himself by thinking, fasting, and waiting. The attempt ended in failure after seven years; it was as if the the dark forces could not be conquered. And yet it did not end in mere failure, but in an insight into failure. As he sat under the fig tree Gotama saw the failure of the worldling to conquer fortune and the failure of the recluse to conquer himself, and in that failure the failure of all conquest, the failure of taking; but at the same time he saw the possibility of another kind of life, a life of simple giving and receiving, and in this he saw the way to wisdom and bliss.

The man we envisioned climbing the mountain did not attain such a simple and transforming insight. He only experienced the failure; he found nothing at the top of the mountain. Then he returned again, coming down the mountain, to find his way in the valley. Reflecting on the lives of Gotama and Jesus, he can begin to grasp the significance of his own experience, the significance of his withdrawal and its failure, the significance of his return among men. Although he does not possess the clarity of the enlightenment which Gotama experienced, or that of the revelation which Jesus experienced, he does have the experience of the withdrawal and the return itself. Although he does not have a clear vision of the way, he is on the way somehow by the very fact that he returns among men. He does not see fully what Gotama saw or what Jesus saw, but he can see what they did once they had attained insight. They spent the remainder of their lives, a very short time for Jesus and a very long time for Gotama, sharing their insight with others. Whatever they said about the way, this is how they themselves walked it. He sees that he could spend his life too sharing what insight he has and attaining what insight he can. It occurs to him that he may be able to discover the way step by step as he travels it.

Discovering the way by traveling it is a lifelong process. Walking the way in this fashion, one finds that the life of insight and sharing insight with others is indeed disproportionate to the dark forces at work in one's life. Lacking enlightenment like Gotama's which would penetrate all the way through the dark forces, one is always in the process of transforming the darkness into light and is never at the point of full integration and complete inner peace. It is only in the moment of passing over into other lives that one has a glimpse of what full enlightenment would be. For in that moment one's self and its habitual standpoint disappear and one sees what it is like to care for others in their own right, instead of caring for them only insofar as they have a role in one's own life. In passing over into other lives one can see what Gotama means when he speaks of "no-self." This, it seems, is what one would see if one really saw through the illusion of conquest, the conquest of others and the conquest of self. One can see too what the Upanishads mean when they speak of Atman as a universal self, what Krishna means in the Gita when he speaks of acting without seeking the fruits of action, and what Jesus means in the Gospel of John when he speaks of doing what he sees the Father doing.

In all these instances there is a disappearance of the self and its standpoint, just as there is in the experience of passing over to lives other than one's own. The "no-self," the universal self, action without seeking the fruits of action, doing what God is doing, all seem to go with the conviction "You are what man is" and "You are what God is." In the experience of coming back to oneself, however, the self and its standpoint reappear. The self, its individuality, the fruits of action, one's doings as one's own, all reappear at once. In passing over, when one becomes conscious of oneness with other men and with God—it seems that every man, as the Gita teaches, is really an incarnation of God. In coming back to oneself, when one becomes conscious of uniqueness and distinctness, it seems credible rather that the Man, as the Gospel teaches, is the incarnation. Still one does bring back with one the insight gained in passing over, and this tends to put one's life on a new basis. Something does happen to the relationship between one's self and its cares, to that between one's action and its fruits, and to that between what one is doing and what God is doing. It seems that one is on the way towards the vision one has seen in passing over.

On the way, on the journey in time, one's vision is always bounded by a horizon. It is like walking along a road and looking ahead towards the horizon. In the moment of passing over, on the other hand, the horizon disappears. It is like pausing on the road and looking directly up into the night sky where there is no horizon and the stars can be seen receding into greater and greater distances. Vision is bounded looking towards the horizon, but it is unbounded looking upwards into the sky. The one kind of vision approaches the other, nevertheless, if one is moving towards the horizon and not standing still. For then the horizon itself recedes.

The bounded vision becomes like the unbounded vision because the boundary is constantly changing. Thus the experience of living by insight, living one's life as a voyage of discovery in which one is constantly going on from one horizon to another, is comparable to the experience of passing over to God. The one experience seems to be leading into something like the other.

As the stars recede into greater and greater distances in the night sky they become fainter and fainter. This shows that one's vision, as one looks up into the night sky, is not actually infinite. It has no visible boundary but it is finite; it is, like Einstein's universe, "finite and unbounded." Something similar is true of the experience of passing over to God. It is an experience of boundless depths and yet it is finite. The realization of this fact, we surmised, is what sets a prophet apart from a mystic. Both experience the boundless depths, but the mystic is prone to think that the experience is incommunicable, while the prophet, realizing that it is finite, realizes also that it is communicable and sees in this a call to communicate it to others. Realizing that his vision, though unbounded, is finite, a prophet like Mohammed would never agree to a statement such as the one we made, "You are what God is." Such a statement rises out of the unboundedness of the experience of passing over to God; it takes no account of the finiteness. Instead he will speak of a God like Allah who reveals himself to man but who always remains above and beyond man.

If man's experience of God is always finite, however, there is a journey here too, from one revelation to another. It is like falling into the boundless depths of the night sky. There are historic experiences of enlightenment and revelation which have given rise to the world religions, and these experiences can be shared by being re-enacted in individual lives. But the journey into the boundless depths of God is unceasing. Malraux asked the question "How many centuries is it since a great religion shook the world?"[4] The answer would have to be "Many," for the last great religion to arise was Islam. It has been thought, moreover, in Islam that Mohammed is the "seal of the prophets," the last prophet and the consummation of prophecy. If the essence of Mohammed's experience, however, is a sense of the finiteness of man's experience of an infinite God, as we are saying, then there is no end of revelation. Each time man passes over into God he can see wonders that have never been seen before. If each experience of God is finite, then no man has seen all there is to see.

The journey towards the horizon and the journey into the boundless depths are not only comparable, it seems, but equivalent. The journey of the individual man through life and the journey of mankind through time, we have suggested, are images of one another. The journey of the individual man through life is a journey towards the horizon; the horizon of his awareness is constantly changing throughout his life. First he is an immediate man, a child whose awareness is bounded by the here and now; then he is an existential man, a youth whose awareness reaches to the confines of his own life, birth, and death; and then he is an historic man, a man whose awareness goes beyond his own life to the time of mankind. Then he may return again from the horizon of time to that of life within time and to that of the moment in life and time. At every point he is re-enacting the story of mankind. The change from immediate to existential to historic awareness is like the transition from prehistory to history. The return from time to life and to the moment is like the withdrawal and return which led to the world religions. Beyond this he is able to pass over from his own life into other lives, and thus from his own history into other histories and from his own religion into other religions. This is like the transition from history to world history which has been taking place in our own times.

The turning points in life seem thus to correspond to the turning points in time. The journey of the individual man seems to be heading in the same direction as the journey of mankind. If we try to draw the moral of the individual life story, we find that we must draw a different one for each turning point. Or if we draw a general one it would have to be "Act on insight," since each turning point means new insight. The expansion of consciousness from the immediate to the existential to the historic realm, the return from time to life and to the moment, the passing over to other lives and times, the coming back to one's own life and times—each of these movements of the mind means new insight. They are also movements of the heart. To act upon them transforms one's life story from a story of behavior into a story of action. The term "behavior" we can define as "activity prior to insight," the term "action" as "activity based on insight." To transform the story of behavior into a story of action is in effect to transform the dark forces at work in one's life. This is the transformation we have been looking for. It occurs, according to this, not at any one single turning point, but step by step as one goes from one turning point to another and one's life becomes less and less a story of behavior and more and more a story of action.

This is how the transformation occurs in the life of a man who is discovering his way step by step as he travels it. No matter how great the realm of action in his life there is always a realm of behavior still untransformed. This seems generally true of the journey of mankind in time. It is to some extent a story of action, but it is very largely a predictable story of behavior. The moral we could draw from history, the lesson we could learn from it, is not to control human behavior, not to promote this or that kind of behavior, not to encourage desirable behavior or to discourage undesirable behavior, but to transform the story of behavior into a story of action. This, to judge both from life stories and from history, can only be done step by step, and since insight is what makes the difference between action and behavior it can be done only by communicating insight. The kind of life it calls for is the kind that Socrates and Gotama and Jesus lived, a life of insight and sharing insight with others.

A life of this kind is the noblest and simplest a man can live, and also the most helpful to mankind, but if one actually tries to live it one may find it very incomplete. One may find it lacking in intimacy, lacking in power and glory, lacking in some of the things man most desires. The lack makes itself felt very strongly and insistently. It is as though there were some power at work in one's life and in history too which calls for something more. This power one could see simply as the dark forces of sexuality and violence still incompletely transformed. One's unassimilated sexuality makes one feel the lack of intimacy; one's unassimilated violence makes one feel the lack of power and glory. Actually, though, the power at work here is a power which will not let one be satisfied as long as there is still some realm of behavior, sexual or violent or otherwise, which has not become part of the realm of action. It is a creative rather than a destructive power, though the destructive forces of untransformed sexuality and violence serve its purpose.

It seems to work from a vision of man which man himself does not have, a vision which is always richer and more comprehensive than man's own. At any given point in life or in time man's activity is divided into action and behavior, into activity based on insight and activity apart from insight. Man can see both realms: he can see the purpose of his action and the probable course of his behavior. What he cannot see is what it would be like for his behavior to be transformed into action; he cannot see what he himself would be like acting where he is now behaving. He can see this only when he has actually attained it, only when he is in actual possession of the insight on which it would be based. His vision always depends on where he is in his journey through life and through time. His life project, what he intends to be, is based on his own vision of life, and his historic purpose, what he intends man to be, is based on his own vision of time. His plans necessarily fall short of the creative purpose at work in life and time. The best he can do, it seems, is to be aware of this, give his consent to the creative purpose at work in human existence, come to know it as it gradually reveals itself, and as it comes to light make it the basis of his own action.

Thus the statement of the Upanishads, "You are that," would have to be qualified by the question which is posed in the Upanishads, "How can the knower be known?"[5] The statement seems to say "You are what man is" and even "You are what God is." The question seems to ask "How can man know what man is?" and ultimately "How can man know what God is?" The creative power at work in man's life is what God is, we can say, and this power's aim, its vision of man, is what man is. You can say this but we do not fully understand the creative power or its vision of man. Each time I pass over to another person's life I come back with a new vision of man and a new insight into the creative power. Suppose I am giving my life to attaining insight and sharing insight with others, but suppose I pass over to the life of a person who enjoys making things and giving them to others. I may discover a capacity in myself for making, and this simple discovery may be enough to transform my vision of my own life and my vision of man. From seeing man as a discoverer I may come to see him also as a maker, and from seeing the creative power at work only in human discovery I may come to see it at work also in human inventiveness.

It is true, I may see only human creativity in human discovery and in human invention. It may seem obvious to me that in my life I do the discovering and in the other's life the other does the making and that there is no need to invoke some divine creative power. One will see divine creativity in human discovery and invention and generally in human development only if one sees emerging in life and time a vision of man which man himself does not already possess. One will see divine creativity only if one asks oneself the question "How can man know that man is?" By passing over to other lives and making new discoveries about man and the creative power at work in his life, and by realizing that there is no end of passing over and further insight, one comes eventually to see that man can never fully know what he is and what God is. A man can say to himself "You are what man is," meaning that his life contains somehow the riches of all human lives. He can say to himself "You are what God is," meaning that the creative power is at work in his life, the same creative power which is at work elsewhere in the world. Knowing, however, that he does not know what man is, he knows that his life cannot be reduced to his life project. Knowing likewise that he does not know what God is, he knows that the creative power cannot be reduced to his own creativity. His own life project and his own creativity, he can see, are transformed at each turning point in his life.

A man who can say to himself "You are what man is," one who has the experience of passing over to other lives and discovering always some basis in his own life for understanding others, finds in this a kind of well-being, a sense of human completeness. Perhaps this is the wisdom and the bliss of the sage. It is a sense of his completeness as a human being, a realization that he has within himself everything any other man has, that he has all the richness and all the resources of humanity. If this is the wisdom of the sage, then it consists in an appropriately simple insight. It is so simple that it can seem to be no insight at all. It is simply the realization that he is a human being. It is simple, but not common. It is more than knowing that one belongs to the same species as other men. It is knowing that there is something within oneself corresponding to whatever one finds in other men. It is actually feeling and acknowledging the resonance within oneself to whatever one meets in others. It is thus a very vivid realization of one's own humanity and theirs. To come by it a man would have to make a practice of passing over to others through sympathetic understanding; he would have to engage in it until passing over into the unfamiliar became to him a familiar experience.

Ordinarily large portions of the human world will be unfamiliar to him. If he is a traveler like Malraux, if his journey in life is mostly a journey from one situation to another, the inner world and the inner journey will be comparatively unfamiliar. If he is a dweller like Jung, if his journey is mostly an inner journey, a journey in time, the outer journey and the significance of the situation will be unfamiliar. Even after passing over into the unfamiliar has become a familiar experience to him, there will still be vast regions of the human world which he has not yet explored. When he realizes this and realizes that it must be so, it is then that he may ask himself "How can man know what man is?" The question, he knows, is unanswerable. Man can never fully know what man is. At each stage of my journey in life I am what man is, but at no stage do I fully understand what this involves. My vision of man is always changing. Each time I pass over to another's life and come back to my own my vision becomes richer. Each time I pass over and come back the understanding on which my actions are based becomes more comprehensive.

In this growing richness of thought and feeling and action I may see the work of a creative power. If every turning point in my life means a new horizon, a new vision, a new realm of feeling and imagination, a new field of action, then a creative power seems to be at work in my life. Is the creative power at work in my life the same as the creative power at work in the world at large? "Yes" to this question seems to be the meaning of the statement "You are what God is." It means that the principle at work in man's life is the same as the principle at work in the world. It means that I have within me the basis for understanding not only other human beings but also all other living beings and indeed all beings, that the creative power at work in my life is the same power which is at work in other human lives and in all lives and existences. A creative power seems to be at work in my life as I go from immediate to existential to historic awareness, as I return from time to life and to the moment, as I pass over to other lives and come back to my own. The same creative power seems to be at work in time as mankind goes from prehistory to history, as the world religions arise, and as mankind goes on from history to world history. The same creative power seems to be at work as the inorganic world becomes an organic world and as the organic world becomes a human world.

A man can see all this, it seems—he can see a creative power at work in his life, he can see it at work in other lives, he can see it at work in the course of human events, he can see it at work in the world at large. What he cannot see is the end. He does not know what he is becoming, what man is becoming; he does not know where the creative power is leading. This is the meaning of the question "How can man know what God is?" To know what God is would be to know the creative power, to understand its working, to know where it is leading. Without knowing what man is, man cannot know what God is, and without knowing what God is, man cannot know what man is. One response to this is that of Gotama, to keep silence about Atman and Brahman, to keep silence about what man is and what God is. Another response is that of Mohammed, to speak of what man can know about it, to say that the power is creative rather than destructive, that it leads man to being rather than nothingness. Another response is that of Jesus, to see what the creative power is doing in life and time, to do what one sees the creative power doing, and thus to reveal the creative power to man.

Silence goes with the realization that man does not know what man is and what God is. Living in silence like this would be quite different from living in doubt or in disbelief. Instead of doubt and disbelief there is in this silence a sense of boundless depths. It is like the experience of the man who looks up into the night sky and sees that there is no horizon there. Speech does not really break this silence if it does not pretend to penetrate those depths. Rather it is like the experience of the man who realizes that although he sees no boundary in the night sky his vision is nonetheless limited and the most distant stars fade from his view. Action arises when a man sees that if he acts on his insight he will be led from one insight to another. It is like the experience of the man who journeys towards the horizon, who sees the night sky as it comes up over the horizon, who sees the earth as the horizon recedes before him.

The round earth has no final horizon and the night sky is boundless, but man's journey in life comes to an end in death. Birth and death seem to mean that life does have bounds and final horizons. Man's experience during life of boundless depths and changing horizons seems nevertheless to point beyond birth and death, beyond even the beginning and end of the time of mankind. It is as though time were an infinite sphere, its center everywhere, its circumference nowhere. The infinite sphere is a metaphor with a long history.[6] Once it was a metaphor of God, an image of his presence everywhere and his absence nowhere. Then it became a metaphor of space, the image of an infinite universe in which the earth was no longer the only center. Now let it be a metaphor of time and of God in time. Let the past, the present, and the future be the dimensions of time. Let the moment be the center where past and present and future meet. Every moment then is a center, even the moment of death. The center is everywhere, the circumference nowhere.

NOTES

1. *Chandogya Upanishad,* VI, 12 ff.
2. Terence, *Heauton Timorumenos,* I, 1, 25 (*Homo sum; humani nil a me alienum puto*).
3. Here I am summarizing Chapter One, and in the following paragraphs I summarize Chapters Two to Seven, one by one.
4. Malraux, *Anti-Memoirs,* tr. by Terence Kilmartin (New York, Bantam, 1970), p. 3. Cf. my discussion of this question at the beginning and end of Chapter One.
5. *Brihadaranyaka Upanishad,* II, 4. Cf. Chapter Seven, note 5, and also the discussion of this question in Chapter Seven.
6. For the history of this metaphor, how it was first a metaphor of God and then a metaphor of space, cf. Jorge Luis Borges, *Other Inquisitions,* tr. by Ruth L. C. Simms (New York, Washington Square Press, 1966), pp. 5 ff. Borges ends with the sentence (p. 8) "Perhaps universal history is the history of the diverse intonation of a few metaphors."

Index